LOCOMOTION PAPERS

The Bristol-Radstock-Frome Line

by
Colin G. Maggs

THE OAKWOOD PRESS

© Oakwood Press & Colin G. Maggs 2013

British Library Cataloguing in Publication Data
A Record for this book is available from the British Library
ISBN 978 0 85361 726 6
Typeset by Oakwood Graphics.
Repro by PKmediaworks, Cranborne, Dorset.
Printed by Berforts Information Press Ltd, Eynsham, Oxford.

All rights reserved. No part of this book may be reproduced or transmitted in any form or by any means, electronic or mechanical, including photocopying, recording or by any information storage and retrieval system, without permission from the Publisher in writing.

About the Author

Colin Maggs has been writing railway books for almost 50 years. He had been writing magazine and newspaper articles for about 10 years prior to the publication in 1963 of his first book, *The Weston, Clevedon & Portishead Railway*.

Not wishing to produce a manuscript and then not find an interested publisher, he contacted both David & Charles and the Oakwood Press asking whether they would be likely to publish such a book. They both replied in the affirmative, but Roger Kidner, the gentleman who had the foresight to found the Oakwood Press, clinched the matter by lending him two photographs.

Published in 1964, that book proved a success and has been in print for most of the intervening years, a second edition appeared in 1990. Colin remembers that Roger's letters to him were marvels of brevity, consisting of only one or two short sentences.

That first title was followed by *The Bristol & Gloucester Railway and the Avon & Gloucestershire Railway* and many others, including three on tramways – Bath, Weston-super-Mare and Newport.

Colin warns, 'Potential authors beware. Writing books is like a drug, when you've finished one you want to write another, then another and another, you just can't stop!'

Front cover: '45XX' class 2-6-2T No. 4536 heads the 5.55 pm Frome to Bristol Temple Meads Channel Island boat train at Hallatrow in the early 1950s. Note the express headlamps. The fireman and signalman are exchanging tablets.
R.J. Cannon/Author's Collection
Title page: '57XX' class 0-6-0PT No. 8744 leaves Clutton with the 2.53 pm Saturdays-only Bristol to Frome train on 25th July, 1959. The driver's left hand is on the regulator as he leans out of the cab listening for the engine's response to the admission of steam into the cylinders.
Michael Jenkins
Rear cover, top: 'Hymek' class type '3' diesel-hydraulic No. D7001 crosses Pensford viaduct with a goods train on 10th June, 1968.
Revd Alan Newman
Rear cover, bottom: Railway Clearing House Map of the Bristol-Radstock Frome line and its surroundings.

Published by The Oakwood Press (Usk), P.O. Box 13, Usk, Mon., NP15 1YS.
E-mail: sales@oakwoodpress.co.uk
Website: www.oakwoodpress.co.uk

Contents

	Introduction	5
Chapter One	The Wilts, Somerset & Weymouth Railway	7
Chapter Two	The Bristol & North Somerset Railway	12
Chapter Three	Description of the Line	45
Chapter Four	Locomotives	171
Chapter Five	Timetables and Train Working	187
Chapter Six	Signalling and Permanent Way	203
Chapter Seven	Regeneration?	211
Chapter Eight	Mishaps	215
Chapter Nine	The Camerton Branch	219
Appendix One	Footplate trip from Bristol East Depot to Radstock 12th April, 1961	229
Appendix Two	Traffic dealt with at branch stations 1903 to 1933	235
	Bibliography, Sources & Acknowledgements	238
	Index	240

An 0-4-2T heads an up passenger train at Radstock *circa* 1905. The first vehicle is a four-wheeled brake van with two passenger compartments. The engine's buffers are burnished and the brass dome shines. By the entrance gate a poster warns off loiterers and trespassers.
Chapman

Gradient profile *circa* 1924

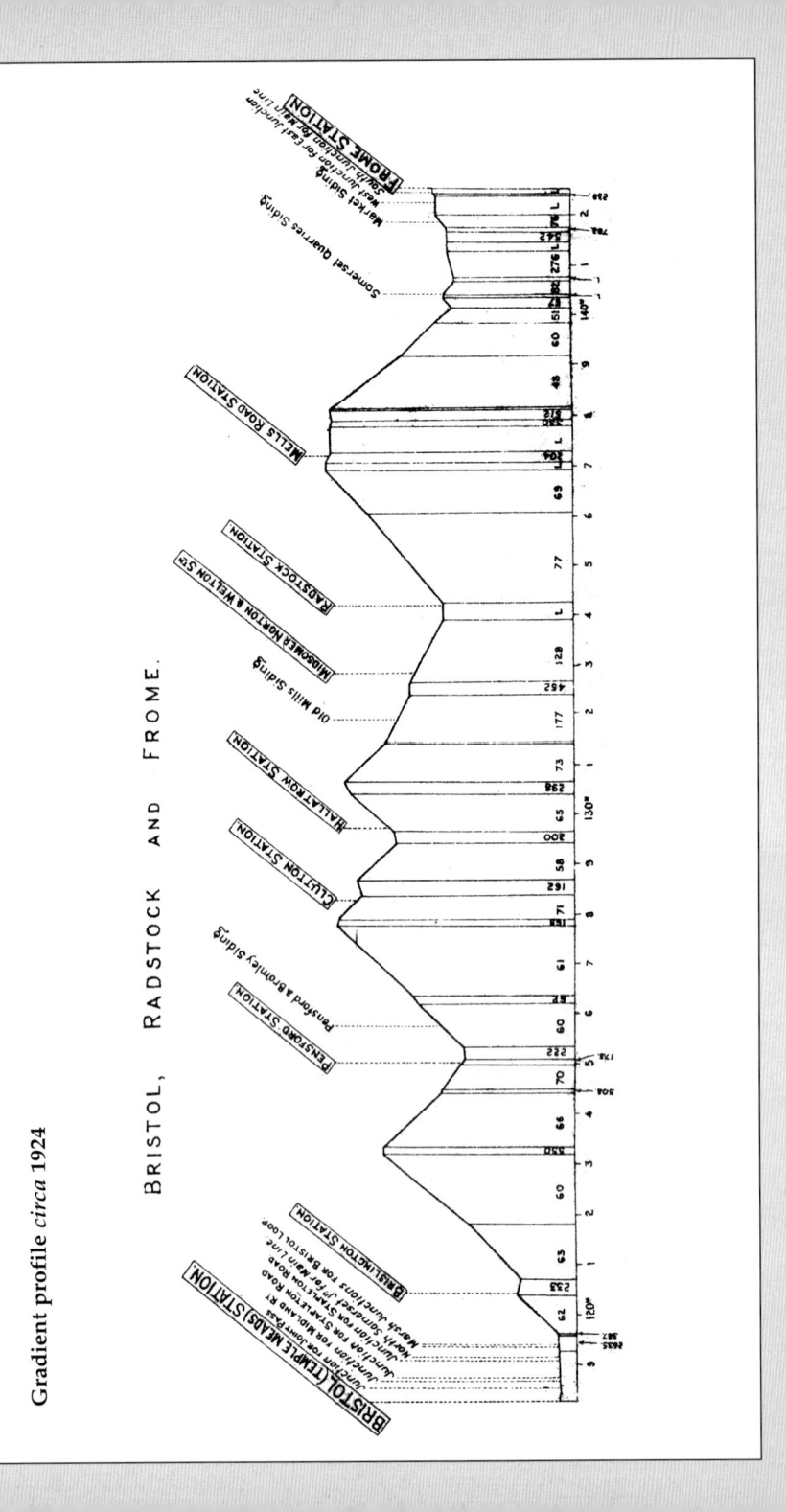

BRISTOL, RADSTOCK AND FROME.

Introduction

Initially coal was at the heart of it; now stone provides the only traffic. The apparently simple line from Frome to Radstock and Bristol had a fairly complex history: first just a broad gauge mineral branch from Frome to Radstock; then a standard gauge passenger/goods/mineral railway linking Radstock with Bristol. Although the broad gauge Frome to Radstock branch had been converted to standard gauge before the line to Bristol had opened, through passenger traffic could not immediately be run as the former line was not adapted to carry passenger traffic.

The whole line was closed to passengers in 1959, but the profitable goods and mineral traffic continued. In 1966 it was decided to split the branch into two sections: Mells Road to Frome and Kilmersdon Sidings to Bristol. Fortunately the intervening 2½ miles remained *in situ*, so when a flood washed away the embankment north of Pensford, the Radstock to Bristol line was closed and Kilmersdon Sidings to Mells Road re-opened.

Kilmersdon Colliery, the last pit in the Radstock coalfield, closed in 1973. Marcroft's wagon works closed in 1988 and the branch was cut back to Hapsford Loop where stone trains offered traffic. The Radstock to Hapsford section was retained out of use. The Somerset & Avon Railway Association hoped to reopen it to commuter traffic but did not get the necessary support. Nevertheless, a requirement for re-opening has been recognized and the route between Radstock and Frome registered in the 2010 Great Western Utilisation Strategy.

Two trains cross at Hallatrow *circa* 1910. The coaches are 4-wheelers. The up train carries a tail lamp and two side lamps, as was standard on passenger trains until 1933. The 2-4-0T on the down train has shiny buffers and passengers are in abundance. *Chapman*

Above: William Ashman, engineer of Clandown Colliery, who built a locomotive which ran on the Somerset Coal Canal tramway from Radstock to Midford in 1826. *Author's Collection*

Left: South portal of Somerset Coal Canal tramway tunnel, Wellow on 11th August, 1998. It is now in a private garden. *Author*

Chapter One

The Wilts, Somerset & Weymouth Railway

The Radstock coalfield was sited awkwardly. Its main markets, Bristol and Bath, lay only a few miles distant, but hills intervened, seriously restricting the load a horse could pull. The Somerset Coal Canal opened in November 1801 and joined the Kennet & Avon Canal at Limpley Stoke offering a roundabout route to Bath and Bristol. One horse could draw 25 tons on the canal, compared to only one ton on a road. The canal only served collieries in the Cam Valley, but a branch canal was constructed to serve Radstock, terminating immediately south of the present Waldegrave Arms Hotel. Collieries were linked to the canal by tramroad.

To avoid an expensive staircase of locks at Midford linking the Radstock branch with the main arm, a mile-long tramway linked the two levels. The Radstock branch of the coal canal opened in 1804, but proved far from ideal due to the trouble and expense of quadruple transhipment: from tramway to canal at Radstock; from canal to tramway at Twinhoe; from tramway to canal at Midford and finally from canal to road at Bath.

This Radstock arm was probably disused by 1812 and at a meeting on 1st October, 1814 it was agreed to construct a 3 ft 2 in. gauge tramway along the towpath thus halving the number of transhipments: from tramway to canal at Midford and canal to road at Bath. The rails were flanged plates, the wagons having plain wheels capable of running on ordinary roads or a tramway with equal facility.

The tramway opened in July 1815, three horses drawing trains of eight or nine wagons, each containing 27 cwt. The return journey from Radstock to Midford and back took five hours, which allowed two double return trips to be made daily. At the height of the tramway's fortunes, no less than 28 return trips were made daily.

It was a single line, with passing loops set at 600 yd intervals. In the event of trains meeting head-on between loops, it was the practice for drivers to take their coats off and fight, the winner taking precedence!

On Saturdays, Radstock market day, some wagons were cleaned, boards placed across them and were used to carry passengers from Midford, Wellow and Single Hill to and from Radstock. It was one of the first passenger-carrying lines in the country.

In August 1826 William Ashman, engineer to the Clandown Colliery, constructed a steam locomotive to draw nine loaded wagons between Clandown and Midford, reaching a speed of 3¾ mph on the level. Unfortunately it proved a failure, not mechanically, but because its weight of 2 tons 3 cwt broke the cast-iron rail plates. It finished life as a stationary engine at Clandown.

Subsequently much of the tramway's traffic was siphoned off by the Wilts, Somerset & Weymouth Railway's (WSWR) Frome to Radstock mineral branch and by 1866 'was not used by Radstock Collieries at all, and not much by any other', according to James McMurtrie's (the Radstock Collieries' Manager) evidence on the Bristol & North Somerset Railway (BNSR) Bill. The canal proprietors were pleased that the Somerset & Dorset Railway's Evercreech to Bath Extension Act of 21st August, 1871 authorized that company to purchase the moribund tramway for £20,000 to be used as a trackbed.

The broad gauge Wilts, Somerset & Weymouth Railway was formed to link the Great Western Railway (GWR) at Thingley Junction, near Chippenham, to Weymouth, with branches serving Devizes, Radstock and Salisbury. When stating the 'advantages' of the WSWR's branch to Radstock, Mr Cockburn, representing the opposing London & South Western Railway, cited evidence of Mr Paine, a Salisbury coal merchant who sold Newcastle coal at £1 13s. 0d. a ton and Radstock coal for £1 3s. 0d. but sold more of the former because it was of better quality. Cockburn continued:

> For all purposes of domestic convenience this Radstock coal is an intolerable article, that as regards pictures and furniture, it would be impossible to burn it, owing to the dust and smoke which arise from it.

Mining it was difficult. He continued:

> The deepest coal mine in the Field is stated to be at Radstock, near Bath; it is 409 yds from the surface, there are several small seams of coal ... some exceeding 3 ft; they would scarcely be deemed worth working were it not for the scarcity of coal in that part of England.

Opposition overcome, the authorizing Act, 8 & 9 Vict. cap. 53 was passed on 30th June, 1845. On 7th October Isambard Kingdom Brunel reported to the WSWR Directors that he had examined possible routes from the WSWR to Bath and considered a link from just east of Bradford-on-Avon to Bathampton, preferable to one from Radstock to the GWR at Twerton, just west of Bath, though the former route would be more costly at approximately £150,000.

Due to a slump following the 'Railway Mania', investment in the WSWR was slow. Thingley Junction to Westbury opened on 5th September, 1848, but the remainder of the 120 miles of railway had finished, or incomplete bridges and earthworks. In many cases the land remained in the hands of the former occupiers, or was let. In preparation for constructing the Radstock branch, on 31st January, 1848 the WSWR purchased almost two miles of the unfinished Dorset & Somerset Canal. The purchasing agreement made provision for the railway company 'to be at liberty to deposit spoil in the old canal so as to fill up the same or any part thereof without money payment'.

Progress with the construction of the WSWR was so tardy that the GWR Directors realized that the line's only hope was to take over the WSWR, so offered four per cent guaranteed stock in lieu of their ordinary shares. As the GWR had already guaranteed four per cent on the WSWR's capital, it was just a paper transaction. The GWR took over the WSWR on 14th March, 1850, this transfer confirmed by Parliament the following year by an Act 14 & 15 Vict. cap. 48 of 3rd July, 1851. The line reached Frome on 7th October, 1850.

Early in 1851 eight contractors tendered for making earthworks for the Radstock branch:

C.E. Lansdell	£19,680
Roach & Pilditch	£21,380
Messrs Fowler	£21,334
William Fitzpatrick	£22,491
William Few	£23,041
Henry Clark	£23,700
Joseph Diggle	£27,500
William Baker	£34,000

The cheapest did not always prove to be the best and Roach & Pilditch's was accepted. R.J. Ward was appointed Resident Engineer. Barnes & Taylor laid the permanent way, the total cost of the finished line working out at approximately £11,000 a mile. One interesting feature still to be seen in Willow Vale, Frome, is that No. 17 had to be partly demolished and some windows and doorways blocked on the railway side of the building. The remaining part of the structure was sold in 1858 and renovated. It was described in a conveyance of 1871 as 'recently erected'. When the branch was completed Captain Yolland made his report to the Board of Trade:

Frome, 23rd October, 1854

Sir,

In obedience to the instructions contained in your letter of the 19th instant, I have this day inspected the Radstock Branch of the Great Western Railway (Wilts, Somerset & Weymouth) and have the honor [sic] to report for the information of the Lords of the Committee of the Privy Council for Trade, that the whole of the permanent way on this line of about 8½ miles in length, is laid with a single line of rails, and the works appear to be in good order throughout: but no arrangements have yet been made for working the line for Passenger Traffic at Radstock as no station accommodation or platform for Passengers has yet been provided and the station is not yet entirely inclosed - Some slight portions of fencing also require to be completed and some Policemen's Boxes have to be placed at Public crossings, but I am informed that the fencing and the placing of the Policemen's boxes will be attended to without delay.

I learn also that there is no present intention to commence working the Line for Passenger Traffic.

I am therefore of [the] opinion that taking into consideration the incompleteness of the works that this line cannot be opened for Traffic, without danger to the public using the same.

I have the honor [sic] to be, Sir,
    Your most obedient servant
        W. Yolland
        Capt. R. Engs
        & Brevet Major

The line did not see passenger traffic for another 21 years, but was opened to minerals on Tuesday 14th November, 1854.

Lady Waldegrave's Ludlows Colliery was directly linked to the GWR, but other mine owners could only gain access to the GWR by using the Somerset Coal Canal tramway to Ludlows and her new tramway to a coal tipping dock serving the GWR. For using this facility each proprietor paid an annual rent of £20 plus a royalty of 6*d*. per ton carried in excess of 1,000 tons annually and a minimum of 1,800 tons. Colliery owners sought ways of avoiding these charges and planned various alternative lines, the most promising of which was the

Radstock Collieries 1858

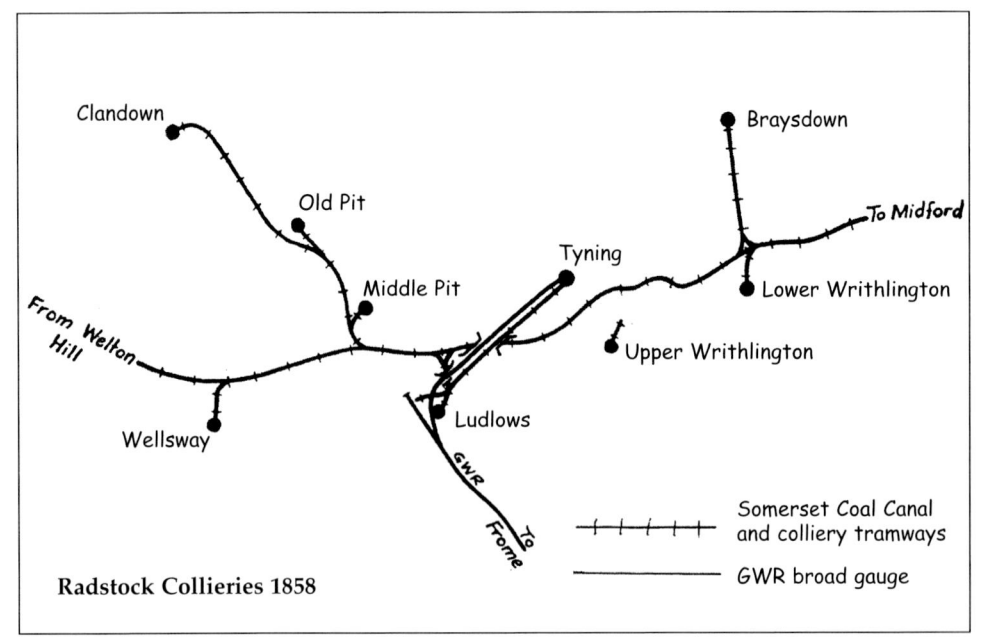

Somerset Coal Canal and colliery tramways

GWR broad gauge

An edge rail tramway wagon with reconstructed body. This vehicle is similar to that used on the Somerset Coal Canal tramway. It is seen here at Haydon Museum, Radstock, 28th October, 1995.
Author

THE WILTS, SOMERSET & WEYMOUTH RAILWAY

Bristol & North Somerset Railway. The BNSR Bill which came before the Parliamentary Committee on 17th June, 1861 was strongly opposed by the GWR, the Bristol & Exeter Railway, the East Somerset Railway and three landowners. Several coal mine proprietors in Gloucestershire and Bedminster were called to prove that Bristol was already adequately supplied with coal. The Bill was lost, the *Bath Chronicle* of 4th July, 1861 commenting:

> The rejection of the measure which would have provided a railway of great accommodation for this district is to be regretted, and we trust that some arrangements may, before another Session, be come to with the opposition in order to secure the passing of the Bill.

Somerset Coal Company,
GREAT WESTERN RAILWAY, FROOME.

F. BENDLE

Begs respectfully to inform the inhabitants of Froome and neighbourhood that he has always on hand

BEST FOREST OF DEAN COAL,

For Drawing-room and Parlour purposes.

Best Radstock Screened Household Coal.

SMALL COAL,

For Engines, Kitchen Stoves, Lime-burning, &c.

Also a FIRST-CLASS COAL from the celebrated NEWBURY and MELLS COLLIERIES, admirably adapted for Threshing Engines, Brewing, Brick-burning, Baking, and other purposes.

ORDERS ADDRESSED TO
F. BENDLE, at the COAL DEPOT,
WILL MEET WITH EVERY ATTENTION.

A Froome (old spelling) coal merchant's advertisement.

Chapter Two

The Bristol & North Somerset Railway

A meeting held at Paulton on 15th June, 1862 expressed the opinion that either the GWR mineral branch should be extended as a mixed gauge line, or that the Somerset Central Railway reach Bristol, with a branch serving collieries in the Paulton area, passenger traffic being a secondary consideration.

On 23rd September, 1862 a meeting in Midsomer Norton market hall chaired by Prebendary Milward, the Vicar of Paulton, proposed that a railway be built from Radstock to Bristol including a branch from Temple Meads to the floating harbour, then unserved by rail. From Radstock the line would link with the Somerset & Dorset Railway near Bruton. (The Somerset Central Railway ran from Burnham-on-Sea to Cole where it linked with the Dorset Central Railway, the two combining as the Somerset & Dorset Railway on 1st September, 1862.) These meetings resulted in the Bristol & North Somerset Railway Bill being deposited in November 1862.

Chaired by Prebendary Mayne, Vicar of Midsomer Norton, on 23rd March, 1863 another public meeting was held in the market hall, Midsomer Norton, for planning the success of the Bill in the Lords as it had passed the Commons despite GWR objection. John Bingham, the BNSR agent, had acted for a London & South Western Railway (LSWR) 1861 scheme to Bristol which had been dropped. Although now acting for the BNSR, the GWR believed Bingham was still in the LSWR's employ. Later on 23rd March, 1863 a similar meeting was held at Chew Magna.

The necessary Act of Parliament 25 & 26 Vict. cap. 168 was passed on 21st July, 1863 permitting £275,000 to be raised by shares and an additional loan of £91,000. The Act authorized a mixed gauge line from Bristol to Radstock and a branch from Hallatrow to Camerton.

The first Directors were John Colthurst, William Adlam, Joseph Cary, David Charles Wait, Robert Jameson, Charles Mullins and James Thatcher. James G. Fraser was Engineer and Bethell & Walton, contractors, had been appointed on 24th June, 1863.

On 21st July a dinner for 200 was held in the market hall, Midsomer Norton to celebrate the Act's passing. Bells were rung throughout the day and the town was decorated with flags. The West Mendip Brass Band played. In a speech Prebendary Mayne, hitherto a supporter of the GWR, remarked that when a company like the Great Western said: 'We will do nothing for you' it was time for them to promote the best interests of the neighbourhood. He believed that all parish priests supported the BNSR.

The GWR, miffed at having to share its profits with the BNSR, refused to consider working the new line and also turned down the notion of opening its Radstock to Frome line to passenger traffic on completion of the Bristol to Radstock line. The BNSR then opened negotiations with the Somerset & Dorset Railway (its Evercreech to Bath extension had yet to be built), but these were concluded due to the financial crisis of May 1866 when the bankers Overend &

Gurney crashed and caused both the BNSR and Somerset & Dorset serious problems.

The BNSR's first meeting was held on 2nd September, 1863 at the Warwick Arms, Clutton. Chairman John Colthurst reported that James Fraser, assisted by Benjamin Piercy, was completing the permanent survey because land could not be purchased until the survey had been undertaken and the contractors could not enter land until the solicitors had arranged for its purchase.

Piercy, born at Trefeglwys, Montgomeryshire, had prepared other railway surveys, mainly in north Wales, including Barmouth bridge. Following his time with the BNSR, he was Chief Engineer on the Sardinian Railway and the Napoléon-Vendée Railway in France. He died in 1888 working for an Indian Railway.

The Directors hoped that 'the energetic and spirited contractors' could begin work in September 1863 and said that the contract was 'on most advantageous terms'. The Directors felt that there was a need to increase the local subscription list. John Bingham was appointed Secretary and an unnamed chief clerk was to come from the Manchester, Sheffield & Lincolnshire Railway. At the meeting Colthurst praised Prebendary Milward for his great zeal in getting the Act through Parliament. When Milward succeeded, one of his opponents, Sir Frederick Slade, shook his hand and said: 'You have fought a good fight, you have done your work well and I wish you a hearty success in your undertaking'.

On 5th October, 1863 a meeting was held at Shepton Mallet to propose an extension of the BNSR from Farrington Gurney through Shepton Mallet to the Somerset & Dorset Railway at Evercreech, and also to build a branch from Camerton to Twerton, west of Bath. These and subsequent schemes thrusting to Evercreech and Bath proved abortive.

At the Directors' meeting on 12th September, 1863 it was agreed that the ceremony of cutting the first sod would be held at Clutton at 1 pm on 7th October. Lord Warwick would be invited to officiate, with Lady Waldegrave as first reserve and Mrs Milward, wife of the vicar of Paulton as second reserve. Milward had been Chairman of the BNSR Provisional Committee. The first turf would be ceremonially lifted on the Bristol Dock Tramway at 2 pm on 8th October by Mrs Hare, Mayoress of Bristol.

At the Directors' meeting on 24th September it was announced that no reply had been received from Lord Warwick: that Lady Waldegrave was in Ireland, so Mrs Milward had been asked to turn the first sod. Mrs Milward and Mrs Hare had both sent letters of thanks at being invited to perform the ceremony and most unusually, both letters were recorded in the Directors' Minute book. Miners had also been invited to the Clutton ceremony, but colliery owners suggested that their dinner be postponed as the colliers were just getting into full work following the lower demand of the summer season. The BNSR Directors had to explain that this suggestion had come too late as the men were already aware of the invitation to a meal.

The first turf of the BNSR was turned at Clutton on 7th October, 1863. The field where the ceremony took place was owned by the Earl of Warwick and leased by Mr Gibbons. Tents had been erected to feast colliers and children,

Mrs Milward, wife of the vicar of Paulton, lifts the first sod into the wheelbarrow at Clutton, 7th October, 1863. Notice the rain, umbrellas and stiffly blown flags. Schools and their banners are on the far right; those of the miners are on the left; the gentry stand in the centre.

Author's Collection

The wheelbarrow and spade used for turning the first turf of the BNSR at Clutton on 7th October, 1863. *Author's Collection*

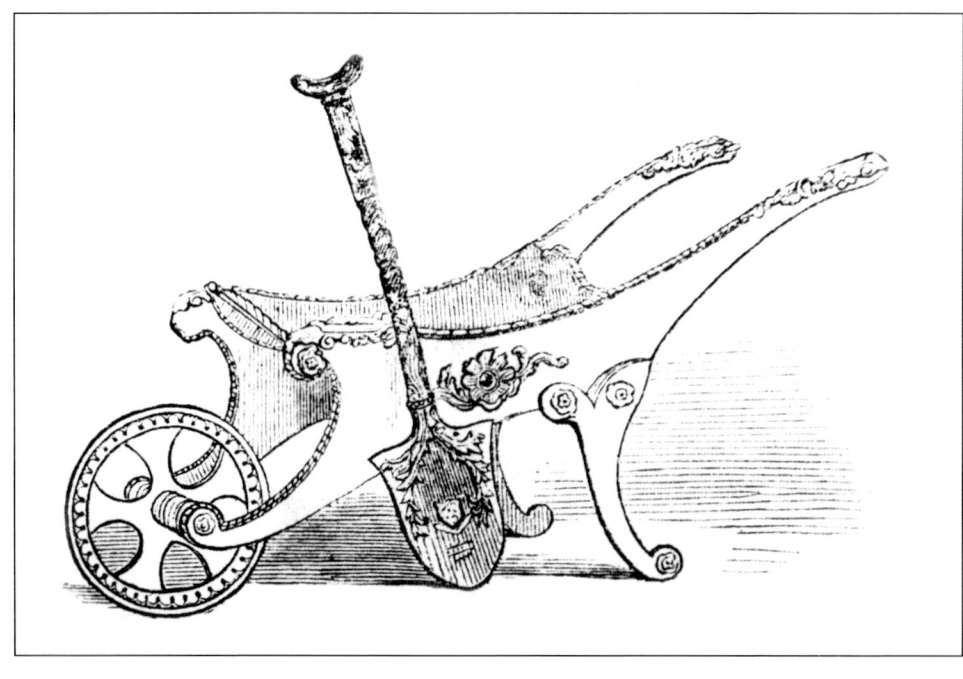

while another marquee was provided for the Directors and friends. All the miners in the district had been invited. Those accepting came from Bishop Sutton, Camerton, Clandown, Clutton, Farrington Gurney, Fry's Bottom, Grey field, Paulton Engine, Paulton Old Mills, Radstock, Timsbury, Old and New Welton. Men from several collieries declined: Braysdown, Foxcote, Huish, New Rock, Sweetleaze and Writhlington. Miners arrived in groups headed by a banner denoting their colliery and took a position to the right of the platform. Children similarly had banners and came from Bishop Sutton, Chewton Magna, Clandown, Clutton British School, Clutton Workhouse School, Farrington Gurney, High Littleton, Hinton Bluett, Midsomer Norton, Paulton Wesleyan School, Publow, Stanton Drew, Stowey and Timsbury. Children and teachers were placed on a piece of ground lower than the field so that they could view the proceedings. Many thousands of people attended and were entertained by a band conducted by J.O. Brooke.

At first the sun shone and it was warm, but then, the *Bath Chronicle* for 8th October, 1863 commented:

> Alas that such a splendid picture should so soon be destroyed - we had almost said *dissolved*. Within a quarter of an hour of the time fixed for the ceremony, the clouds assumed an ominous look, a few drops of rain fell, followed by a soaking shower. Delicate silk dresses dripped with water and bonnets were 'totally destroyed'.

About 1.15 pm Mrs Milward appeared and due to the inclement weather, most of the ceremony took place beneath umbrellas. Psalm 100 was sung by all and a prayer offered by Prebendary Osmaney, Rural Dean and Vicar of Chew Magna, in the unavoidable absence of the Diocesan Bishop.

The BNSR Chairman, John Colthurst, presented Mrs Milward with a silver spade with an oak handle, which she used with the assistance of two navvies, to place several sods in a highly-polished, silver-mounted oaken wheelbarrow. She wheeled this barrow to the end of the platform where it was tipped and a bottle of champagne broken over it. Another prayer was said and three cheers given for Mrs Milward, three for the Sheriff, three for the Directors and three for Prebendary Milward. The National Anthem was sung. The spade and barrow were supplied by Messrs Mappin Brothers of London who inscribed Mrs Milward's crest and the text: 'Presented to Mrs Eliza Milward, October 7th, 1863'.

The 4,000 miners then proceeded to the tent and were given 1 lb. of bread, 1 lb. of beef and a quart of beer supplied by Mr Clarke of the Farrington Inn; Mr Combes, Bell Inn, Radstock; Mr Selway, Chewton Inn and Mr Willcox, Waldegrove Arms, Radstock. Children were supplied with tea and cake, while the Directors and friends partook of a *déjeuner* supplied by Mr Keen of the Greyhound Inn, Broadmead, Bristol. 'During the whole of the proceedings the rain descended with great violence, soaking through the tent, and literally casting a "damper" upon the gathering'.

The following day Mrs Sholto Vere Hare performed a similar ceremony at the Floating Harbour Tramway, Bristol. It was known as the 'floating' harbour as lock gates contained water so that vessels could float at all states of the tide. A platform had been erected for guests and nearby ships were well-filled with

Mrs Hare wheels the first turf of the tramway to the Floating Harbour, Bristol, 8th October, 1863. The first rail is on the artist's side of her. Terrell's rope works is in the background.

Author's Collection

Details of the BNSR in *Bradshaw's Railway Manual, Shareholders' Guide and Directory*, 1865.

47.—BRISTOL AND NORTH SOMERSET.

Incorporated by 26 and 27 Vic., cap. 168 (21st July, 1863), to construct a line from the Great Western, at Bristol, to Radstock, with a branch to Camerton. Length, 16 miles. Capital, 275,000*l.*, in 20*l.* shares, and 91,000*l.* on loan. Extra land, twenty acres; compulsory purchase, three years. Completion of works, five years. Mixed gauge. Works in rapid progress.

CAPITAL.—The receipts to the 30th June, 1864, 53,287*l.* 10*s.*; expenditure, 39,912*l.*; balance, 22,375*l.* 4*s.* 6*d.*

No. of Directors—8; minimum, 6; quorum, 5 and 3. *Qualification*, 400*l.*

DIRECTORS:

Chairman—JOHN COLTHURST, Esq., Chew Court, and the Mall, Clifton.
Deputy-Chairman—THOMAS HARRIS SMITH, Esq., Midsomer Norton, Bath.

Henry Box, Esq., Chewton Mendip, Bath. | James Thatcher, Esq., Midsomer Norton, Bath.
Joseph Langford, Esq., Timsbury, Bath. |
James Perrin, Esq., Temple Cloud, Bristol. |

OFFICERS.—Sec., John Bingham; Engs., Benjamin Piercy, C.E, 28, Great George Street, Westminster, S.W., and James Fraser, C.E., 19, Duke Street, Westminster, S.W.; Solicitors, John Rees Mogg, High Littleton, Bristol; T. A Hill, Paulton, Bristol; and Bingham and Co., 17, Parliament Street, Westminster, S.W; Bankers, Stuckey's Banking Co., Bristol, or any of their Branches; and the Union Bank of London, Temple Bar, London.

Offices—9, Clare Street, Bristol.

spectators. Rows of flags were displayed on various buildings and ships' rigging. All were entertained by the artillery band and peals of bells from St Mary's Redcliffe. The Mayoress used an ornamental spade and barrow identical to that used the previous day. Mrs Hare filled the barrow with earth, wheeled it along a plank and overturned it to the crowd's applause. A large group then adjourned to Mr Hyde's decorated sail loft where an elegant *déjeuner* was served and speeches delivered. Mrs Hare's spade bore her family crest and the word: 'Presented to Mrs Elisabeth Hare, Mayoress of Bristol, October 8th, 1863'. To complete the story of the Bristol Harbour Railway, which had little subsequent association with the BNSR, the GWR and the Bristol & Exeter Railway opened it on 11th March, 1872. Following the demise of the city docks due to larger ships not being able to reach Bristol, the line closed on 11th January, 1964.

In October 1863 the BNSR Directors received a deputation seeking a branch from the BNSR to Writhlington and Braysdown collieries and also to those in the Nettlebridge Valley, but Lady Waldegrave was against building a line to pits which competed against hers. Writhlington and Braysdown were eventually served by the Somerset & Dorset Railway when it opened its Evercreech Junction to Bath extension in 1874 which also partly served the Nettlebridge Valley.

In December 1863 the BNSR Directors agreed to subscribe £30 annually for a chaplain for workmen engaged on the line's construction. That month Bethell & Walton required an advance of £1,000 cash and £1,000 in shares, but the Directors only agreed to advance the shares. Two months later the contractors were given £1,000 cash and £7,500 bonds. Fraser, the Engineer, reported on 29th January, 1864 that plans and sections had been prepared, but that there was an unexpected delay in obtaining possession of the land. He said that the masonry of Pensford viaduct had been commenced.

The second half-yearly meeting took place at the Warwick Arms, Clutton, on 2nd February, 1864. T.H. Smith, the vice-chairman presided. Bingham reported steady progress since the work began on 7th October. A considerable quantity of land had been obtained, working plans and sections prepared and masonry started for the heaviest works - Pensford viaduct and the Avon bridge, Bristol.

By 19th March, 1864 it was said that hitherto 'energetic and spirited contractors' had failed to provide the necessary sureties, whereas the truth was they refused to continue the contract unless paid cash and this was a commodity the BNSR lacked. On 16th April, 1864 the Directors were told that Lawrence & Fry were willing to take over the contract if it was free from any dispute with the previous contractors. Bethell & Walton agreed to settle amicably for £25,000 and ceased work in April 1864. Lawrence & Fry undertook to carry out the contract for £40,000 shares at 30 per cent discount and debentures at 10 per cent discount. Bethell & Walton were paid £13,000 for shares and plant, the £13,000 having been received from Lawrence & Fry in return for £31,000 in bonds and £40,520 in shares.

Lawrence & Fry signed the contract on 22nd April, 1864, but unfortunately all was not plain sailing; for on 27th June the Secretary reported to the Directors that a notice had appeared in *The Times* of 23rd June, 1864 saying that Lawrence

& Fry had suspended payment. The Directors resolved to take action against their new contractors for recovery of the shares and debentures in their hands. They found that the contract itself had been tampered with. Although executed on 22nd April, 1864, it was dated 7th January, 1864 and the date on the stamp obliterated. Many other alterations had been made.

In July counsel advised that the contract was illegal and that the Directors could not recognize it. They wished to avoid costly litigation so were prepared to settle with Lawrence & Fry on payment for the shares already advanced. While undergoing negotiations to find a contractor to build the line, and in order to take advantage of the fine weather, the BNSR itself carried on building Pensford viaduct. On 11th August the Directors were informed that Thomas Brassey had offered to complete the line. Unfortunately for the cash-strapped company, he was wise enough to require cash payment and was not prepared to accept shares.

At the half-yearly meeting held at the Red Lion Inn, Paulton on 30th August, 1864 Bingham revealed that the GWR's suspicion of him was correct. He said that the aim of the BNSR was to create a new line to London in competition with the GWR and the London & South Western Railway's Engineer had been examining property on the site required for a Bristol station. 'It is not that Mr Brassey, the new contractor of the North Somerset line, is acting upon a agreement or understanding with the authorities at Waterloo'. Fraser reported that the piers of Pensford viaduct had been commenced and the foundations of the Avon bridge started, while several small arches and culverts had been built and some road bridges begun in addition to erecting three miles of fencing.

The BNSR did not gain much support from the contemporary authors G.C. Greenwell and J. McMurtrie, for in *On the Radstock Portion of the Somerset Coalfield* published in 1864 they wrote: 'The line is now in the course of construction and at present rate of progress may be completed some time during the next century'.

At the Directors' meeting on 29th September, 1864 William Lawrence, now on his own, offered to complete the works for one-third cash, one-third shares and one-third debentures; meanwhile discussions with Brassey continued, but he was adamant regarding his terms and said he would not touch an inch of the line until the land was paid for, so on 11th October, 1864, talks with Brassey ceased.

William Lawrence took over the contract in Mid-October and the Directors' meeting of 1st December, approved his sureties. The BNSR's finances were in a very unhappy state as most of its authorized capital had not been subscribed. On 18th February, 1865 the Directors learned that £35,000 had been loaned by the Imperial Mercantile Credit Association and £35,000 by Messrs Baillie, Cave & Co. at 10 per cent interest, This was illegal as loans should not have been taken until all the authorized capital had been subscribed. At the general meeting the same day the Directors reported that one difficulty facing the company was the extravagant claims of landowners who had originally supported the railway. Fraser reported that several of the cuttings had been proceeded with and 40,000 cubic yards completed; that all the piers, except one, at Pensford were concreted and the stonework built for some feet.

In March 1865 James Fraser discovered errors in the plans and sections not of his making, but the Directors held the view that he should have checked them so punished him with dismissal. From 6th April Benjamin Piercy, hitherto Fraser's assistant, became sole engineer, but resigned, not wishing to be associated with a troubled company. In June actions were brought against the BNSR by Fraser and Piercy, with a counter action by the BNSR against Fraser.

In August 1865 John Furness Tone was appointed Engineer, a man who had had considerable experience of mineral railways in the north of England. On appointment he discovered that the contractor and resident engineer were almost entirely devoid of proper information and working drawings. At the half-yearly meeting on 17th August, 1865 the Directors ambitiously hoped that 'a large length of the line will be ready for opening next summer'.

On 9th September, 1865 the Board wisely resolved not to contract for the Camerton branch unless and until the proprietors of the Camerton and Timsbury pits signified their intention to find a portion of the capital required for its construction. Excitement was caused at the meeting on 21st September when the Chairman John Colthurst refused to vote on the resolution that the contractor be paid entirely in cash instead of on-third cash and two-thirds shares. Cash payment would have reduced the line's cost by eight per cent. Colthurst was asked to resign but remained in the Chair. The next Board meeting demanded Colthurst's resignation, but he remained adamant and remained seated.

The Secretary, Bingham, revealed that at Pensford 10 navvies were living in one cottage room and asked that more accommodation be made available and teachers provided for navvies' children.

At the half-yearly meeting on 29th March, 1866 Tone reported that all the works were in course of construction between Farrington Gurney and Bristol, many approaching completion. He proposed an amended route from Farrington Gurney to Radstock which offered a saving of considerable expense by rendering unnecessary the destruction of homes in Radstock and avoided interference with the house and grounds of Radstock parsonage.

The Board meeting of 4th April, 1866 heard that severe and wet weather had caused delay to the works generally, while those in the Radstock area had been put back by plans for the deviation, but were to be recommenced at once. Part of the deviation was within the area allowed by Parliament, but a further Act was required for the remainder and for a branch to Writhlington, that colliery's proprietor subscribing a considerable sum to build such a branch. Tone observed that these works were very light and could be finished simultaneously with the heavier works required north of Farrington Gurney.

A colliery owner, the Earl of Warwick, became BNSR Chairman on 18th April, 1866. He had a short reign as John Colthurst was re-elected on 13th July, 1866.

By an Act of 29 & 30 Vict. cap. 262 of 23rd July, 1866 the BNSR was authorized to raise an additional £100,000 in shares and £33,500 on loan.

The year 1866 was a poor one for finance in Britain as 11th May was Black Friday when the bankers Overend & Gurney collapsed. In lieu of cash, that summer Lawrence was paid in bonds. Tone's report to the half-yearly meeting on 31st August revealed that little construction had been carried out due to the unexpected financial crisis preventing them from procuring funds; so the contractors, with the consent of the Directors, ceased work in early summer. Tone said that two-thirds of the line was 'well done'; that the incomplete works would be undamaged by the weather; that the Directors anticipated an early resumption of work and that the line would open the following summer. Colthurst observed that while the fine dry weather could not be used for building, some banks had started to slip and that enforced rest would settle them. He said that the BNSR had within its Bill an extension to join the Somerset & Dorset and also to enter into an agreement with the Great Western whereby that company lay down standard gauge on the Wilts, Somerset & Weymouth Railway between Radstock and Salisbury. Additionally this agreement enabled improved and cheaper junctions to be made at Bristol and Radstock. It was 'one in the eye' for the Somerset & Dorset when Bingham remarked that in his dealings, the GWR 'stood out, in the most marked contrast as to fairness and gentlemanly conduct, with that of the Somerset & Dorset'.

Bingham's agreement with the GWR was found ambiguous and disadvantageous to the BNSR. The following year, with the assistance of J.S. Forbes, General Manager of the London, Chatham & Dover Railway, a supplemental agreement was made whereby the GWR guaranteed £5,500 per annum on BNSR debenture stock as the first charge on the entire gross receipts and the BNSR was given free use of GWR stations at Bristol and Radstock.

In February 1865 Colthurst and his fellow Directors had applied to bankers Montague Baillie for a loan of £35,000 in return for fully paid up, or preference shares in the company to an amount of £6,000. On 21st February, 1866 the loan expired, but Baillie was prepared to extend it for three months provided he received £10,000 by 31st March, 1866. At their meeting on 13th March, 1866 the Directors believed the banker might resort to legal proceedings to recover the money, so met him on 17th March and persuaded him to defer his demands until October.

At the half-yearly meeting on 31st August, 1866 Colthurst told shareholders that their Directors had borrowed large sums which required early repayment. Bingham admitted that he had persuaded the Directors to obtain these loans because he believed that the line would have been completed before the date of repayment, but the recent financial panic had wrecked his prediction.

In November 1866 Bingham was told to produce the accounts so that they could be investigated by a committee of Montague Baillie (the largest shareholder) and two Directors. This committee was to negotiate with the company's creditors and try to persuade them to suspend proceedings for repayment until the line was complete and the BNSR receiving an income. The outcome of these efforts was that the principal creditors suspended litigation in return for four creditors being elected to the Board. At the shareholders' half-yearly meeting at Clutton on 28th February, 1867 Colthurst announced that a committee had been formed to investigate the accounts and that two new Directors would be elected, one of whom would represent the creditors - rather different from what had been agreed the previous November. The meeting reconvened on 13th March, T.H. Smith taking the Chair, Colthurst having resigned due to his bankruptcy. The Engineer, Tone, said he believed that the line could be completed at a cost of £100,000 to £110,000 and optimistically stated that if work restarted immediately, the line would be open by late autumn that year and the company able to accept the profitable coal traffic. The meeting continued on 4th May, 1867 when the Directors revealed that the company was in the hands of creditors who were 'suing from one end of the line to the other' and no funds were available to meet their demands.

The investigating committee placed advertisements in local papers:

> A Committee having been appointed by the Shareholders to Investigate this Company's Affairs, all Persons having CLAIMS against the Company are requested to forward full particulars of the same to the Office of the Company, No. 9, CLARE STREET, Bristol, on, or before TUESDAY next, the 26th Inst. By Order of the Committee.

It was dated 18th March, 1867.

This committee found a dire situation. Its report of 6th June, 1867 revealed that of the 13,750 shares authorized by the 1863 Act, only 804 had been applied for and distributed. In addition 355 shares had been issued to pay for land. A further 2,026 had been issued to Bethell & Walton to pay for work done. Three thousand paid-up £20 shares had been issued to the Imperial Mercantile Credit Association in return for a loan of £30,000. Other shares had been disposed of for payment to solicitors and Parliamentary agents. In total, 3,049 shares had been issued in total. Although the £275,000 authorized by the 1863 Act had *not* been raised by the issue of ordinary shares, the Directors had illegally proceeded to borrow money by giving promissory notes, shares, debentures or bonds for loans totalling £215,000. The debentures had not been issued from the company's office, nor registered in any book. Loans had been taken out by some Directors for a total of £180,000 using their own promissory notes as security. The BNSR's receipts totalled £220,000, yet the amount spent on construction was £124,000 and the company owed over £275,000 in addition to bills of an unclear nature as 'one of the accounts not given is that of the late Secretary (Bingham) whose repeated promises to furnish it remain unfilled'.

Late in May 1867 Bingham oddly replied to the Directors via a letter he sent to the Bristol newspapers saying that illness had prevented him from attending the half-yearly meeting on 4th May and that he had been unable to meet the investigating committee due to the illness of his eldest son.

On 7th June, 1867 a special meeting of shareholders was held at the Warwick Arms, Clutton, to consider:

1. The agreement with the GWR.
2. The heads of agreement between the creditors and the company.
3. The report of the Committee of Investigation.

The meeting believed that the Great Western had acted fairly in the joint management of traffic on the BNSR and that the BNSR should offer 2*s.* 6*d.* in the pound to its creditors. The meeting was adjourned till August when it was hoped to produce a plan for the line's completion.

What happened to John Bingham? On 7th June 1870, at Bristol Central Criminal Court he pleaded guilty to having forged and altered an endorsement for £536 17s. 6d. with intent to defraud William Baillie. He was sentenced to 12 months' hard labour.

An Act 31 & 32 Vict. cap. 178 of 31st July, 1868 authorized the BNSR to make several deviations and also gave an extension of time for completion until July 1871. Two influential and well-attended meetings were held at Stone's Cross Inn, Midsomer Norton on 28th and 29th April, 1870. The first meeting moved:

> That this meeting desires to express its decided opinion that nothing short of a direct narrow gauge railway communication, simultaneously with the completion of the North Somerset Railway, will meet the wants of the Somerset coalfield. An amendment carried was: That in the opinion of this meeting the existing arrangements between the Bristol & North Somerset Railway Company and the Great Western Railway Company, as regards the laying down of the narrow gauge, and assuming that a junction with the Somerset & Dorset Railway at Bruton is effected, are satisfactory, and nothing short of these arrangements would meet the requirements of the district.

It was then carried unanimously that the chairman, W.B. Naish, communicate with Lady Waldegrave in favour of the BNSR Bill of 1870. He was also empowered to communicate with the GWR with a view to fix a period for laying down narrow gauge to Bruton. The Earl of Warwick was thanked for extricating the BNSR from pecuniary difficulties and able to be in a position for early completion.

The meeting on the 29th concurred with that on the 28th and heard with regret petitions against the Radstock deviation by the Somerset Coal Canal, the Rt Hon. Chichester Fortescue, the Countess Waldegrave and the GWR. The canal company's suggestion that it be converted to a steam railway was 'not deserving of consideration'.

By the summer of 1870 William Clarke had been appointed BNSR Engineer. His first appointment had been with the Shrewsbury & Crewe Railway; 1859-1862 he was resident engineer of the Lahore Division of the Punjab Railway; in 1863 he completed the Tenbury & Bewdley Railway and the Ludlow & Clee Hill Mineral Railway. In May 1866 he became a member of the Institute of Civil Engineers and the same year was appointed assistant chief engineer of the London & North Western Railway.

Clarke had inspected the BNSR back in the summer of 1869 and recommended a deviation at Radstock for which a further Act had to be sought. His route was slightly north of that authorized and needed less demolition; was cheaper and offered a better junction with the GWR. It required the diversion of the Frome Turnpike road which was shifted away from Victoria Square to join the Bath to Wells turnpike near the Waldegrave Arms, leaving only a pedestrian subway to follow the original route to Victoria Square. Apart from one small building, no other required demolition whereas the original route needed valuable buildings to be destroyed. The new route also placed the station in a better position. The Act 31 & 32 Vict. cap. 178 of 30th November, 1869 allowed the creation of £124,500 debenture stock (on which the Great Western was paying £5,500 per annum interest), while the consolidated stock issued to creditors was anticipated to amount to approximately £400,000. As the BNSR possessed the advantages of 'an inexhaustible coalfield, a district rich in agricultural produce, a large population, and the important City of Bristol for a terminus' the outlook seemed rosy. With the prospect of standard gauge communication to Salisbury and beyond, the BNSR Directors anticipated a minimum dividend of 2½ per cent, the average dividend of mineral railways in the United Kingdom, and the Directors said that they would be disappointed if this was not exceeded. They hoped to open from Bristol to Pensford in the spring of 1871 and complete the line by that autumn.

Under the 1869 Act, all claimants on the BNSR were required to deliver particulars of their claims by November 1869. Between November 1869 and January 1870, £320,966 of undisputed claims were received and disputed claims of £65,909, the latter being settled by Court of Chancery. All valid claimants were entitled to consolidated BNSR stock. In addition to these creditors were the former engineers Fraser and Piercy.

In May 1870 the Directors met colliery owners and the GWR. A figure was offered for a minimum amount of coal guaranteed to be carried between Radstock and Bristol when the line had been completed. The GWR agreed to work the BNSR and also convert its Radstock to Salisbury line (to give access to the LSWR) within a year of the BNSR's opening. At the shareholders' meeting on 21st July, 1870 the Chairman was Gwinnett Tyler, also a Director of the Bristol & South Wales Union Railway and the Carmarthen & Cardigan Railway.

In July 1870 the Board sought tenders for the railway's completion. The offer of Messrs John Perry & Sons, Stratford, London, was accepted at £90,000, a sum less than Clarke's estimate. Messrs Perry was a reliable firm which had constructed lines for the London, Brighton & South Coast Railway and were contractors for St Thomas' Hospital, Westminster. Contract No. 1 was from Radstock to Cloud Hill, just north of Hallatrow, and No. 2 from Cloud Hill to Bristol. Perry's contract was signed by the end of October 1870, but little work was carried out by him during the winter due to shortage of BNSR funds.

At the Directors' meeting on 31st May, 1871 regret was expressed that the works were not proceeding as fast as the Engineer had led them to expect. Clarke submitted plans for stations at Brislington, Pensford, Clutton, Welton and Radstock and said that the inhabitants of Whitchurch and Farrington Gurney had urged the company to provide them with stations. He also reported that at its own expense the Great Western was laying extra sidings at Bristol to accommodate the BNSR.

It the half-yearly meeting held that month, the Directors reported that financial difficulties had been settled, but constructional problems had begun due to the heavy rain in the winter of 1870 to 1871 causing frequent landslips. Work was now proceeding satisfactorily with opening expected before or during June 1872. Of the £124,000 debenture stock authorized by the Arrangement Act of 1869, £69,321 had been placed, of which £35,281 issued at par was fully paid up. The remaining £33,500 would be issued as the company required funds. £55,179 of stock remained to be appropriated. The Earl of Warwick had guaranteed the completion of the line and the payment of interim interest and but for him it was doubtful if the line would have been completed.

William Clarke reported that,

All land was in the possession of the railway except for a small portion at Radstock for which arrangements are being concluded. Between Cloud Hill and Bristol, 11 miles, bridge works are far advanced and should be completed before winter sets in. Pensford Viaduct for half its length is carried up to springing height of the arches. This work is the key to the opening of the line as after the viaduct is completed, 45,000 cubic yards of earthwork will be run over it to the north side. The viaduct is hoped to be finished in March 1872. Works were light on the Radstock section. Ballasting and permanent way laying to be carried out during the construction of the viaduct and embankment and will be ready simultaneously with those works. Junctions at Radstock and Bristol have been settled with the Great Western and arrangements are being made to lay down a third rail on the Great Western at Bristol to allow BNSR traffic to use Temple Meads. [This was done on 1st August, 1873.]

The 1871 census recorded 45 railway construction workers at Pensford. At the Directors' meeting held 30th August, 1871 at the Inns of Court Hotel, London, it was reported that satisfactory progress was being made and the line would open by midsummer 1872. On 30th June the amount of unappropriated debenture stock was £81,679 and of this amount £6,500 had since been issued.

The Directors arranged to place £26,500 as they required funds, leaving a balance of £48,679. Clarke reported that the contractor had experienced great difficulty in getting workmen. All land was in the company's possession and the Radstock section was so far advanced that it was believed it could be completed earlier than anticipated. Although the GWR had agreed to lay standard gauge between Radstock and Salisbury within 12 months of the BNSR opening, colliery owners memorialized the GWR to have standard gauge ready for the BNSR's opening.

Only about half a dozen shareholders were present at the BNSR half-yearly meeting held at Paddington on 20th March, 1872. They were informed that earthworks were almost complete from Pensford to Radstock. Work was needed on Pensford viaduct as the piers were insufficiently substantial and four additional piers were required to strengthen it. This would require 'a considerable amount of money'. It was anticipated that the line would open that midsummer. The meeting was then made 'special'. Two deeds of covenant were read: one between the Earl of Warwick and debenture stock holders, and the other between the company and the Earl of Warwick . The Earl undertook to fund any of the company's deficiencies and in return he would be reimbursed from the first receipts of the company following payment of interest on debenture stock.

In March 1872 tenders were sought for constructing the stations. On 9th July, 1872 five men were injured, none seriously, when a ballast train 'upset' between Whitchurch and Bristol, while on 26th July, Dale, a navvy, was killed when a wagon of spoil passed over him. Pensford viaduct builders struck on 23rd July, 1872.

In November 1872 the junction at Bristol was effected, Colonel Yolland inspecting it the following month. He found that only the up GWR line connected with the BNSR and even on that, a rail had been taken out to prevent mishaps. At the time of his visit it was only intended to use the junction to take material onto the BNSR and nothing off. The signal box had been erected, but as the signals and points were not connected, he was unable to test them. The BNSR was not now expected to open until February or March.

Rains in December 1872 hindered progress and at the half-yearly meeting in January 1873 shareholders were informed that completion of the line faced two problems: the scarcity of labour back in the summer of 1872 and the recent wet weather rendering it almost impossible for the men to work. In that summer the contractors required 1,000 men, but could only obtain 150, even though they offered higher wages than they could earn in Bristol. Clarke explained that the men they employed were uncontrollable 'going to work and leaving off when they liked'. That winter the contractor had enough men but he required fine weather. The line was only sufficiently complete at that moment to run a locomotive from Bristol to Pensford and from the south end of Pensford viaduct to Radstock. The viaduct was finished except for the 'backing' (the filling above the arches and below the track), and the parapets. The line would have been more forward but for a serious slip of 40,000 to 50,000 tons of earth near the viaduct.

In January 1873 it was said that it was unlikely that the line would be opened until the summer and that for the second time, the bridge near North Somerset Junction near Bristol had been taken down for rebuilding. In April it was announced that the opening date had again been put back to the late autumn.

In January 1873 the Earl of Warwick had concerns regarding the construction, so arranged for an inspection of the line by an independent engineer, Thomas E. Harrison. He had been employed by Robert Stephenson in 1830 and 1831 preparing plans for the Wolverton to Rugby section of the London & Birmingham Railway. He was then appointed to the post of Engineer of the Stanhope & Tyne Railway and in 1849 Chief Engineer of the York, Newcastle & Berwick Railway. On the formation of the North Eastern Railway in 1854 he became its Engineer. One of his most outstanding achievements was York station, completed in 1877.

Harrison closely inspected the BNSR on 16th and 17th January, 1873 and noted that the piers of Pensford viaduct were constructed on an unusually thick bed of concrete. The original design had been modified to give a broad effect to the base and he noticed slight symptoms of settlement in the facework at the bases of some of the piers. Two slips had occurred nearby: one in a cutting and one on an embankment. The slip in the cutting was very heavy and required earth to be taken out and placed on the embankment north of the station. The embankment itself had been formed on very treacherous ground, the strata lying at a considerable angle. Large stone drains had been laid to lead the water away. Time proved that these two locations continued to cause trouble throughout the working life of the line. Harrison reported that he had seen more slips than on any other line of similar length. He observed that the line had a poor finish, but believed that if a great effort were made, it would be possible to open in three months.

Acting on Harrison's advice, at the Board meeting on 6th February, 1873 it was stated that in order to hasten the opening, John MacKay, Shrewsbury, would complete Perry's No. 2 contract, but Pensford viaduct would be excluded. Perry would complete Contract No. 1 and Pensford viaduct. Perry agreed to complete his work by 1st May, and MacKay said that for £9,000 he would complete his length of line by the end of May 1873.

By the end of March 1873 earthworks were almost finished and by early July an advertisement appeared in *The Builder*:

Bristol & North Somerset Line

T. Melhuish for J. Perry & Co. of Tredegar Works, Bow: to auction on 22/23rd July 1873 at Hallatrow Depot, remainder of plant used in the construction of the above line, including two 6-wheel saddle tank locomotives.

Perry had moved his headquarters from Stratford to Bow in 1872.

Another accident occurred on 5th August, 1873 when a young man named Crane, aged about 17, was uncoupling wagons from a contractor's engine at Clutton, was caught between the buffers and received fatal injuries.

The half-yearly meeting in March 1873 was told that the only assets of the BNSR were £375,000 of unissued shares and creditors refused to take these in lieu of claims and cancel the debt. Completion of the line had been guaranteed by Lord Warwick promising five per cent to debenture holders until the line was completed. Warwick had already advanced £30,000 and was expected to contribute a further £20,000. The GWR promised to work the line and subscribe £40,000. By two Acts the BNSR had been empowered to raise £375,000 in ordinary capital and £124,000 by loans. The BNSR was now asking Parliament for a further £100,000 capital and borrowing powers of £33,300. The cost of the line to date had been £33,300 per mile. James William Dawson, clerk to the BNSR's solicitor, admitted that this money had not been spent in cash 'but has been squandered away. I do not know how. No doubt in the earlier stages Mr Bingham was the company. The company had actually no funds whatsoever'. Sir Dordaunt Wells QC for the Somerset Coal Canal, read a report of a BNSR meeting at which a Director stated that only £20,000 had been subscribed to the BNSR. £400,000 had been raised in loans and creditors paid in shares.

When the Directors met on 5th August, 1873 Clarke reported that the line was complete and arrangements made for a visit by the Board of Trade inspector. This was carried out on 28th and 29th August, 1873 by Colonel Rich who reported:

Railway Department
Board of Trade
2nd Sept 1873

Sir , I have the honor [sic] to report, for the information of the Board of Trade, that in compliance with the instructions contained in your Minute of the 15th ultimo I have inspected the Bristol and North Somerset Railway from a Junction with the Great Western Railway near Bristol to Radstock.

The new line is single, land has been enclosed & the bridges and viaducts have been built for a double line , but the permanent way for a double line, has only been laid over one bridge which is at Pensford.

The new line is 15 miles 13 chains long. The guage [sic] is 4 ft 8½ in. The intervals between the line & the sidings are 6 ft. The ruling gradient is reported to be 1 in 52 & the sharpest curve to have a radius of 13 ch.

The railway is connected with the Great Western Railway from Bristol to London, by a double junction, which is situated about ¾ of a mile from Bristol, on the London side.

The stations are Brislington, Pensford, Hallatrow, Clutton, Whelton [sic] and Radstock – all of these except the last, are on gradients of 1 in 71 to 1 in 200, *but as they are placed in the hollows at the bottom of the inclines* and that it would be difficult to alter them, I recommend that they be permitted to remain as they are. The line was commenced a long time since.

The permanent way consists of a Vignoles pattern rail, that weighs 72 lbs per lineal yard. It is fished and fixed with fang bolts and dog spikes to sleepers laid transversely, at an average distance of 3 ft apart. The sleepers are 9 ft long 10 in. x 5 in. The line is well ballasted.

There are turntables at Radstock and at Birmingham [sic - he meant Bristol] which are terminal stations.

The works consist of twenty over bridges - nineteen are built of stone with Bk arches and one has wrt iron girders.

Twenty six under bridges - fourteen consist of stone & brick. Eight have cast iron girders & four have wrt iron girders.

There are two viaducts – one upon the River Avon has stone piers & wrt iron girders and the one at Pensford consists of sixteen semicircular brick arches on stone piers. Fourteen arches have spans varying from 51 ft to 51 ft 10 in & two have spans of twenty eight feet. The widest span [on the line] is 100 feet [in height].

There are vertical deviations beyond the Parliamentary limits at

m.	ch.		m.	ch.
3	50	to	3	65
4	25	"	4	63
5	65			
7	70	to	8	75
9	50	"	10	76
13	50			

The gradients are in most cases somewhat worse in consequence of these deviations, but I was informed that the landowners have made no objections to the alterations.

There is a level crossing of a public road at Radstock. The gates close across the road & railway. They are worked from the adjacent signal cabin and are interlocked with the signals.

All the signals & points on the railway are worked from signal cabins and interlocked; the arrangements for working the line on the block telegraph system were very nearly completed. The following works required to be done –

Several bridges showed slight settlements. The cracks should be pointed & they should be carefully watched for some time.

One of the three sets of facing points should be taken out at Pensford station.

The rails on the Avon Viaduct & Pensford under bridge require fastening with through bolts.

The bolt lock on the loop line at the junction with the Great Western Railway was badly fixed by Messrs Saxby & Farmer & did not work effectually.

The gates at Radstock required bolts & one line of rails on the level crossing required to be taken up & the crossing should be packed.

Clocks were required in some of the signal cabins & shelves for the telegraph instruments interfered with the view of the signalmen & with the working of the levers & required to be fixed at the sides of the cabins. Diagrams of the lines of rails & signals were required in the signal cabins. The locking of the signals & points at Radstock, which were arranged for working up & down lines at the station required to be changed for working the station as a single line, until such time as the railway is opened to Frome & Radstock & the station is used as a passing place.

The Engineer (Mr Clarke) undertook to have these services completed at once & I trust that the Board of Trade may sanction the opening of the Bristol & North Somerset Railway, as soon as a satisfactory undertaking as to the proposed mode of working is sent in.

The Great Western station at Bristol is in process of reconstruction.

This very necessary work appears to progress very slowly indeed.

   I have etc.
     F.H. Rich Colonel RE

* * * * * * * * * * * * * * *

BRISTOL AND NORTH SOMERSET RAILWAY
STATEMENT TO ACCOMPANY TABULAR FORMS AND PLANS ALREADY FORWARDED

Permanent way. The Rails single headed, flat bottomed, 72 lbs per yard and fastened with Spikes & Fang bolts as on the Tracing showing the Plan of Road & Section or Rail and fastenings.

The Sleepers are of best Memel Timber about 3' 0" centre to centre and 9' 0" x 10" x 5" rectangular.

The Line is single throughout excepting at the Bristol Junction and at Pensford Station where there are two Platforms and a double line of Rails as a passing place for Trains. The length of double line at these points as well as sidings at other Stations are all shown on the Tracings of Station Plans as well as the signalling arrangements and position of home and distant Signals.

The width of Line at formation level is various, the minimum being 18 feet. The whole of the land is purchased for a double line of Rails throughout.

The gauge of the line is 4' 8½".

The distance between lines of rail where double is 6' 0" and between main line and Sidings 8' 0" and 10' 0".

The points are made by Ramsden of Leeds and are provided with double connecting rods.

Engine Turntables are provided at Bristol and Radstock.

The Ballast is of broken Limestone and Ashes and is 1 foot deep below the under surface of Sleepers.

Fences Between Radstock 0M.00 and 3M.32 Chs wire fencing with wood-posts and Iron Strainers are provided.

Between 3M.32 Chs and 4M.00 wire fencing with Iron posts and Iron strainers are provided. The details are shown on Tracings. The remainder consists of Larch fencing as shown on Drawing.

Drainage No difficulty has attended the drainage. The usual side drains in Cuttings and at boundaries of the Line at foot of Embankments and on tops of Cuttings have been adopted.

The drainage of Slips is described in the Tabular printed forms.

Stations The names and positions are shown on the longitudinal Section of the Line and the position of the Signals and details of Sidings are shown on the Station plans & diagrams.

Width of Line, Bridges &c The widths of Line at narrowest points are indicated by Tracings of Bridge Plans. There are no retaining walls 2' 6" above rail level and no pillars at any of the Stations supporting roofs. No Girders stand 2' 6" above Rails.

The Great Western Company will work the Line.

  (signed) William Clarke

45 Parliament St, S.W.

Opening was announced for Tuesday 2nd September,1873, but as insufficient time had been allowed for making the arrangements, it was deferred until the next day, however 'a considerable number' turned up to catch the 7.40 am from Temple Meads on 2nd September because they had not seen the postponement notice in that morning's paper .

The first train was in the up direction and left Radstock at 6.15 am on Wednesday 3rd September, 1873 with no ceremony and almost a score of passengers. The first down train was the 7.40 am from Temple Meads. The second up train was well patronized and on the first day a total of about 500 passengers were carried. The *Bath & Cheltenham Gazette* reported that no mishap occurred; there was the usual large number just going for the ride and that there were 'a crowd of natives at the stations as the first trains passed through the different villages'.

Early on 16th September a serious landslip occurred in the deep cutting of loose shale 100 yds on the Clutton side of Pensford viaduct. About 5.30 am, due to heavy rain, the upper side of the almost perpendicular cutting gave way for about 120 ft causing several hundred tons of rotten shale to bury the permanent way to a depth of several feet. Fortunately the slip was discovered before the 6.15 am from Radstock was due. Passengers alighted before the obstruction, walked over the debris to a train waiting on the other side, this delay causing trains to be ½ to ¾ hour late. Forty to 50 navvies worked all day to clear the line and in relays throughout the night. Traffic resumed on 17th September. The previous evening the locomotive of the last down train became derailed while running round its train at Pensford, but suffered no serious damage. It was re-railed after two hours.

On 9th December, 1873 Elijah Whitlock of Midsomer Norton placed a sleeper lengthways on the right-hand rail near his home. The locomotive was almost derailed when it cut through the sleeper, damaging the guard irons. The driver said he left Midsomer Norton at 5.35 pm and on passing Old Mills coal works, his engine hit an obstruction. He stopped and found the stone guard knocked off and believed that but for this protection, the engine would have been derailed. Whitlock was committed to the Winter Assizes.

At the BNSR half-yearly meeting held in the Great Western offices, Paddington on 23rd December, 1873 (it had been adjourned from 30th August), Gwinnett Tyler, Chairman, said that although the line had been opened to passengers on 3rd September, owing to incompletion of facilities, it had not been available to goods until the end of October. He said that goods and mineral traffic could not be developed until the GWR had narrowed the gauge on its mineral branch which it was under agreement to do by 3rd September, 1874, but undertook to do voluntarily in May. He did not state the reason for this, but probably the GWR wanted standard gauge to reach Radstock before the Somerset & Dorset Railway's Evercreech Junction to Bath extension opened on 20th July, 1874. Gwinnett Tyler reported that the Bill for making the Camerton branch and confirming the agreement with the Earl of Warwick for the reimbursement of his outlay for completing the line and the creation of stock for that purpose, received Royal Assent in July. The final accounts for the line's construction were still not ready. The Engineer informed shareholders that various colliery proprietors had applied to connect their pits with the BNSR and the necessary steps were being taken to carry out these works.

Opening the BNSR affected Bath shopkeepers. D.H. Gale in *Tourists' Descriptive Guide to the Somerset & Dorset Railway* published 1874, wrote regarding Bath:

> It is well known among tradesmen of this city, whose merchandise was patronised by the inhabitants of the coal field, that since the North Somerset line to Bristol has been opened, the colliers and their families have forsaken the Bath road, with its uncertain and uncomfortable conveyances, and carried their money to Bristol. Ask any of the traders likely to be affected by such a diminution in customers, and they will tell you that the falling off has been serious. To Bristol, the increase of business has been correspondingly great.

The Somerset Coal Canal and the BNSR had been in contention on 7th May, 1873. The object of the suit was to make the BNSR carry out work at Midsomer Norton which under a previous order of court it was obliged to have done. The BNSR had been empowered by its Act to redirect the coal canal tramway and convey free of cost the site of a substitute line 'which shall be constructed by the company and delivered to the Canal Company in full and perfect order before the present tramway shall be taken or interfered with'. The BNSR had, indeed, made the tramway, but it was not 'in full and perfect working order'. The BNSR's defence was that no time had been fixed for the conveyance of the site of the substituted line.

The matter continued in contention and the *East Somerset Telegraph* of 26th February, 1876 reported:

> This was a suit which had been brought to restrain the defendants from continuing in possession of a tramway at Radstock, Somersetshire, before they had delivered to the plaintiffs a substituted tramway in full working order. The defendants were entitled under their Acts to take a tramway belonging to the plaintiffs and to hand over to them one in substitution.
>
> It was alleged by the plaintiffs that the defendants had neglected to complete the substituted tramway but had nevertheless taken possession of the original one. On the matter before the court on a previous occasion an eminent engineer was appointed to report on the state of the tramway. He reported adversely to the defendants and a money payment of £207 7s. had been adjudged to the plaintiffs in compensation. They now expressed themselves willing to put an end to the litigation on the payment of this sum and the costs of the suit. On Friday the Master of the Rolls after hearing counsel decided that the plaintiffs were entitled to the £200 and the costs of the suit.

Gauge Conversion

Back in 1871 the GWR Directors contemplated laying a standard gauge line at a cost of £54,000 beside the existing broad gauge Frome to Radstock line and continue it to a junction with the LSWR at Yeovil from where Salisbury could be reached over standard gauge lines, but no active steps were taken to further this idea.

The last broad gauge train left Radstock on 13th June, 1874. Local permanent way men were insufficient to carry out the task of conversion which included the rest of the Wilts, Somerset & Weymouth Railway, so others were drafted from other parts of the system, arriving in special trains. Each workman was expected to bring a shovel, rug, great coat or other covering, a coffee or tea can and enough food for three days, after which he was promised the opportunity of purchasing food locally. The men lodged in huts supplied by the GWR. Before starting work, each man had to sign an undertaking not to absent himself without permission and to work from daylight to dusk – as the work was carried out in late June, this entailed working 18 hours at a stretch. The men were prohibited from smoking, and drinking spirits, but an oatmeal drink was supplied free by the GWR.

The men were set in gangs of 20 under a ganger who was responsible for a mile, or a mile and a half of track. One man in each gang was deputed to boil the oatmeal and serve it out *ad libitum*, 1 lb. oatmeal being sweetened with 1 lb. of sugar. This GWR drink was found to allay thirst better than beer, cider or spirits and give the men more stamina. Packers were paid 3*s*. 3*d*. a day and 1*s*. 3*d*. ration money plus 5*d*. an hour overtime, while gangers received 4*s*. 6*d*., 1*s*. 3*d*. and 6*d*. respectively.

Ballast had been cleared away previously and alternate transoms cut, so conversion involved removing strap bolts, shortening the remaining transoms, slewing the rail and the longitudinal timber to which it was secured, replacing the strap bolts and packing the rail. Finally the ganger checked the gauge. The Radstock branch was converted in a day. It reopened with the rest of the WSWR as standard gauge on 26th June, 1874.

Colliery proprietors necessarily had to provide themselves with standard gauge stock, but many wagons had been built for easy conversion. This made the wagon works at Radstock very busy. Two large fields were covered with stock of both gauges and scores of men converted wagons to standard gauge, quite a number of men having travelled a distance to obtain this work.

Colonel Yolland inspected the newly-converted branch and issued a report:

RAILWAY DEPARTMENT ,
Board of Trade,
Whitehall, Lond., S.W.

Bristol 25th June 1875
Sir, I have the honor [sic] to report for the information of the Board of Trade, in compliance with the instructions contained in your Minute of the 4th Instant That I have re-inspected the Radstock Branch of the Great Western Railway which was first inspected by me, in the year 1854, but the notice with intention to open was subsequently withdrawn (as a Passenger Line), and it has been worked since that date as a mineral Line.

This Line, which is now on the narrow gauge commences at the North side of the Frome Station on the Wilts, Somerset and Weymouth Branch, and terminates in the Radstock Station yard a short distance to the East of the Radstock Passenger Station of the Bristol and North Somerset Railway, and its length is returned as 8 miles 4.6 chains independent of a short Junction Line, 23 chains in length, joining the Wilts , Somerset and Weymouth Branch at what is called the North Junction, still further to the North than the Junction close to Frome Station, this Short Junction Line was not ready for Inspection, and I did not in consequence look at it, and I have therefore to state that by reason of the incompleteness of the works its opening for Traffic would be attended with danger to the Public using the same. I would suggest that the notice of the intention to open this short Junction Line should be withdrawn, and another one given, when the works are complete.

As regards the main Line between Frome and Radstock I have to state that the details received from the Great Western Railway Company, no longer represent the present state of the Line, as it is described as a Single Line throughout, whereas the Line has actually been doubled between Radstock and Mells for upwards of 3 miles, and I would suggest that the Great Western Railway should be requested to supply correct details of the present state of the Line as requested on the 1st June.

I understand that the Line was relaid in 1861, and the Company has been engaged lately in taking out a good many of the worn rails and replacing them with new ones – portions of the Line are laid with an entirely different description of permanent [way] which I am unable to particularise from the details having made out for the state of the line in July 1874, but both kinds are substantial.

The gauge is 4 feet 8½ inches and the intervening space where there are two lines, is 6 feet; the steepest Incline is 1 in 48.29 and the sharpest curve for a length of 15.6 chains has a radius of 10 chains close to Frome station – this curve is protected by check or guard rails on each Line inside the inner rails of the curve of each Line.

There are 11 over and 11 under Bridges besides 5 Viaducts on this Line. The largest openings in the over Bridges are 28 feet on the square and 32½ feet on the skew: among the under Bridges, the greatest openings are 27 feet on the Square and 31$\frac{5}{12}$ feet on the Skew - and among the Viaducts, the largest opening is 42 feet on the Square and 46 feet on the Skew. I have no drawings of any of these bridges or viaducts, but although they have now been constructed for upwards of 20 years they are standing well, with the exception that in some, the stone has suffered from the action of the weather, and repairs have been required and in some places are still in hand and with respect to the under bridges and viaducts where Timber is used for supporting the permanent way, they did not present any unusual deflections under a rolling load. The Viaducts will require to be carefully looked after, as they are mostly of wood and after such an interval of time, decayed portions will continually require from time to time to be taken out.

There are no Stations on the Line. Frome Station at one end and Radstock Station of the Bristol and North Somerset Railway (which is worked at the other, by the Great Western Railway), are to be made use of.

There are 3 authorised Level Crossings of Public Roads on the Line, but I understand that the Great Western Railway Company, are seeking powers in Parliament at this Session to do away with these 3 Level Crossings, and under such circumstances, it is not necessary to ask the Railway Company to put up Lodges or Stations at them – they are protected by Signals in each direction.

The requisite arrangements have been made for working the Traffic on the absolute Block System and on the single portion of the Line in conjunction with the Train Staff, but I have not received any undertaking of the Co. as to the mode of working intended to be adopted.

The requirements of the Board of Trade have also been complied with in reference to the interlocking but the Points and Signals are not yet generally connected with the Levers in the Signal Boxes and in some instances which were pointed out on the ground, the facing point locks required closer adjustment. Clocks have also to be placed in these Signal Cabins. At the Junction of a Coal Siding near the west Signal Box at Frome, a single throw-off point is to be changed into double switches with a dead end. At Huish's Coal Siding an Electric communication is to be Established between Nos. 1 and 2 Signal Boxes.

There is a steep Incline for tram cars from a Colliery on a hill near Radstock (Whittenson & Hewits) down to a colliery siding north of this Line, where if a tram car or cars were to break away, they might be projected across the Passenger Lines – and a stone buttress is to be erected between the Colliery Siding and these Passenger Lines, to prevent accidents from occurring to the Trains.

The Line required to be very carefully gone over and all worn or damaged rails, should be taken out, and be replaced by new ones, but I am unwilling to recommend that the opening of this Line for Passenger Traffic should now be postponed on this account, or from the connecting up of the points and Signals with the Levers in the Signal Boxes not having been yet completed if it be understood that these things will at once be completed another Inspector of the Board of Trade, may if thought necessary again go over the Line, when these few requirements have been attended to – and provided also that a satisfactory undertaking as to the mode of working be received from the Company.

I have the honor to be,
    Sir,
        Your most obedient Servant,
           (signed) W. Yolland
           Colonel

The line opened throughout from Frome to Radstock to Bristol to passengers on Monday 5th July, 1875, the *Western Daily Press* of 6th July commenting:

The opening of this branch of the GWR (Radstock-Frome) took place yesterday, the first train leaving Frome at 7.20 am, in charge of Messrs Graham (District Superintendent) and Morrison, Liddiard and Robson (inspectors). The engine employed was driven by Mr Dennis Haycroft, and was profusely ornamented with flowers, evergreens and small coloured flags. The boon confered upon the travelling public by the opening of this small branch is considerable. Improved communication is opened between Bristol and the Weymouth branch, in which Frome will especially benefit. Hitherto the journey to Bristol from Frome has occupied two hours; via Radstock it can be accomplished in an hour and a quarter, without change of carriage. There is now a double line of rails between Radstock and Mells, and it is intended to continue the second line to Frome.* The difference in the distance between the old and new routes to Bristol from Frome is nine miles only; the saving in time between the two is due to the train running direct between the two places.

The GWR Take-over

The BNSR gross receipts from 1st July, 1874 to 30th June, 1875 were £11,967 – a poor return for the outlay and offering no dividend to ordinary shareholders. At the meeting on 23rd October, 1877 with James Grierson, the GWR's General Manager, the BNSR proposed that the GWR took over the company, paying off debenture shareholders and the Earl of Warwick at 4 per cent and giving a small increasing dividend to consolidated shareholders . The GWR was to pay £10,000 in the first year and an increased sum subsequently. Negotiations were protracted: the GWR only offering a low figure for the line and shareholders reluctant to sell for a pittance. For the next few years, at each half-yearly meeting the Secretary informed shareholders that there was as yet no result from negotiations with the GWR. In November 1880 the BNSR Secretary informed shareholders that daily an answer was expected from the Great Western. In 1881 the GWR's Bill before Parliamentary Committee included an

---

* The line from Mells to Frome was never, in fact, doubled.

BRISTOL, RADSTOCK, AND FROME.

WEEK DAYS.

Fares from Bristol.						STATIONS. Class between Bristol and Frome.	1,2,3 A.M.	1,2.P. A.M.	1,2,3 A.M.	1,2,3 P.M.	1,2,3 P.M.
Single.			Return.								
1Cl.	2Cl.	3Cl.	1Cl.	1Cl.	2Cl.						
s. d.	s. d.	s. d.	s. d.	s. d.	s. d.						
0 0	0 0	0 0	0 0	0 0	0 0	BRISTOL .... dep.	6 50	9 15	12 30	2 35	
0 4	0 3½	0 3	0 6	0 10	0 6	Brislington .... ,,	6 57	9 22	12 42	2 42	
1 0	0 9	0 6	1 6	2 0	1 6	Pensford .... ,,	7 10	9 35	12 45	2 55	
1 6	1 0	0 9	2 3	2 9	1 9	Clutton .... ,,	7 20	9 45	12 55	3 10	
2 0	1 6	1 0	3 0	3 6	2 3	Hallatrow .... ,,	7 25	9 56	1 0	3 20	
2 6	1 9	1 3	3 9	4 3	3 0	Welton (For M.N.) .. ,,	7 35	10 0	1 10	3 25	
3 0	2 0	1 6	4 6	5 0	3 4	RADSTOCK .... ,,	7 40	10 5	1 15	3 25	
3 9	2 9	1 9	5 6	6 3	4 3	FROME .... arr.	8 5	10 30	1 40	3 50	
5 6	3 3	2 2	9 0			Frome (For Chipp'm) dep.		10 50		2 18	6 50
4 9	3 3	2 4	8 0			Westbury .... ,,		11 5		2 28	7 17
4 9	3 2	2 4	8 0			Trowbridge .... ,,		11 37		2 40	7 17
4 5	3 0	2 2	7 5			Chippenham .... arr.		12 7		3 7	7 52
8 6	6 0	3 6				Frome (for Weymouth) dep.	8 15	11 35		1 50	4 2
10 6	7 0	4 16				Yeovil .... ,,	9 25	12 50		2 55	5 15
14 3	10 0	6 17				Dorchester .... ,,	10 20	1 43		3 40	6 10
15 6	11 0	6 10				WEYMOUTH .... arr.	10 40	2 0		4 0	6 30

SUN.

	12.P. A.M.	1,2,3 P.M.
	5 50	
	5 57	
	6 10	
	6 20	
	6 25	
	6 35	
	6 40	
	7 5	
	7 10	
	7 20	
	7 35	
		12 50
		1 0
		1 17
		1 50
	7 30	9 40
	8 25	10 36
	9 20	11 30
	9 40	11 53

WEEK DAYS.

STATIONS. Class between Frome and Bristol.	1,2.P. A.M.	1,2,3 A.M.	1,2,3 A.M.	1,2,3 P.M.	1,2,3 P.M.
WEYMOUTH .... dep.		8 10	0 12 10	4 35	
Dorchester .... ,,		8 20	12 28	4 52	
Yeovil .... ,,	6 5	9 25	1 15	5 45	
Frome .... arr.	7 10	10 45	2 15	6 50	
Chippenham .... dep.		7 10	10 20	1 0	2 55
Trowbridge .... ,,		7 45	10 53	1 25	3 30
Westbury .... ,,		7 58	11 5	1 35	3 45
Frome .... arr.		8 15	11 35	1 50	4 2
FROME (For Bristol) dep.	7 20	10 50	12 55	3 0	7 10
RADSTOCK .... ,,	7 45	11 15	1 20	3 25	7 40
Welton (For M.N.) .. ,,	7 50	11 20	1 25	3 30	7 45
Hallatrow .... ,,	8 0	11 30	1 30	3 40	7 55
Clutton .... ,,	8 5	11 35	1 40	3 45	8 0
Pensford .... ,,	8 15	11 45	1 50	3 55	8 10
Brislington .... ,,	8 27	11 57	2 2	4 7	8 25
BRISTOL .... arr.	8 35	12 5	2 10	4 15	8 30

SUN.

12.P. A.M.	1,2,3 P.M.
	8 35
	8 52
	9 45
7 4	
9 21	
9 35	
9 45	
9 4	
9 45	740
10 10	8 10
10 15	8 15
10 25	8 30
10 30	8 35
10 40	8 45
10 55	8 55
11 0	9 0

Working timetable April 1875.

arrangement that the BNSR be transferred to the Great Western for an annual payment of £5,840 in 1881, £8,540 in 1882, £8,950 in 1883, £9,635 in 1884, £9,910 in 1885, £10,820 in 1886, £11,280 in 1887, £11,555 in 1888, or in lieu of money payment, secured stock or shares to the shareholders.

Then on 19th May, 1881 a special meeting of GWR shareholders was held at Paddington. Some BNSR shareholders, doubtful whether their line was profitable or not, were told that it was not, and had not been worked in the interests of ordinary shareholders. The BNSR shareholders met on 23rd May, no Directors were present and the accounts were severely criticized. This resulted in a motion refusing to adopt them. The BNSR shareholders also expressed disapproval of the GWR take-over Bill before Parliament.

In the summer of 1881 the Earl of Warwick took legal action to recover the £113,125 owed him by the BNSR. Although in January 1882 the court upheld his claim, the destitute BNSR was unable to pay. This resulted in the Court of Chancery taking over the BNSR and it appointed three BNSR Directors to be receivers and managers.

As the GWR had almost a monopoly of Bristol to London traffic, Bristol merchants were supportive of a proposed rival line. In 1882 the Bristol & South Western Junction Railway was planned to link the LSWR at Andover with the BNSR at Radstock. Its Bill provided for doubling the BNSR and gave the LSWR running powers to Bristol where a new line would have been built to a central station. After a hard struggle in the House of Commons Committee, chiefly due to Midland Railway opposition, the Bill was rejected.

BNSR income was	Main line			Camerton branch		
	£	s.	d.	£	s.	d.
1st January, 1882-30th June, 1882*	7,309	3	9	84	14	9
1st January, 1883-30th June, 1883	8,192	15	4	403	11	0

The Camerton branch had failed to make a profit and on the main line the increase was exclusively in minerals and merchandise, passenger traffic actually showing a slight decrease.

At the half-yearly meeting held in the Grand Hotel, Broad Street, Bristol on 29th September, 1883, the Chairman Joseph Wethered reported that the BNSR had seen greater numbers of passengers travelling to and from Weymouth and the Channel Islands. The GWR, realising the value of the BNSR to a competitor such as the Bristol & South Western Junction Railway, decided to take it over. At their half-yearly meeting on 14th February, 1884 GWR shareholders approved a Bill to absorb the BNSR, the official date for the take-over being 1st July, 1884. This move was authorized by an Act 47 & 48 Vict. cap. 235 of 7th August, 1884. Holders of the £110,000 North Somerset 5 per cent debenture stock received Great Western 5 per cent consolidated preference stock exchanged at par.

On 16th August, 1884 the BNSR held an extraordinary meeting at the Grand Hotel, Bristol, to consider the resolution 'That the Bristol and North Somerset Railway Company be wound up voluntarily under the provisions of the Great Western Railway Act, No. 1 1884, and of the Companies Acts of 1862 to 1880' – and to determine the amount of remuneration to be paid to liquidators.

---

* The Camerton branch was only open for four of the six months. It opened on 1st March, 1882.

MARCH 1st, 1882, and until Further Notice.

BRISTOL TO RADSTOCK AND FROME.—NARROW GAUGE.

The Line from Bristol to Radstock is single (Pensford is the intermediate Crossing Station, but Hallatrow is a Staff Station), from Radstock to Mells double, and from Mells to Frome Junction, single. The single portions are worked by Train Staff and Auxiliary Disc Telegraph. The following are the particulars of the Staffs and Tickets.

SECTION.   **Form of Staff and Tickets.**   **Colour of Ticket.**
BRISTOL AND PENSFORD. — Square. — Red.
PENSFORD AND HALLATROW. — Round. — White.
HALLATROW AND RADSTOCK. — Triangular. — Blue.
MELLS AND FROME JUNCTION. — Round. — White.

For Special Instructions for working the Inclines on this Branch see Circular dated April 21, 1881.

DOWN TRAINS.—WEEK DAYS.

Distance.	STATIONS.	1 Goods A.M.	2 Coal A.M.	3 Passenger A.M.	4 Passenger A.M.	5 Coal A.M.	6 Goods and Coal A.M.	7 Coal A.M.	8 Coal A.M.	9 Passenger A.M.	10 Coal A.M.	11 Coal P.M.	12 Coal P.M.	13 Coal P.M.	14 Passenger P.M.	15 Goods & Coal P.M.	16 Coal P.M.	17 Passenger P.M.	18 Passenger P.M.
	Bristol .... dep.	6 45	...	6 30	7 55	...	8 30	...	...	10 12	...	...	...	...	12 15	2 30	...	4 30	7 25
2¼	N. S. Junction... „	—	...	6 37	8 — 2	...	8 55	...	...	10 18	...	...	...	...	12 21	3 —	...	4 37	7 31
2¾	Brislington ...... „	7 10	...	6 49	×	...	9 15	...	...	10 30	...	...	...	...	12 31	3 0 ×	...	4 48	7 42
6¾	Pensford { dep. arr.	7 20	...	6 50 7 —	8 15 8 30	...	9 40 10 20	...	...	10 32 10 42	...	...	...	...	12 32 12 42 ×	3 25 3 45	...	4 50 5 —	7 43 7 52
10	Clutton .... „	7 45	...	7 —	8 —	...	10 20	...	...	10 47	...	...	...	...	12 47	4 10	...	5 —	7 57
13½	Hallatrow ...... „	—	...	—	8 40	...	C E 10 40	...	...	10 55	...	...	...	...	12 55	4 30	...	5 15	8 —
13¾	Old Mills Siding „	—	...	7 15	—	...	—	...	...	—	...	...	...	...	—	4 50	...	—	8 5
14¼	Welton .... „	—	...	—	—	...	—	...	...	11 0 ×	...	...	...	...	1 2 5	—	...	5 20	8 10
	Old Welton Siding „	—	...	—	—	...	—	...	...	—	...	...	...	...	—	—	...	×	×
	Wells Way ...... arr.	—	...	—	—	...	—	...	...	—	...	...	...	...	—	—	...	5 22	8 12
16	Radstock { dep. arr.	—	6 0 6 20	7 20 7 22	8 45	8 5 8 25	10 45 A	...	9 30 9 50	11 1	2 11 30 11 50	12 20	2 0 2 20	2 45 3 5	1 4 Coal P.M.	3 45 4 5	5 33 5 45	8 20 8 35
19	Mells .... „	—	—	7 33	...	...	...	9 15 9 40	...	11 12 11 25	...	12 20 12 45	...	...	1 13 1 25	4 30 4 50			
24	Frome .... arr.	—	—	7 45 ×	...	...	...	—	...	11 25	...	—	...	...	—	—			

SUNDAYS.

	1 Passenger A.M.	2 Passenger P.M.
Bristol	8 15	5 50
N. S. Junction	8 22	5 57
Brislington	8 33	6 8
Pensford dep.	8 35	6 10
Pensford arr.	8 46	6 20
Clutton	8 50	6 25
Hallatrow	9 0	6 35
Radstock dep.	9 5	6 40
Radstock arr.	9 7	6 42
Mells	9 15	6 50
Frome	9 30	7 5

A ST No. 133. This Train to leave Goods Yard at 8.30, and be at N. S. Junction to start sharp at 8.35. **Y** This mark indicates where Trains cross each other. **E** When necessary a second Engine can go to Radstock coupled to 2.30 p.m. Goods, and Station Masters, Signalmen, and others concerned must understand that it will return as a Special at 8.20 p.m. as per Time Table, and arrange staff working accordingly. Mr. Walton must be advised the day before.

Working timetable, down trains, 1st March, 1882.

RADSTOCK AND FROME TO BRISTOL—continued.

UP TRAINS—WEEK DAYS.

Distance	STATIONS		1 Coal A.M.	2 Passenger A.M.	3 Coal A.M.	4 Coal A.M.	5 Passenger A.M.	6 Coal A.M.	7 Passenger A.M.	8 Coal A.M.	9 Goods & Coal A.M.	10 Coal noon	11 Coal P.M.	12 Coal P.M.	13 Passenger P.M.	14 Coal P.M.	15 Coal P.M.	16 Passenger P.M.	17 Goods P.M.	18 Goods & Coal P.M.	19 Passenger P.M.	20 Goods & Coal P.M.
	Frome	dep.	..	7 15	..	..	..	..	10 45	11 45	..	..	1 40	2 45	2 20	3 50	..	5 0	..	..	7 45	..
5¾	Mells	{ arr.	8 30	X 7 33	8 30	8 35	..	10 0	11 0	12 5	..	12 0	2 0	3 0	2 35	4 10	4 20	5 14	..	ST	8 0	..
		{ dep.	6 45	7 40	8 55	8 50	..	10 15	11 8	..	11 20	12 15	..	..	2 43	..	4 35	5 23	..	5 40	8 10	8 20
8¾	Radstock	dep.	..	7 45	..	..	9 10	..	11 10	..	..	..	..	..	2 45	..	..	5 25	..	6 5	..	..
...	Wells Way		..	..	..	..	..	..	..	..	11 55	..	..	..	2 50	..	..	5 30	..	CR	8 15	8 35
10½	Old Welton Siding		..	7 50	..	..	9 15	..	11 15	..	CR	..	..	..	..	..	..	..	..	6 45	8 26	..
11¼	Welton		..	8 0	..	..	9 25	..	11 25	..	12 10	..	..	..	3 0	..	..	5 38	6 25	6 45	8 30	8 55
13¾	Old Mills Siding		..	8 5	..	..	9 30	..	11 30	..	..	..	..	..	3 5	..	..	5 43	..	7 10	8 38	..
14¾	Hallatrow		..	8 13	..	..	9 39	..	11 40	..	12 20	..	..	..	3 12	..	..	5 50	6 48	7 25	X	..
	Clutton		..	..	..	..	X	..	..	..	X	..	..	..	X	..	..	..	..	X	..	..
18	Pensford	{ arr.	..	8 15	..	..	9 40	..	11 41	..	12 50	..	..	..	3 15	..	..	5 51	6 50	7 50	8 40	9 20
		{ dep.	..	8 27	..	..	9 45	..	..	..	1 10	..	..	..	3 28	..	..	6 3	..	8 10	8 53	..
22½	Brislington	»	..	..	..	..	..	..	..	..	..	..	..	..	..	..	..	..	..	X	..	..
24	N. Som. Junction		..	..	..	..	..	..	..	..	1 20	..	..	..	..	..	..	..	..	..	9 0	9 40
24¾	Bristol	arr.	..	8 35	..	..	10 5	..	11 55	..	..	..	..	..	3 35	..	..	6 10	7 20	8 20	9 0	9 40

SUNDAYS.

	1 Passenger A.M.	2 Passenger P.M.
Frome	10 0	8 15
Mells	10 16 / 10 23	8 30 / 8 35
Radstock	10 25	8 40
Welton	10 30	8 45
Old Mills Siding	10 40	8 55
Hallatrow	10 45	9 0
Clutton	10 54	9 7
Pensford	10 55	9 10
Brislington	11 8	9 22
Bristol	11 15	9 30

CROSSING INSTRUCTIONS.

The 6.30 a.m. Bristol Passenger crosses the 7.15 a.m. Frome Passenger at Mells.
The 8.30 a.m. Bristol Goods crosses the 8.10 a.m. Rad-tock at Pensford.
The 7.55 a.m. Bristol Passenger crosses the 7.16 a.m. Frome at Pensford.
The 10.12 a.m. ex Bristol, crosses the 10.45 a.m. ex Frome, between Mells and Radstock.
The 12.15 p.m. Bristol Passenger crosses the 11.20 a.m., Goods at Pensford.
The 2.30 p.m. Bristol Goods crosses the 2.20 p.m. Frome Passenger at Pensford.
The 4.30 p.m., ex Bristol, crosses the 5.0 p.m., ex Frome at Radstock.
The 7.25 p.m. ex Bristol, crosses the 6.40 p.m. Goods at Pensford.
The 7.25 p.m. ex Bristol crosses the 7.45 p.m. ex Frome at Radstock.

ST No. 150.

Working timetable, up trains, 1st March, 1882.

Pensford viaduct dominates the village. *Author's Collection*

Sandy Park Road overbridge, Brislington, *circa* 1890. Since this date the land has been developed. *M.J. Tozer Collection*

Joseph Wethered in the Chair explained that as the company had been sold to the GWR it existed only as a company for winding-up purposes. He said that it had been suggested that those who had carried on the affairs of the company should continue to act as liquidators and their remuneration be 1 per cent on the stock of the company. This resolution was put and carried.

The branch prospered under GWR control and little of note occurred until industrial trouble raised its head in the 20th century. A meeting arranged for members of the Amalgamated Society of Railway Servants was held at Radstock on Sunday evening 20th August, 1911, to publicize the grievance of long hours for inadequate pay. The average wage of a signalman was £1 3s. 2d., a porter 17s. 5d., carman 19s. 11d. and goods porter 19s. 8d. The meeting had been arranged before the settlement of the national 2-day strike on 19th August. Had the strike lasted much longer, collieries would have had to have closed as no wagons were available to remove the coal lifted. Kilmersdon Colliery and Middle Pit (the latter linked to the Somerset & Dorset), closed on 21st August due to a shortage of wagons. Farrington Gurney closed by the 18th, but reopened on the 22nd, but this had been caused by a miners' and not the railway strike.

A blizzard at the end of March 1916 caused telegraph poles between Radstock and Midsomer Norton to lean.

The branch provided an alternative route in the event of main line damage. On 24th October, 1940 at 1.30 pm, high explosive bombs damaged all four roads at Huish Crossing, west of Yatton and traffic had to be diverted Bristol-Radstock-Frome until two lines were opened at Huish at 7.15 pm. On 6th December, 1940 three coaches of the 5.57 pm for Frome, standing at platform 2 at Temple Meads , were set on fire by incendiary bombs. Also that evening block instruments for the Marsh Junction to Pensford section failed, so passenger trains temporarily terminated at Brislington.

At 9.30 pm on Saturday 1st March, 1941 Whitchurch Airfield was attacked unsuccessfully, but high explosive bombs fell on the branch line near Whitchurch Halt. A bus substitute was inaugurated from Pensford to Bristol for one Sunday train until the line was cleared at 11.30 am. On the night of 11th and 12th April, 1941, two high explosive bombs damaged the line between Whitchurch and Pensford, but normal working was resumed within a few hours – which was fortunate as on that occasion Bristol Tramways & Carriage Company was unable to supply substitute buses. A few days later an unexploded bomb was detonated *in situ* on 18th April, 1941 at 11.00 am, buses conveying passengers from Bristol to Pensford until 3.25 pm. In the Bath blitz on 25th and 26th April, 1942 the main line was blocked, so some Weymouth trains ran over the Radstock line to Frome. Thicket Mead bridge, west of Midsomer Norton, 10 miles 17 chains from Frome, was destroyed by enemy action and replaced with way beams and temporary hand rails.

On 24th March, 1959 British Railways (BR) announced the withdrawal of passenger and parcels services on the branch. During one week in January 1959 the number of passengers using the line only totalled 363. Midsomer Norton was the busiest station, 52 passengers joining and 47 alighting, followed by Clutton with 52 and 29 respectively. Hallatrow had but eight in each category. Sunday services only operated in the summer and a census during five Sundays

'45XX' class 2-6-2T No. 4567 arrives at Radstock with the 10.50 am Temple Meads to Frome service on 8th April, 1958. *R.E. Toop/Author's Collection*

'8750' class 0-6-0PT No. 9615 heads the 4.05 pm Frome to Bristol by Frome New Quarry North ground frame on 8th August, 1959. *Michael Jenkins*

in August 1958 revealed each of the three trains each way only carried an average of nine passengers. Midsomer Norton and Radstock stations each dealt with an average of four passengers on a Sunday, while Pensford was not used by a single passenger. British Railways claimed that the branch lost £8,313 annually on gross receipts and that closure would save £20,103 a year. The cost of £42,500 to introduce diesel-multiple-units (dmus) was not therefore an option. The branch was to remain open for freight and mineral traffic which was still healthy – the collieries at Old Mills and Kilmersdon were still producing, while Whatley Quarry provided a significant amount of traffic.

The withdrawal of passenger services was planned for Sunday 13th September, 1959, the end of the summer timetable, but as a strike of print workers that July delayed the issue of the winter timetable, closure was delayed until Monday 2nd November, 1959. Sunday services had ceased with the expiry of the summer timetable, so the last scheduled trains ran on 31st October, 1959. As a party of RCTS members travelled on the 2.53 pm Bristol to Frome, the normal 2-coach 'B' set was strengthened with three corridor coaches, the train worked by '4575' class 2-6-2T No. 5532 from Frome shed. They returned in the same stock on the 5.55 pm express with BR Standard class '3' 2-6-2T No. 82035 piloting No. 5532. The same rake was used for the 7.45 pm, the last down train. The 9.25 pm return working was with Ivatt class '2' 2-6-2T No. 41203, assisted to Mells Road by Frome's 0-6-0PT No. 9612 coupled 'inside' the train engine. It was estimated that the train exploded over 100 detonators when it left Clutton. Brislington closed to goods traffic on 7th October, 1963 as did other stations on 15th June, 1964, except for Radstock which closed on 29th November, 1965 having been a coal depot only from 17th May, 1965.

From October 1960 supplementary operating instructions ruled that all signal lamps between Frome and Pensford should not be lit from 1st April to 30th September, but that all signal lamps must be filled, trimmed and stored in the lamp huts ready for use in the event of trains having to run during hours of darkness.

On 15th August, 1966 the Radstock to Mells Road section closed, Radstock coal being sent out via Bristol. Mells Road continued to deal with bitumen traffic and stone traffic from Whatley was healthy. On 12th June, 1968, H.C. Sanderson, divisional manager, West of England, said that the single line would be reopened between Mells Road and Radstock West to permit the line being closed between 8 miles 45.2 chains at Radstock and 22 miles 61.6 chains at Bristol, Marsh Junction, the effective date for this being 1st July, 1968. Non-completion of signalling and telegraph work delayed the reopening and this was amended to 15th July. However, on 10th July an unusually violent rainstorm caused a very serious slip to the embankment north of Pensford which had always given trouble. A special last passenger train to have run from Bristol to Frome on 29th June, 1968 was cancelled due to a 'work to rule'. This meant that the RCTS 'Thames & Avon' railtour on 6th April, 1968 was the last passenger train to run over the whole of the branch.

In 1968 the double track from Mells Road to Radstock was reduced to a single operating line, though the second track remained in place. The up line was used for approximately ½ mile from Mells Road and then the track was slewed across to the down line for the remainder of the section to Radstock. This proposal had

BR Standard class '3' 2-6-2T No. 82042 heads the 12 noon Frome to Temple Meads on the last day of Sunday service, 13th September, 1959 at Radstock. It is a very pleasant weather and the passengers appear to be going for a day out. *Michael Jenkins*

'2251' class 0-6-0 No. 2273 at Mells Road with a down goods on 19th April, 1963. The engine looks as if a clean-up would not go amiss. No. 2273 went new to Carmarthen, then Landore and finished at Westbury being withdrawn in December 1963. The fourth vehicle is a bulk grain wagon. *Author*

A 4-car dmu works an RCTS special from London on 6th April, 1968. This was the last passenger-carrying train over Pensford viaduct. *Clutton History Group*

The 'Somerset Quarryman' special at Radstock on 28th September, 1974. This railtour was organized by the Dean Forest Railway Preservation Society. The wagons are awaiting repair, or have been repaired. *W.H. Harbor/ Author's Collection*

Class '117' Pressed Steel 3-car suburban dmu set No. C469 and class '119' Gloucester Railway Carriage & Wagon Co. 3-car Cross-Country set No. C590 at the east end of Mells Road layout with a Great Western Society special on 28th October, 1978.   *W.H. Harbor*

been made as early as June 1948. By the disused Radstock South signal box a large stencilled notice read: 'Stop. Start of OEIS Line'.* Although Midsomer Norton closed to goods on 15th June, 1964, the line from Radstock was not closed until 31st December, 1968. The track from Marsh Junction to Radstock was lifted in April and May 1969.

The last coal was wound at Kilmersdon Colliery on 31st August, 1973 and at Lower Writhlington on 28th September, 1973, the final coal train leaving on 16th November, 1973. Approximately once a week a train continued to run to Radstock with wagons for repair at Marcroft's wagon works. In the spring of 1977 trial trains removed spoil from Kilmersdon, but were soon discontinued. Work at Marcroft's eventually ceased and the last train left on 29th June, 1988, No. 47370 heading the final train. The branch was officially closed, but the track from Radstock to Hapsford Loop was left *in situ* and still remains 25 years later.

A view from outside the former Radstock locomotive shed looking towards the buffers at Radstock on 30th March, 1983.   *Author*

---

* OEIS = one engine in steam.

Chapter Three

Description of the Line

Passenger trains normally started from Bristol, Temple Meads and ran over the main London line for ¾ mile to North Somerset Junction (23 miles 26 chains from Frome). The first signal box here opened in February 1873 to deal with construction trains and was replaced by a new box on 22nd March, 1886. This box closed on 20th July, 1970. A powerful stench from the adjacent Coles' glue factory penetrated the box. It was slightly less pungent in the centre and at the Bath end, rather than Temple Meads end. The smell seemed worse on humid summer nights.

Priority at the box was to avoid delays to trains on the main Temple Meads to Bath line. The art of achieving this lay in the timing of trains to and from South Wales and the North of England from Dr Day's Bridge Junction signal box across the main line and round the Bristol Avoiding Line (which also commenced at North Somerset Jn). The location on the main line of a higher class train had to be checked by telephoning various boxes in order to avoid it being delayed by another train crossing the main line and rounding a speed-restricted curve. The box had about 13 telephones and 93 levers.

Since about 1892 branch goods trains normally left from Bristol East Depot down yard and immediately after crossing the Avon bridge, at East Depot Junction curved south to join the line from North Somerset Junction at Marsh Junction north. Between North Somerset Junction and Marsh Junction (23 miles 6 chains), a facing siding off the up line served Bennett's Colliery siding from November 1898 until June 1924. Marsh Junction signal box was where the lines from North Somerset Junction and East Depot Junction converged and those to the Avoiding Line (also known as the Relief Line) and the Radstock branch diverged. Marsh Junction had a new signal box on 2nd March, 1959, but was closed on 20th July, 1970. As the box was on the driver's side of the line, when he collected a staff this necessitated taking his eyes off the curving road. On one occasion this resulted in a death. The inquiry showed that if the fireman had been responsible for collecting the staff, that person would have been noticed and the accident prevented.

The construction of the relief line incurred re-aligning the BNSR. To the east of Marsh Junction were Marsh Pond Carriage Sidings opened in the spring of 1917 to store empty coaching stock of ammunition workers' trains. At the south end of these sidings the track became single, the parallel line being a shunting neck.

The BNSR crossed the 72 yds-long Avon viaduct (22 miles 71 chains). This was replaced between 10.30 pm Saturday 26th September, 1959 and early Monday morning 28th September, by a concrete and steel span with a flood arch on each side. The steel was supplied by the Fairfield Shipbuilding & Engineering Co. Ltd. When the Radstock branch closed, this bridge remained as it carried a headshunt for the carriage sidings.

The BNSR climbed at 1 in 62 passing beneath the A4 Bath Road by an unassuming bridge. To cope with increased traffic it was widened on its

'45XX' class 2-6-2T No. 4551 with a B-set, leaves Temple Meads, Bristol, for Frome in May 1956. A 'Britannia' class 4-6-2 can just be seen in the background. *P.Q. Treloar Collection*

BR Standard class '3' 2-6-2T No. 82042 with the 12 noon Frome to Temple Meads train approaches North Somerset Junction on Sunday 13th September, 1959 - the last day of Sunday working. The bridge spanning the Feeder (a canal which takes water from the River Avon to the floating harbour) is to the left of the signal box, as is Coles' glue factory. *Michael Jenkins*

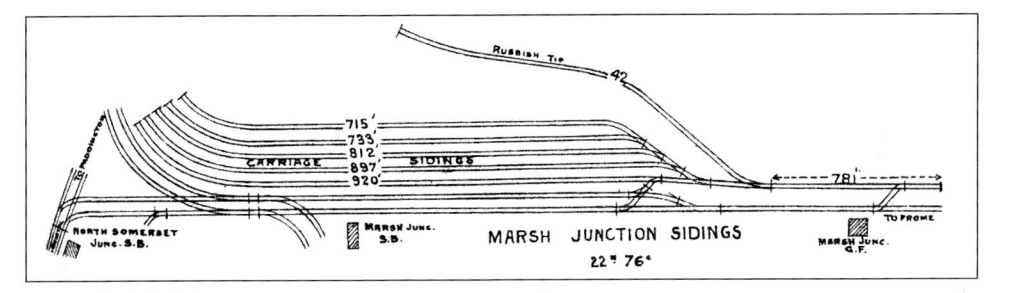

A view of Bristol East Depot looking westwards, probably just prior to its opening in 1890. The main line on the far right is mixed gauge. Bristol No. 1 Tunnel signal box, shown in the centre of the photograph, closed with the opening of the depot. *Author's Collection*

Bristol East Depot, view west, August 1936. *M.J. Tozer Collection*

An 0-6-0PT heads the 7.45 pm Saturdays-only service over the 73 yds-long River Avon viaduct on 18th July, 1959. The B-set has been strengthened with a corridor coach. *Michael Jenkins*

View across the River Avon viaduct towards Marsh Junction in 1959. The dmu depot is in the distance at right-angles to the branch. Just to the right of the modern flat-roofed Marsh Junction signal box is an 0-6-0PT with coaches. Only the running line (*left*) has viaduct guards, note the shunting neck on the right. *John Mann Collection*

Reconstructing the River Avon viaduct, 19th November, 1959. *John Mann Collection*

southern side in 1937 by W.T. Nicholls Ltd. The cutting here is now used as a vehicle park for a Mormon church. Although latterly a suburb of Bristol, the single-platformed Brislington station (22 miles 01 chains) retained its rural village appearance. Originally having just a single siding, on 18th August, 1906 a second siding was brought into use. Its signal box probably closed by 1900 and was replaced by a ground frame. On 14th April, 1908 the sidings were extended at their northern ends to form goods loops. The points at the Bristol end of the sidings could only be used by up trains. Both sidings and their ground frames were taken out of use on 14th June, 1964.

The passenger platform was extended to 365 ft at its northern end on 25th April, 1908. The building, constructed of brick and stone, was designed by the BNSR Engineer William Clarke who favoured the use of a standard building. Single-storey in design, the main building had three chimney stacks serving respectively the booking office, general waiting room and ladies' waiting room fires. Each chimney had two or three vertical stone deflectors. A flat-roofed extension contained a coal house, store and lamp room, gentlemen's urinal and WC, the ladies' toilet being accessed from their waiting room. The whole of the beautifully proportioned building was about 55 ft in length and 16 ft wide. A flat-roofed canopy supported by brackets sheltered the platform in front of the booking office and waiting rooms. At Brislington the station was set on the east side of the line. In 1955 BR proposed to replace oil lamps with electric lighting, but this work was never carried out. The opening of the electric tramway to Brislington in 1900 drew many passengers from the station.

Circa 1900 a station master and porter were employed, but a report of 15th January, 1921 revealed that Brislington then had a station master and two porters and that no reduction in staff could be made. By 1959 the station was only staffed from 6.45 am until 3.15 pm, after which it was treated as an unstaffed halt.

The goods yard dealt with coal traffic and in the 1950s much scrap was handled. Although Messrs Robertson's marmalade and jam factory, opened in 1915, was adjacent, apart from workers, latterly it did not put much traffic on the line. In 1920 it was reported that a decrease of £1,133 in annual receipts at the station was due to the reduced output of jam owing to fruit and sugar problems. The goods yard closed on 7th October, 1963 and by 11th June, 1967 the former passenger platform was caged-in as the property of a coal merchant. Brislington was one of the rare GWR stations which had neither goods shed nor a loading bank.

In April 1958 two chassis of 4-wheeled diesel 6-cylinder Gardner-engined railbuses were constructed at the nearby Bristol Commercial Vehicles' factory. After completion, they were given running tests from Marsh Junction to Pensford between 10.30 pm and 2.00 am – a period when the branch was normally unused – Pensford signal box being kept open for these runs. On trials these vehicles were operated by Bristol Commercial Vehicle drivers accompanied by a BR driver and inspector. Following tests, the chassis were sent by road to Eastern Counties Coachworks, Lowestoft, for bodies to be fitted. The railbuses which became SC79958 and 79959 worked on BR until 1968.

By mile post 22 at Brislington station was a stop board for up goods trains. It read: 'All Up Goods And Mineral Trains Must Stop Dead At This Board'. When

Ivatt class '2' 2-6-2T No. 41249 approaches Sandy Park Road bridge with the 5.20 pm Temple Meads to Frome service on 12th September, 1959. Railwaymen's allotments can be seen on both sides. *Michael Jenkins*

'1813' class 0-6-0ST No. 1819 and 2-4-0T 'Metro' No. 632 approach Brislington with a down train in 1908. The North ground frame is to the left of the leading engine. This view shows the A4 road bridge before it was widened. *Author's Collection*

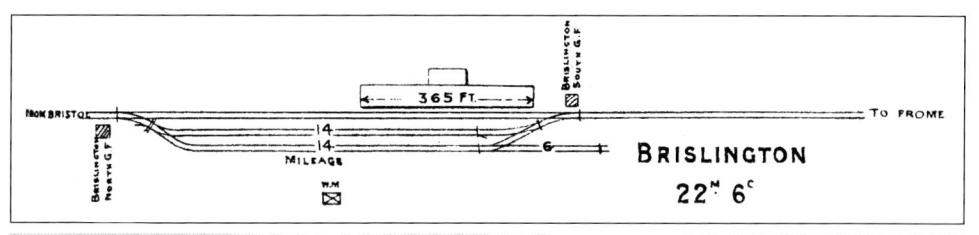

'57XX' class 0-6-0PT No. 7784 leaves Brislington with the 1.10 pm Frome to Temple Meads service on 28th March, 1959.
R.E. Toop/Author's Collection

'8750' class 0-6-0PT No. 3735 leaves Brislington with the 4.05 pm Saturdays-only Frome to Temple Meads train on 25th July, 1959. The coal yard is lower right and the scrap metal yard centre right. Robertson's marmalade and jam factory is visible beyond the station.
Michael Jenkins

Brislington station viewed in the down direction on 18th April, 1959. Notice the gas lamps and also the wires from the chimney stack supporting the generously-dimensioned platform canopy.
M.J. Tozer Collection

Staff at Brislington during World War I. *Left to right:* Mrs Swaine, leading porter; John Royale Williams, station master and Harold Hole, junior porter. An enamel advertisement publicizes Brooks' dye works.
Collection Mrs M. Mitchell

DESCRIPTION OF THE LINE 53

Brislington station and Robertson's jam factory *circa* 1920. A down passenger train with clerestory coaches leaves the station. Wagon loads of partly sheeted timber stand in the yard.
Author's Collection

Brislington station on 28th March, 1959. The jam factory is on the right. A steel-bodied coal wagon waits to be unloaded.
R.E. Toop/Author's Collection

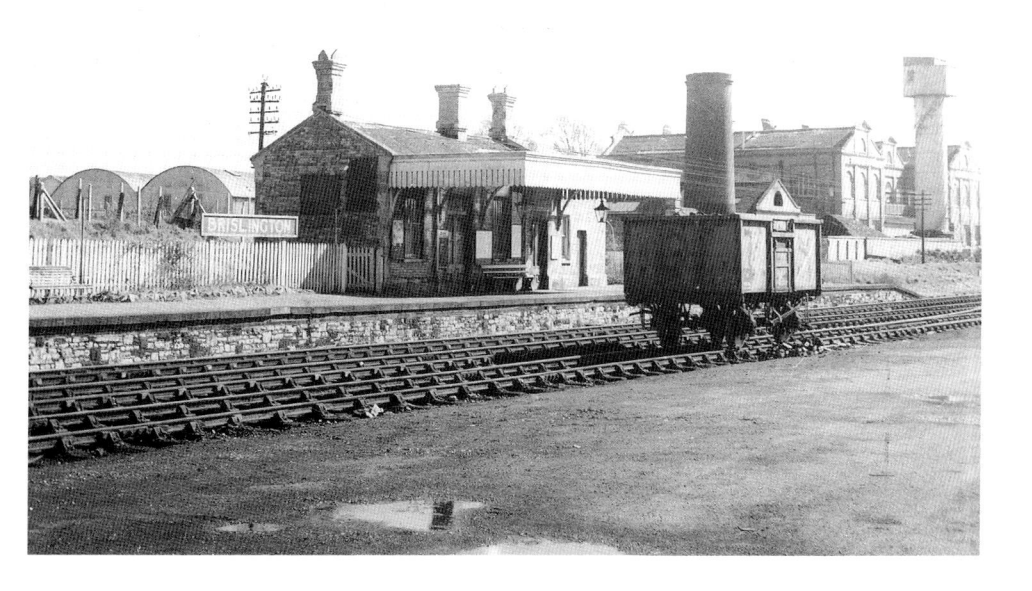

54 THE BRISTOL-RADSTOCK-FROME LINE

Brislington station pre-1906 with just a single siding. *M.J. Tozer Collection*

'4575' class 2-6-2T No. 5536 at Brislington with a Temple Meads-Frome service on 22nd May, 1959. The track dips sharply downwards at 1 in 62 at the rear of the train. *R.J. Sellick*

Brislington viewed in the down direction on 11th June, 1967. The sidings have been lifted and the former passenger platform belongs to a coal merchant - coal is stacked on the platform. The merchant is mechanized and has a tractor with a shovel for loading coal into the hopper. The former goods yard is utilized by the scrap metal merchant who owns a Ford 'Thames Trader'.
Author

Brislington *circa* 1965. Notice the caged former building in use by the coal merchant. The scrap merchant's yard is to the right.
Lens of Sutton Collection

56 THE BRISTOL-RADSTOCK-FROME LINE

'57XX' class 0-6-0PT No. 5757 arrives at Whitchurch Halt with the 2.53 pm Saturdays-only Temple Meads to Frome service on 18th April, 1959. It will pick up at least three passengers.
Michael Jenkins

BR Standard class '3' 2-6-2T No. 82040 passing Whitchurch Halt with the 10.50 am Frome-Temple Meads service on 31st October, 1959, the last day of passenger services.
Hugh Ballantyne

a train halted, the guard came forward and began pinning down the wagon brakes as the train moved forward at about 4 mph. When the driver was satisfied that sufficient brake levers had been dropped, he gave the guard two short blasts on the whistle and the guard would return to his van. Safely aboard, he waved his green flag. At the foot of the gradient the train stopped and the guard unpinned the brakes.

South of Brislington station the line fell at 1 in 233 for ¼ mile before rising at 1 in 63/60 for 2½ miles. West Town Lane overbridge was struck on several occasions by double-decker buses.

Whitchurch Halt (19 miles 73 chains) on a rising gradient of 1 in 63, opened on 1st January, 1925, south of the village and south of the A37 stone overbridge. Until the halt opened, villagers going to Bristol walked two miles to Knowle to catch an electric tram. Initially tickets at Whitchurch were sold at the post office or a nearby cottage. Later, staff at Brislington or Pensford were required to issue excess notes to passengers joining at the halt. The 150 ft-long platform had a typical GWR corrugated iron pagoda shelter and the total cost of constructing the halt was £358 12s. 6d. It was sited on the west side of the line. Latterly a Brislington porter caught the 1.38 pm from Brislington (the 1.30 pm Temple Meads to Frome), trimmed and filled lamps at Whitchurch and swept the platform before returning on the 2.01 pm (1.10 pm ex-Frome). The guard of the last train turned out the lights, but sometimes a passenger offered to do it.

The rise continued beyond the halt to a stop board for down trains at the foot of Maes Knoll (19 miles 08 chains) in preparation for the 1 in 66/70 falling gradient, while at 19 miles 20 chains was a similar board for up trains.

Pensford (17 miles 29 chains) had the only original passing loop between Bristol and Radstock. Its signal box was renewed in 1898 when the loop was extended, but closed on 14th June, 1964, replaced by a ground frame. This in turn was closed on 6th March, 1966 when the goods shed (containing a 1 ton 5 cwt crane) and siding were taken out of use. The loop had been taken out of use in August 1960, the withdrawal of the passenger service having rendered it superfluous. In the early 1950s the goods shed was de-roofed because, with the introduction of zoning for small deliveries, freight was now delivered from Hallatrow. By 1959 the goods shed was given a corrugated iron roof and Gas Purification Ltd used it for manufacturing.

The station building, like all the others on the BNSR, was a standard William Clarke design in brick. The platform on the down side had a small timber shelter bearing a fretted canopy. The up platform was 253 ft long and the down 240 ft. The down home signal at the up end of the up platform, for easy sighting, was placed very high. Its lamp was raised and lowered on a chain, much better for members of staff who had no head for heights, as the signal was on an underline bridge.

Circa 1900 staffing consisted of a station master, signalman, signal porter and porter, but by 1st January, 1921 had increased to station master, four signalmen, a signal porter, parcel porter, porter and lad porter. Two of the signalmen were employed in the station box from 5.15 am to 1.15 pm and 3.45 pm to 11.45 pm, the period from 1.15 pm to 3.45 being covered by the signal porter. (The other two signalmen worked at Pensford & Bromley Colliery Sidings signal box.) When not

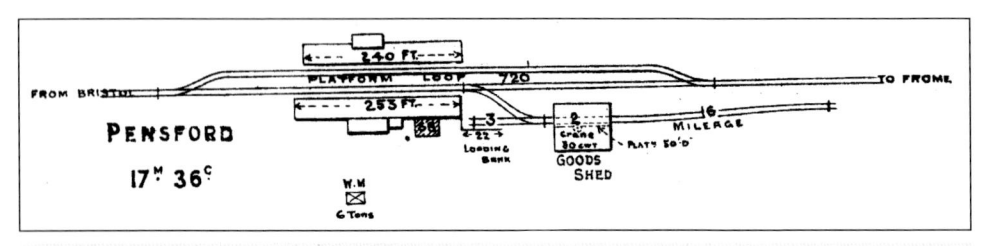

Pensford viewed in the up direction following the removal of the down platform loop in September 1960. The parapet of the new underline bridge can be seen by the signal. Notice that the height of the up platform has been doubled. The signal box closed on 14th June, 1964.
Lens of Sutton Collection

Pensford viewed in the down direction *circa* 1961.
Lens of Sutton Collection

DESCRIPTION OF THE LINE

Pensford station and goods yard *circa* 1910. *Author's Collection*

'4575' class 2-6-2T No. 4593 calls at Pensford with the 10.50 am Frome-Temple Meads service on 10th October, 1959. The train comprises two corridor coaches in carmine and cream. The signalman holds the single line token. *Hugh Ballantyne*

Two views of Pensford *circa* 1910: to the right of the viaduct (*in the lower picture*) low-sided wagons stand to the left of the goods shed. The road, later to become the A37, winds through the village. *(Both) Author's Collection*

signalling, the signal porter carried out clerical work. The parcel porter and porter took early and late turns and were in charge in the absence of the station master. Their chief duties were to shunt goods trains; check outwards goods traffic and obtain signatures for it; invoice outwards goods traffic; keep wagon and milk books; book parcels and milk traffic. The lad porter attended to the 47 signal lamps – including those at Pensford & Bromley; cleaned the lavatories and platform; attended to the fires and made up all collected tickets daily. ('Making up' involved sorting tickets into first/third; singles/returns or blank cards, so that the recorded destination in the Register of Blank Cards could be checked to see that it accorded with what was actually on the ticket.) Some voluntary assistance was given by signalman Westcott from the station box who made out coal invoices and assisted in entering up some goods books. Statistics for September 1920 were 2,299 passengers, 26 season tickets, 102 parcels forwarded, 4,372 cans of milk forwarded, 221 parcels received, 573 goods invoices forwarded and 177 received.

During World War II Mary Jewell was appointed signalwoman at Pensford after successfully passing a colour blindness test and a week's signalling training. Her sister Daisy joined the station as a porter. In 1942 Mary began her working day at 5.30 am with the arrival of the goods from East Depot. About 20 trains passed until the last working of the day, the Pensford & Bromley coal train which left for Bristol at about 10.30 pm. At that date the signal box was worked in two shifts: 5.30 am to 1.30 pm and 1.30 pm to 10.30 pm, six days a week. There was no Sunday working. The district inspector annually tested her knowledge of the rule book and signalling. When an air raid warning was announced by phone, the Aladdin paraffin lamps were turned low and a hand lamp used when making entries in the train register. A radio, officially not permitted in a signal box, was hidden in a cupboard and helped to brighten dark evenings.

From the outset stations were capable of dealing with livestock, horse boxes, carriages and cars, as could all branch stations except Brislington and Mells Road, while Midsomer Norton was not able to deal with horse boxes, cars or carriages. The use of a tow rope, although generally banned, was authorized to be used at Pensford. *Circa* 1910 a GWR 'Design C' cottage was erected by Elijah Love for the station master.

North of the loop the embankment was prone to slipping, so was subject to a permanent 5 mph restriction. Over the years tons of ashes were tipped. Just before Christmas 1960 the underbridge at 17 miles 33½ chains, just north of the station, was replaced by one of a pre-stressed concrete beam type from the Taunton concrete depot. Work at an estimated cost of £6,400 was carried out over about three weekends, a '53XX' class Mogul with a 45 ton steam crane assisting the operation. As the crossing loop had been taken out of use, only a single-line bridge was required.

South of the station is the Grade 2-listed 330 yds-long Pensford viaduct 95 ft high. It has 16 semi-circular arches, the 14 largest each spanning 50 ft, are constructed of quarry-faced stone, said to be from Cloud Hill Quarry near Hallatrow. Four arches are followed by a pierced pier forming a small arch; then follow six arches; a pierced pier and another four arches. It was wide enough for double track, but only a single line was ever laid. The viaduct in recent years has received repair grants of over £700,000.

No. 3440 *City of Truro* crosses Pensford viaduct on 28th April, 1957. '4575' class 2-6-2T No. 5528, as assistant engine, in true GWR fashion is placed 'inside' the main engine. No. 5528 is in the green lined livery permitted that year to many classes hitherto black, or lined black.

Hugh Ballantyne

An 'ROD' 2-8-0 heads a train of mainly empty wagons across Pensford viaduct *circa* 1950. It has plenty of steam for the climb ahead.

Colin Roberts Collection

DESCRIPTION OF THE LINE 63

BR Standard class '3' 2-6-2T No. 82035 heads the 10.00 am Sundays-only Temple Meads-Frome service over Pensford viaduct on 28th June, 1959. The B-set is strengthened with a BR non-corridor coach. *Michael Jenkins*

'5101' class 2-6-2T No. 5104 heads across Pensford viaduct with an up freight on 2nd May, 1959. *R.E. Toop*

Pensford & Bromley Siding
16m 59c

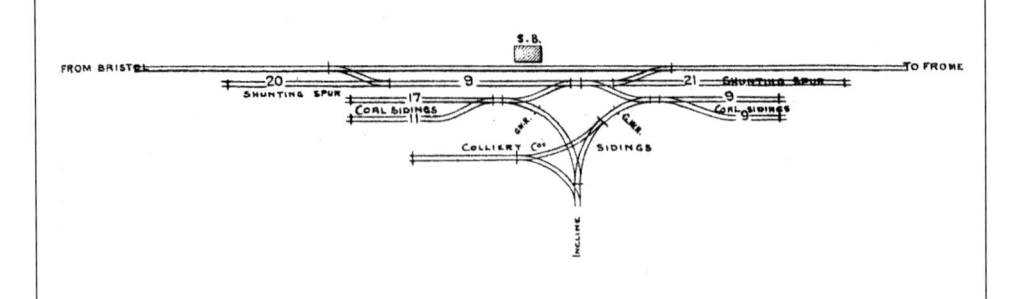

Pensford & Bromley Colliery sidings on 8th September, 1953. An empty end-door mineral wagon with its end doors secured out of use is hauled by steel cable to the colliery from the empty wagon spur. Loaded wagons are in the siding on the far right. *Author*

DESCRIPTION OF THE LINE

From a catch point at the foot of the gradient, the line rose at 1 in 60 to Pensford & Bromley Colliery signal box (16 miles 52 chains), opened on 27th August, 1911 to control the entrance to four sidings and a goods loop. At Pensford & Bromley, two goods trains, or a goods and a passenger train could cross, but not two passenger trains. From 1st May until 30th September its signal lamps were unlit as the box was closed during the hours of darkness.

Bromley Colliery itself had opened by 1893 and rumour tells that it only became a mine by pure chance and was only intended to be a well for watering cattle, the shaft was certainly very small. It was also rumoured that at one time, Bromley Colliery, in debt to the GWR, settled finances by supplying the railway with coal. The results was many rough trips for locomotives as the coal supplied was of very poor quality.

Although work on a siding and a new shaft at Pensford started in 1910, due to great problems coping with an influx of water, regular coal winding could not start until 1917. The colliery was sited about 100 ft above the level of the GWR. An agreement was signed on 9th September, 1910 for a self-acting incline, terminating right at the pithead. As this layout would have made working difficult, plans were amended on 15th March, 1911 making the incline longer and less steep. The method of working was changed from self-acting, to haulage engine.

The 400 yds-long incline was constructed and open by 1912, small quantities of coal being raised in January that year, but until 1917, when the colliery came into full production, it is likely that a greater tonnage was hauled up the incline than was lowered down it. An agreement dated 7th June, 1919 modified the layout.

West of the GWR line was a loop from which two sidings ran uphill for holding empty wagons, another two sidings running downhill for loaded wagons; both pairs of sidings had a capacity of about 43 wagons each. A spur was provided for each pair of sidings in order that shunting operations could take place independently of working over the main line.

A short rake of empty wagons was allowed to run by gravity across the foot of the incline via diamond crossing, momentum causing them to run up into another siding. From there, the wagon's coupling was hooked to the steel cable taken from a wagon just descended, a hawser being looped round the leading axle and also hooked to the cable as a safety precaution in the event of the coupling snapping. When all was ready, a ring was given on the bell signal communicating between the incline winding house and the hut at the foot of the incline. Empty wagons on arrival at the head of the incline were run back by gravity into the pithead sidings, while still attached to the cable.

A loaded wagon was hauled from the pithead sidings to the head of the incline and lowered to its foot where it was unhooked and allowed to gravitate to the lower sidings. It is believed that there was only one accident on the incline, this occurring about 1917 when a wagon became detached from the cable, derailed on the diamond crossing and rolled over three times.

This incline was capable of dispatching up to eight loaded wagons an hour, though the normal daily traffic was about thirty 10-ton wagons.

The National Coal Board issued instructions to its staff to ensure the safe working of the incline. These also appeared in the BR Working Timetable Appendix:

A loaded wagon descends the incline from Pensford Colliery on 8th September, 1953. *Author*

Uncoupling a loaded wagon on 8th September, 1953 by removing the hook fixed to the coupling chain and the wire rope attached to the axle. *Author*

DESCRIPTION OF THE LINE

1. On no account must wagons be sent down the Incline unless the Signal at the top is set to 'clear'.
2. Not more than one loaded wagon or one empty wagon may be allowed to travel upon the Incline at any single journey, either up or down, and every wagon, loaded or empty, must have the safety rope attached to axle of the wagon in addition to the ordinary coupling attached to the rope.
3. The Engineman shall not start the upward journey until he has received the proper Signal from the Shunter in charge at the bottom.
4. The Engineman shall not lower a journey until he has received the proper Signal from the Starter at the bottom that he is in charge of the Catch Points.
5. The Shunter at the top shall signal to the Shunter at the bottom when the journey is ready to be sent down the incline.

The Signalman on duty at Pensford & Bromley Siding signal box must see that these instructions are properly observed, as far as he is able to check them, and immediately report to the Station Master at Pensford any departure therefrom, especially in regard to what is shewn in Clause 2.

Pensford & Bromley signal box with 26 levers and six spares, was opened on 27th August, 1911 to work the new sidings which were not inspected by Lt Colonel Sir H. Arthur Yorke until 2nd March, 1912. He said that the semaphore signal lights from loop to main line were white instead of red. As it was a goods loop, it meant that passenger trains were prohibited from using it. The signal box in later years opened only in the mornings to deal with the arrival of empty and the departure of loaded wagons, the wages of the signalman being paid jointly by the railway and the colliery. The colliery presented signalmen at the box with £3 every Christmas. An electric train staff was in use between Pensford and Pensford & Bromley, and when the latter box was closed and out of circuit, the electric train tablet was in use between Pensford and Clutton, the next box on the south side.

Because of the gradient, a train was not allowed to stand on the main line unless the engine was attached, or a brake van at the Pensford end. A coal washing plant was opened at Pensford Colliery in 1935, for many years it being the only Somerset pit with this facility, but after 1st October, 1953, Pensford coal was sent to the washery at Old Mills Colliery near Midsomer Norton. It was interesting that coal for use at Pensford Colliery had to be sent to Old Mills and then returned after washing. A daily train ran from Pensford to Old Mills, often difficulty being experienced in starting up the gradient of 1 in 60, even though the shunting spur placed the rear of the train on a downward gradient.

Although Pensford was the second largest pit in Somerset, owing to the rise and fall of the seams due to faulting, an above average number of stationary haulage engines were required underground thus making the pit expensive to work. As it was not economic to modernize, the pit closed, the last coal being raised on 13th December, 1958 and the siding agreement with BR terminated on 9th July, 1959. The signal box closed on 22nd March, 1960.

A 2 ft gauge tramway linked Bromley Colliery with that at Pensford Colliery about a mile distant. In 1909 Bromley was bought by the company which was to open the pit at Pensford. It laid a tramway across the fields using embankment and cuttings to give access to Pensford Colliery and the GWR.

Skips on the 2ft gauge tramway between Bromley and Pensford collieries on 23rd August, 1956. The rope returns on the left-hand side of the track. *Author*

Pensford & Bromley slip on 26th January, 1951. In the distance can be seen the excavator used to remove spoil, and beyond are empty wagons in Pensford & Bromley Colliery sidings.
John Mann Collection

An 0-4-0ST was purchased to work the line, *Bromley No. 1*, built by the Avonside Engine Co., Bristol, in 1910 (Works No. 1593). It proved underpowered and prone to derailment. It was sold in 1913 to the Old Delabole Slate Co. Ltd, Cornwall and they resold it to Harper Brothers & Co. for use on construction works at Catterick Camp. It was replaced on the Bromley line by main and tail rope haulage, the cable passing over rollers in the centre of the track and returning by the side. It was capable of moving about 50 tubs at a time. Each tub held 7½ cwt of coal and tared at 3 cwt 35 lb. The rails were in 18 ft lengths fixed directly to wooden sleepers. In 1914 the cost of carrying coal to Pensford Colliery was 2*d*. a ton. Output from the colliery was the lowest in Somerset and it was the last pit in the county to use pit ponies. It closed on 18th May, 1957.

In 1941 Pensford & Bromley collieries with 492 employees had the largest production in the Somerset coalfield, 2,300 tons weekly.

In the evening of 25th November, 1946 the track at 16 miles 40 chains in the cutting south of the colliery lifted about 4 ft for a distance of 120 ft due to presssure from a 100 ft high coal tip on the up side of the line, part of which had slipped. The formation was lowered and the slipped material removed by mechanical excavator. A concrete toe wall was built to retain the bank. Until the line reopened in March 1947 passengers were carried by bus between Temple Meads and Clutton, buses calling at the two intermediate stations and halt.

Only 67 miners worked at Bromley in 1951 when the output was the lowest in Somerset – about 10,000 tons annually. Following the installation of pithead baths at Pensford Colliery in 1931 – the first in Somerset – Bromley miners shared them, being transported along the tramway and back in miniature coaches.

The climb at 1 in 60 away from the sidings on several occasions caused '43XX' class Moguls to slip to a standstill on an 'S'-bend and necessitated the train having to be divided. Near the summit at 14 miles 57 chains was a stop board for up trains while a nearby stone overbridge had a parapet wall only 2 ft high surmounted with a railing of 1½ inch conduit. The line descended at 1 in 71 to Clutton (14 miles 13 chains).

The up platform at Clutton had a Clarke building in brick and stone. It contained, working in the down direction: station master's office; waiting room; ladies' room and gentlemen's urinal and store set side by side. A timber parcels office was added early in the 20th century. Both platforms were 390 ft in length. The down platform, opened in September 1890, had a small waiting shelter with an angled canopy and probably the signal box opened on the same date. Passenger and goods traffic was boosted by the annual Clutton flower show. The goods yard had three looped sidings, a loading dock siding and another terminal siding. The goods shed contained a 30 cwt crane. The permanent way trolley was kept in a hut by the Greyfield to Clutton underbridge. A private siding gave access to the Bristol & Clutton Wagon Co.'s works– necessary due to Fry's Bottom, Burchells, Mooresland and Greyfield collieries being adjacent. All were part of the Earl of Warwick's group.

Fry's Bottom had opened in 1838, and at an estimated cost of £3,872 16*s*. 9*d*. the BNSR built a 1,474 yds-long connection to the colliery. Each cubic yard of excavation cost 1*s*. 2*d*., the permanent way material £1 5*s*. 0*d*. per yard and fencing 2*s*. 3*d*. per yard. Fry's Bottom and Greyfield branches were both built by Frederick George Saunders and Thomas Merriman Ward and opened about

CLUTTON
14ᴹ 17ᶜ

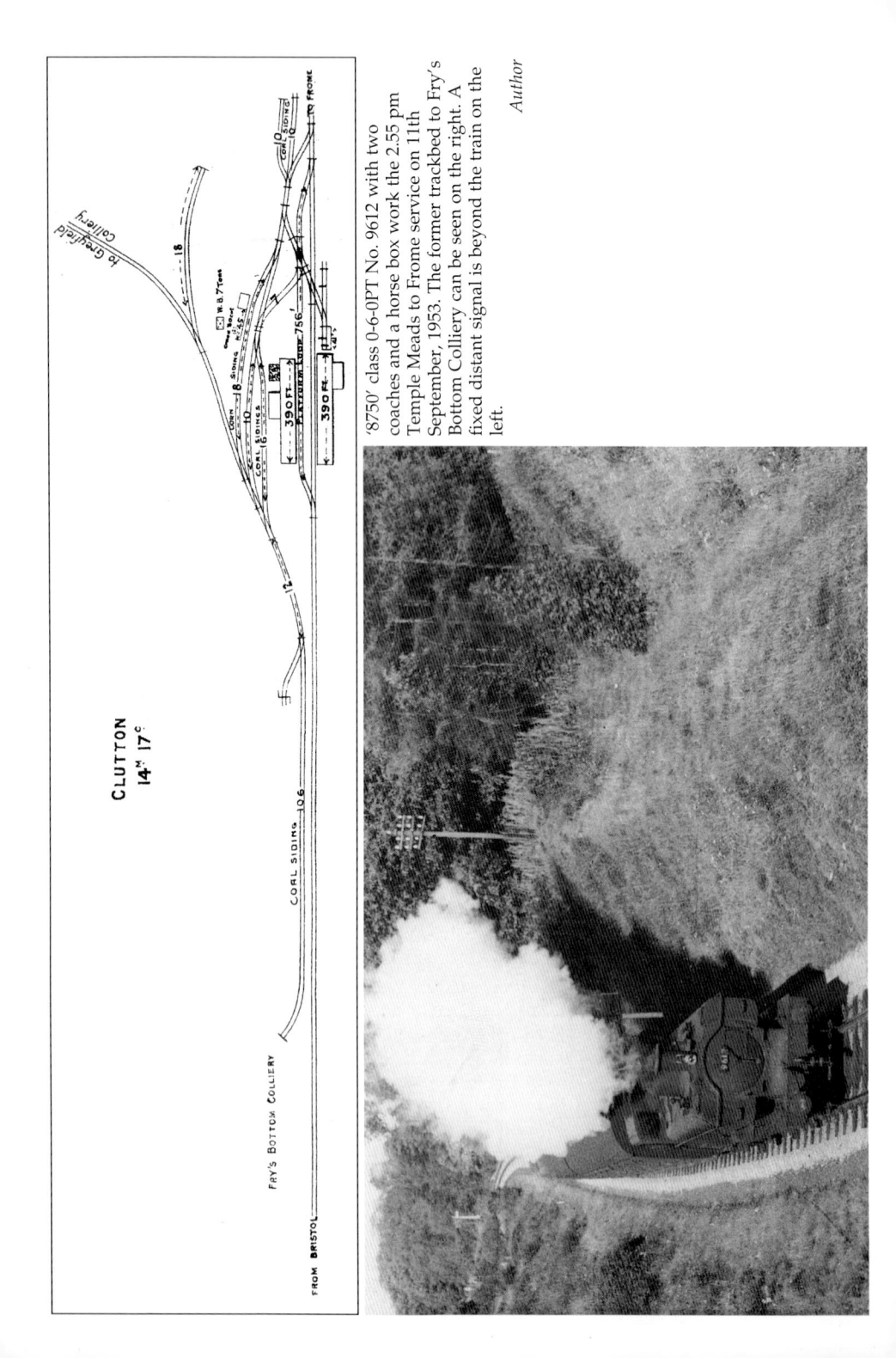

'8750' class 0-6-0PT No. 9612 with two coaches and a horse box work the 2.55 pm Temple Meads to Frome service on 11th September, 1953. The former trackbed to Fry's Bottom Colliery can be seen on the right. A fixed distant signal is beyond the train on the left.

Author

DESCRIPTION OF THE LINE 71

Clutton station was easily accessible to villagers. View *circa* 1905. *Clutton History Group*

'57XX' class 0-6-0PT No. 8744 arrives at Clutton with the 2.53 pm Saturdays-only Temple Meads to Frome train on 25th July, 1959. Each coach has a brake end. *Michael Jenkins*

The station staff near the parcel office *circa* 1930. Mr Gibbs, signalman, is on the left, while on the right is a bow-tie clad shunter with his pole.
Clutton History Group

A typical GWR station house at Clutton. Several low-sided, sheeted wagons are in the yard.
M.J. Tozer Collection

March 1876. Land for the branches was given by the Earl. Fry's Bottom pit closed on 31st May, 1895.

In due course a siding from Burchells Colliery was constructed to join the Fry's Bottom line 200 yards north of Clutton station. Burchells, or Clutton, Colliery, situated west of the station, began lifting coal in 1910 and by March 1912 employed nearly 350. Eventually it produced almost 800 tons per week, but due to flooding and lack of coal, mining ceased on 25th August, 1921. Greyfield Colliery opened south-east of Clutton in the mid-19th century as did Mooresland only 300 yards from Greyfield. The estimated cost of the 1 mile 12 chains-long siding to Greyfield was £6,305 19s. 2d. By 1889 Greyfield was producing about 60,000 tons per annum. As it had no road access, an inclined plane worked by a haulage engine was laid to a coal depot beside the Farmborough to High Littleton road, now the A39. Greyfield Colliery closed on 28th May, 1911 following royalty difficulties.

Originally wagons descended from Greyfield by gravity, horses drawing empties to the colliery. The first locomotive was *Frances*, an 0-4-0ST built by R. & W. Hawthorn (Works No. 2040 of 1885) and named after the colliery owner, the Earl of Warwick. It proved ineffective and was scrapped on site *circa* 1895 being replaced by *Daisy*, named after his wife. This was a Peckett 0-4-0ST (Works No. 581 of 1894). When Burchells Colliery closed on 25th August, 1921, *Daisy* was sold to Wynnstay Collieries Ltd, Denbighshire. *Circa* 1900 when *Daisy* was under repair, *Emlyn* was borrowed from C.D. Phillips of Newport. From about 1906 until closure about 1909, a siding from the colliery line also served Greyfield Brickworks.

The Earl of Warwick built a house, 'Oakdene', at High Littleton for use when he visited his Somerset estates and as a hunting lodge when hosting shooting parties. The Earl travelled by rail from Warwick to Clutton where his private railway coach was coupled to the colliery locomotive and hauled to Greyfield Colliery. The present Greyfield Road was merely a track, so for the convenience of himself and his guests, he had a causeway built along it. From *circa* 1896 'Oakdene' became the residence of the Earl's colliery manager.

About 1900 staff at Clutton consisted of a station master, signalman, signal porter, porter and lad porter, but by 3rd January, 1921 staffing had been increased to station master, lady clerk, two signalmen, a signal porter and two porters. The woman clerk worked early and later turns alternate weeks, booking passengers, invoicing outwards goods traffic, entering inwards and outwards goods books and the milk book, prepared statistical returns and passenger accounts, also assisting with goods and monthly parcels accounts.

The signal porter worked in the box from 1.45 pm to 3.30 pm daily and booked passengers on early and late turns when the lady clerk was off duty. The two porters covered 6.30 am to 10.15 pm, assisting with goods shunting, checking goods traffic, booking milk and parcels, recording inward parcels, attending to all platform and signal lamps and meeting passenger trains. The 1921 report mentioned a heavy decrease in forwarded coal traffic from 1920 due to decreased output, water in the pit and the miners' strike.

When Chew Valley reservoir was constructed in the late 1940s, the station dealt with 1,800 tons of pipes. Latterly containers of glass arrived at the station from Italy and Germany for use at the nearby Franco British Glass Factory.

Clutton viewed in the down direction *circa* 1910. A raft of coal wagons is in the distance while two horse boxes stand in the dock siding. The diamond-shaped plate hanging on the signal box displays a red 'T' on a white background, indicating to a travelling linesman that the telegraph equipment required attention.
Lens of Sutton Collection

Clutton station viewed in the up direction *circa* 1958.
Author's Collection

Clutton, view down, *circa* 1961. A notice at the platform end by the foot crossing reads 'Beware of Trains'. A single wheelbarrow is on the platform, alongside the 4-wheel trolley.
Author's Collection

Clutton, view up, *circa* 1961. As the passenger service has been withdrawn, the waiting shelter on the up platform has been dismantled leaving a gap in the fencing.   *Lens of Sutton Collection*

A scene at Greyfield Colliery, wagons, *left to right*, are: Deane & Son, Winchester; Huntley & Cockram, Lawrence Hill, Bristol; H.J. Pullin; two Clutton Colliery wagons and 0-4-0ST *Daisy*. As the wagons are dumb-buffered, this indicates that the photograph was taken pre-31st December, 1914, after which dumb-buffered wagons were not permitted to run on the main line.

Author's Collection

Right: This Clutton Colliery wagon in the repair yard is newly painted. The legend on it reads: 'Empty to Clutton Somerset GWR. For repairs advise colliery'. It stands on flat-bottom track and sets of wagon wheels can be seen beyond.

Below: Peckett 0-4-0ST *Daisy* (Works No. 581 of 1894) in pristine fully-lined condition *circa* 1900.

(Both) Author's Collection

The Bristol & Clutton Wagon Co.'s works at the station were later taken over by Messrs Marcroft. Cripple wagons were placed in the siding to the erstwhile Fry's Bottom colliery run by gravity to the repair yard. Spruce trees grew by the siding and, one Christmas, a wagon repairer uprooted a spruce, concealed it in a wagon which was then gravitated to the wagon works where he extracted it and took it home. One station master, for a joke, placed a detonator in front of a wagon being pinch-barred into the works. The explosion was frightening. On Saturday mornings, boys took trolleys made from old prams to the wagon works and bought scrap wood which they sold for 2*d.* to local householders, making a profit on the deal.

Clutton goods yard and signal box closed on 15th June, 1964. Due to the gradient, no vehicle without a handbrake was permitted to stand on either loop line. Re-railing ramps were stored in the yard by the signal box.

South of Clutton was a short rise at 1 in 162 followed by a fall at 1 in 58, a stop board at 13 miles 51 chains warning down trains to pin down brakes. As one of the conditions for working the BNSR, the GWR required a station at Hallatrow (12 miles 68 chains). It cost £2,359 16*s.* 5*d.* The original single platform was on the down side, its Clarke building of stone. To cater for the Camerton branch, opened on 1st March, 1882, a very short bay platform was built at the Bristol end, the main line still having only one platform. With the extension of the branch from Camerton to Limpley Stoke, the existing down platform was extended to 454 ft in length and a new, slightly staggered 459 ft-long up platform erected with a red brick slate-roofed waiting shelter, chimney and small canopy. Its junction status warranted a roofed footbridge, the area below the steps enclosed to create lock-ups. In 1912 a timber-built parcels office opened on the down platform at a cost of £55. The erection of a house for the booking porter at an estimated cost of £265 was authorized by the Traffic Committee on 30th July, 1890.

The signal box opened *circa* 1880 and closed on 16th September, 1909, being replaced by a larger box which itself closed on 14th June, 1964. The following day the station ceased to deal with goods traffic. The yard had five looped sidings plus three with dead-ends. A 3-ton crane was provided. One of the loops served the goods shed and cattle pens. Monday was the day of Farrington market. Hallatrow being the nearest station, dealt with this traffic. Cattle tended to be dispatched rather than arrive. Cattle trucks had to be whitewashed. Crates of fowl were sent to London. Farmers packed them in so tightly that their heads protruded and this did not comply with railway regulations. The GWR kept complaining to the farmers and as a result this traffic was lost to road. Messrs Blanning dispatched Cam Valley butter by rail, while a pigeon club at Paulton sent away many baskets. The GWR had three lorries at Hallatrow: two 3-tonners and one 1-tonner. There was also a GWR bicycle, used for delivering accounts, visiting customers or to examine wagons in the sidings at Camerton Colliery.

In addition to ordinary traffic, a large quantity of books, magazines, bus and railway working timetables were dispatched from Purnell's print works at Paulton. When they received their first large order, Purnell's brought hundreds of packets of books at once and Hallatrow ran out of 7*d.* parcel stamps (rate of 7*d.* for 2 lb.). The station then used lower denominations and when these also

Hallatrow goods yard view up, July 1955. Notice the 3-ton Thornycroft parcel vans, right. The former branch to Camerton used the line to the left of the goods shed and curved right beyond the shed. The van to the left of the goods shed has a leaking roof, so to prevent claims for damaged goods, it is covered with a sheet intended for use on an open wagon.
L.B. Sheppard

DESCRIPTION OF THE LINE

'Hallatrow change for Camerton' in the single track, early 1900s. The signal box (*left*) was supplied by McKenzie & Holland when the Camerton branch was built. Beyond the box is the water tank replaced *circa* 1910 by another at the the opposite end of the station. The popular Epps' cocoa sign is apparent.
Author's Collection

Hallatrow viewed in the up direction *circa* 1960. The up inner home signals are, unusually, large disc signals, or 'banjos', because of the lack of space. (Similar signals were used at Worcester and Gloucester.) Notice the store shed beneath the right-hand landing of the covered footbridge. Seven vans can be seen.
Lens of Sutton Collection

Hallatrow looking in the up direction *circa* 1910, showing the footbridge.   *Author's Collection*

Hallatrow, viewed down, in the 1950s. The Camerton branch platform was on the left of the station nameboard.   *T.J. Saunders*

ran out, parcels were stamped 'Hallatrow' and parcel stamps fixed at Bristol until Hallatrow received its new supply. This action ensured traffic was credited to Hallatrow, rather than Bristol.

Parcels were picked up by the GWR parcels lorry almost every afternoon and just before Christmas there would be as many as 2,000 daily, extra staff from Bristol having to be brought in to assist. The normal timetable for the Hallatrow parcels lorry was:

Monday
am: Hallatrow, Farrington Gurney, High Littleton
pm: Timsbury, Tunley, Camerton and Dunkerton

Tuesday
Chewton Mendip, Ston Easton areas

Wednesday
Spare day

Thursday
Timsbury, Tunley, Camerton and Dunkerton

Friday
Chewton Mendip, Ston Easton

In January 1947 when the zonal scheme was introduced, traffic from smaller stations was handled by Bristol, Bath, Hallatrow and Frome. During World War II the Ministry of Food established a buffer depot (now occupied by Bookbarn), for storing corned beef and sugar to be used in an emergency. Traffic was moved in and out by rail. (When first hearing the term 'buffer depot' at a tender age, your author believed it to be a specialized permanent way store!)

From *circa* 1950 calves were dispatched regularly from Hallatrow and in the 1950s horses from a local breeder. Of a total of £28,000 received at Hallatrow for parcels traffic in 1958, £7,000 was for calves, most of the balance being for Purnell's traffic. Although receipts from Purnell were booked to Hallatrow station, they actually left by road to Bristol. When the station closed to passengers and parcels on 2nd November, 1959, calves were sent from Binegar station on the Somerset & Dorset line.

In addition to the traffic mentioned above, there were products of Paulton's three boot (mostly for miners) and shoe factories and also a brickworks. Thirty surrounding farms sent milk from over a wide area: Chewton Mendip, Litton, Paulton, Ston Easton and Cameley. It brought in £300 a month, but this traffic was lost in 1931 when Express Dairies' lorries collected it from 29 of the 30 farms. Most milk went to London, but some went to Bristol and Cardiff. London milk traffic travelled via Frome. The 17-gallon churns weighed 2 cwt when full and were placed into 'Siphon' vans holding 60 churns. The loss of milk traffic caused many of the station's 14 four-wheeled trolleys to be come redundant.

Apart from those shops at Hallatrow, parcels arrived for shops in Paulton, Farrington Gurney, Chewton Mendip, Ston Easton and Litton. A fair number of commercial travellers and their skips of samples used the station.

The detailed 'Hallatrow for Paulton Change for Camerton' station name board *circa* 1909. The footbridge has yet to be built. The smartly-dressed ladies enjoy being photographed. A poster can be seen advertising the new GWR route Wolverhampton and Birmingham to Bristol and the West of England. This opened 1st July, 1908. Another poster advertises the Royal Line ships.
Author's Collection

'57XX' class 0-6-0PT No. 8744 brings the 2.53 pm Saturdays-only Temple Meads to Frome service into Hallatrow station on 23rd May, 1959. The roof of the B-set coach is higher than the locomotive cab.
Hugh Ballantyne

DESCRIPTION OF THE LINE

Hallatrow view up, September 1909 when the up platform opened. The footbridge has yet to be installed. Notice the new water tank, *right*, signal box left and a water column on each platform.
Author's Collection

An 0-6-0ST heads a down train at Hallatrow comprising about a dozen wagons. Note the three headlamps. On the platform is a slot machine for obtaining bars of chocolate.
M.J. Tozer Collection

84 THE BRISTOL-RADSTOCK-FROME LINE

'8750' class 0-6-0PT No. 4607 leaves Hallatrow with the 10.17 am Temple Meads to Frome service on 25th July, 1959. *R.E. Toop/Author's Collection*

'51XX' class 2-6-2T No. 4131 replenishes her water tanks at Hallatrow on 25th July, 1959. The fireman, enjoying a cigarette, will turn off the water when it overflows. The two tank wagons at the end of the train, are probably empty from Mells Road. *R.E. Toop/Author's Collection*

DESCRIPTION OF THE LINE 85

The former very short Camerton bay platform at Hallatrow on 23rd March, 1969. The disused main line has yet to be lifted. *Author*

The former station master's house at Hallatrow, slightly altered, 28th August, 1982. *Author*

An 1871 GWR 'flat-sided' coach condemned in 1894 is seen here as a mission carriage. The postcard it formed was postmarked 23rd November, 1905. The coach's external dimensions were 25 ft x 7 ft 6¼ in. and 7 ft high. *M.J. Tozer Collection*

The interior of Hallatrow Mission Carriage: harmonium, *left*, and pulpit, *right*.
M.J. Tozer Collection

Crowds of passengers travelled from Hallatrow to Bristol for football matches, the platform being absolutely packed and, on at least one occasion, a station seat was placed in a 'Siphon' van to increase a seating accommodation, the seat being returned from Bristol. Crowds also travelled from Hallatrow to Clutton flower show.

Temple Cloud Quarry sidings north of the station were brought into use in June 1886. Pennant stone, including paving stone, was dispatched in GWR 4-plank wagons, six to nine being loaded daily. During the 1920s regular loads were sent to the GWR sea wall defences at Dawlish. The private siding agreement terminated on 31st December, 1941 but a new arrangement was taken up by the Air Ministry on 1st January, 1942 as Parnall Aircraft Ltd set up a shadow factory in the quarry in case its main factory at Yate was bombed. This shadow factory produced parts for Avro 'Lancaster' bombers – the rear turret, a section of the fuselage and wing parts which were taken out by rail. The works had its own fire brigade. A look-out was stationed at the top of the quarry to warn of approaching enemy aircraft. Many girls worked at the factory. It closed when peace was declared.

Circa 1900 staff at Hallatrow comprised a station master, two signalmen, a porter and two signal porters. By 5th January, 1921 this had been increased to a station master, goods clerk, clerk, four signalmen, two shunters, a parcel porter, two goods porters and two porters. Two of the signalmen between them worked the station signal box, while the other two were at Old Mills (located at 10 miles 50 chains), the latter working 8.00 am to 4.00 pm and 2.00 pm to 10.00 pm. During the period 2.00 to 4.00 pm, when the two signalmen were on duty together, one attended to the signal lamps and also assisted with shunting.

The two shunters at Hallatrow worked between them 6.15 am to 10.15 pm shunting and also booking passengers when the clerk was not there. Two porters worked on early and late turn. One cleaned the cattle pens and the other attended to the office, platform and signal lamps. A pumpman came from Bristol daily to work the steam pump supplying the water tank to feed the water cranes. The tank had been installed in 1909-1910 in preparation for the extension of the Camerton branch to Limpley Stoke. Water was pumped from the River Cam. Staff used the tank for bathing on hot days!

The 1921 report suggested that in view of the decreased carted goods traffic forward and return, one of the goods porters would be dispensed with. Parcel deliveries were by an outside contractor who was engaged permanently and used two 2-wheel horse-drawn traps.

In 1906 an ex-GWR flat-sided coach built in 1871 and condemned for railway use in 1894, was used as 'Hallatrow Mission Carriage'. Its inside dimensions were 24 ft 6 in. x 7 ft and 6 ft 9 in. high. It contained a reading desk, harmonium and rows of seats - four to each row.

Beyond Hallatrow the line climbed at 1 in 65 to a summit near 11 miles 60 chains where stop boards were erected. The line fell at 1 in 73 to Farrington Gurney Halt (11 miles 39 chains), opened on 11th July, 1927. A 150 ft-long timber platform with a wooden waiting shelter, it was built at a cost of £500. It was said that on the day it was completed, the Bristol Tramways & Carriage Co. opened a bus route through the village. The halt was famed for passengers

Above: Farrington Gurney ticket office at the rear of the Miners' Arms, September 1936.
Author's Collection

Right: Farrington Gurney ticket office at the rear of the Miners' Arms in BR days. *D.E. Mullins*

DESCRIPTION OF THE LINE 89

BR Standard class '3' 2-6-2T No. 82033 arriving at Farrington Gurney Halt with the 10.50 am Frome to Temple Meads on 8th August, 1959. Notice the reflection in the windows of the grassy bank. *Michael Jenkins*

Farrington Gurney Halt, view up, *circa* 1962, after closure. *Lens of Sutton Collection*

The sharply-curved line at Farrington Gurney Colliery *circa* 1900.

Below: Beyer, Peacock 0-4-0ST No. 1736 of 1877 at Farrington Gurney Colliery. This engine was braked by wooden blocks being applied to the rear wheels.
(Both) Collection A.G. Church

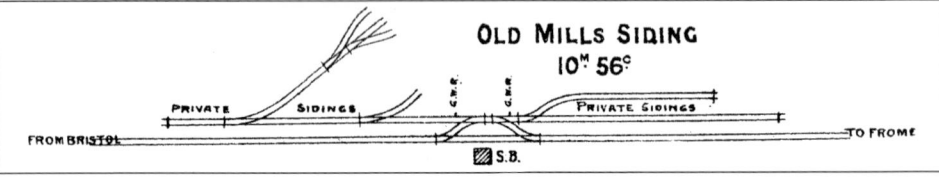

OLD MILLS SIDING
10™ 56°

PRIVATE SIDINGS   G.W.R. G.W.R.   PRIVATE SIDINGS
FROM BRISTOL   TO FROME
             S.B.

having to purchase tickets from the nearby Miners' Arms which was the GWR agent. A notice stated: 'Passengers requiring Tickets up to 7 pm on Weekdays are requested to ring the Bell. After that time and on Sundays Passengers without Tickets should notify the Guard on joining the train'.

When the halt opened, the lady booking clerk at Hallatrow, who had started work during World War I, was sent to the Miners' Arms to instruct the landlady on how to issue tickets. To advertise the opening of the halt, on the first day a return excursion fare to Weston-super-Mare was offered at the cost of 2s. 0d. Three hundred adults and 140 children availed themselves of this bargain. In all, 9,128 passengers used the halt in 1928, its first full year, but the number had fallen to 4,996 by 1934.

One day, in the dark, a lady and child boarded a train at the halt. In helping her into the van with her pram, the guard accidentally knocked his hand lamp to a green aspect. The train smartly accelerated away for Midsomer Norton leaving him on the platform. He went to the Miners' Arms and phoned Midsomer Norton for a taxi to collect him.

Guards were responsible for collecting tickets from passengers alighting at the halt and handing them to the station master at Midsomer Norton or Hallatrow. The Hallatrow station master was responsible for setting the electric time switch for the lights. If a guard found the lights on or off at an inappropriate time, he could gain access to the switch box with a carriage key. The halt dealt with milk traffic and guards were required to hand consignment notes to the person in charge of the next station. The overbridge near the halt was of brick, rather than the usual stone.

Beyond the halt the line continued to fall at 1 in 73 to Old Mills Colliery Sidings laid at 10 miles 56 chains as a result of a private siding agreement of 5th June, 1874. On 8th August, 1882 a private siding agreement was made with Farrington Colliery some distance to the north of Old Mills, the siding there being laid by the contractors Saunders & Ward. The former main line became the line to the colliery and a new main line was added on the west side. The new siding thus paralleled the main line for ½ mile before swinging north-west to the colliery about 600 yds further on. The siding was laid by the BNSR in return for a concession made when the main line was built. Farrington pit closed in October 1921.

Near Old Mills signal box (10 miles 50 chains) was Springfield Colliery. The signal box opened in 1882 and was reduced to a ground frame in 1931. In 1952-1953 it was replaced by three ground frames. Coal winding ceased at Old Mills on 1st April, 1966. For the privilege of using Old Mills Junction, Springfield Colliery paid £250 to Old Mills Colliery, this being believed to be a suitable proportion of the £1,000 the junction had originally cost. Farrington also contributed annually towards the maintenance of the junction. Farrington had three standard gauge locomotives:

Type	Maker	Works No.	Date	Notes
0-4-0ST	Beyer, Peacock	1737	1877	Purchased from Meakin & Dean, contractors, c.1902, following the completion of its Blagdon Reservoir contract. It was probably sold after August 1904.

Type	Maker	Works No.	Date	Notes
0-4-0ST	Peckett	520	1891	Ex-G. Palmer and in use at Farrington by November 1912. On closure of the pit this engine was sent to East Bristol Collieries.
0-4-0ST	W.G. Bagnall	1432	1894	Ex-M.W. Grangebrook Ltd, Netherton, Staffs and advertised for sale on 9th December, 1921 and 7th July, 1922.

These locomotives shunted at the pithead and worked trains of two to three wagons to and from Old Mills siding. When an engine was under repair, horses were hired from a Midsomer Norton timber merchant. One horse drew a wagon from Old Mills Junction to where the siding bore away from the main line and then a trace horse assisted it up the incline to the pithead. The mine was unusual for having an electricity generating station early in the 20th century. Following 1st October, 1953 when Pensford washery closed, coal from that pit was brought in bottom door hopper wagons to Springfield for washing. The washery closed *circa* 1962. As Old Mills sidings were short, before dispatching a train to be shunted there, it was necessary to ascertain that the sidings had sufficient room to accommodate the wagons being sent.

After the signal box closed, an intermediate token instrument was installed in the Old Mills ground frame (former signal box) for the receipt of the Hallatrow to Radstock West token, as the sidings could be used for crossing engines, or short freight trains, or a passenger train (the passenger train being kept on the main line). When a train required to leave the sidings, the man in charge had to inform the signalman in advance to seek permission to move. The Radstock and Hallatrow signalmen would then depress the plunger of the Electric Train Token instruments and the man in charge of Old Mills Sidings was able to withdraw the Electric Train Token.

In the event of a shunting mishap which fouled the main line, colliery staff were required to place, ¾ mile from the obstruction, three detonators 10 yards apart on the rails each side of the obstruction and exhibit a hand danger-signal. Hallatrow and Radstock signal boxes were to be advised by telephone.

The guard of a train shunting at Old Mills, before permitting an engine to be detached, was required to apply his brake tightly, and if an up train, see that the wagon adjoining his van was spragged, or the leading wagon of a down train, to prevent the train, or a portion of it, moving down the gradient.

Old Mills shaft closed for winding in October 1941, but remained connected underground with Springfield. In 1947 the combined Old Mills and Springfield collieries were known as Old Mills Colliery, even though the coal was lifted at the former Springfield pit. Production in the late 1940s was 78,000 tons annually, the second highest in the Somerset coalfield. The mine closed on 1st April, 1966. Old Mills Colliery used a 4-wheel diesel-mechanical locomotive, Ruston & Hornsby (Works No. 200 793), purchased new in 1940.

In the March 1910 Appendix to the Service Time Table, although use of tow ropes was generally banned, they were authorized to be used in Old Mills Sidings. From 1st May until 30th September lamps at the sidings' ground discs could be unlit. Permanent way and engineering staff were warned to watch for subsidence between Pensford and Mells Road. Periodic track alterations were required – for example in 1958 a maximum lift of 5½ in. was made near Old Mills.

Beyond Old Mills, the line descended at 1 in 177. On 30th March, 1949 BR proposed building a 120 ft-long platform at Thicket Mead (10 miles 13¾ chains), but the work was not proceeded with. The halt would have been on an embankment and have a 30 ft x 7 ft shelter. The gradient continued to fall at 1 in 177 to Welton (9 miles 47 chains), the name changed to Welton & Midsomer Norton on 2nd May, 1898 and finally Midsomer Norton & Welton on 1st May, 1904. A Clarke brick building stood on the north side of the line and it also had a timber lean-to building on the 204 ft-long platform. A small wooden signal box was later demoted to a parcels office. West of the station was a looped goods siding, a terminal road serving the goods shed. A small cattle pen was at the west end of the goods shed. It had a 1 ton 5 cwt crane.

As at Old Mills, a guard was required to apply the brake tightly and see that a wagon was spragged. From 23rd August, 1926 until 12th April, 1942, a private siding served the North Somerset Brick & Tile Works. These works closed *circa* 1940, but from 28th November, 1942 R. Blatchford & Co. used the siding for steel and scrap metal traffic and on 5th December, 1946 extended it. It remained in use until 6th July, 1968 although other goods traffic ceased on 15th June, 1964. The siding was on a gradient of 1 in 40 and special care was required at the end of shunting operations to ensure that wagons were securely braked and the two wheel-stops padlocked across the rails, the keys being kept by the station master.

The goods yard dispatched portable timber buildings such as greenhouses and garden sheds manufactured by Pratten's and material from the Standard Cheque Works at Welton, but the ASLEF footplatemen's strike in 1955 lost this traffic. Inwards goods included purchased cattle food imported at Avonmouth for Shearn's and stored in wagons at Bristol until space at Midsomer Norton was available. There was a rush to avoid a demurrage charge and the staff had aching backs after stacking sacks 10 to 12 high on Shearn's lorries. Passenger porters were required to keep their uniform smart so when they assisted with goods, wore a protective sacking apron, especially when handling such products as Aberthaw and Blue Circle sacks of cement. These required double-handling as they were stored in old van bodies to keep the contents dry. Explosives arrived for use in collieries and quarries. Timber and glass were delivered for Pratten's buildings.

Pratten's sometimes sent teams of men away to erect its larger buildings. Films for showing at the Palladium cinema arrived at the station at 6.20 pm for showing at the 7 pm performance. As delivery carmen finished work at 5 pm, a porter was paid 1*s*. to take the film cans to the cinema by bicycle.

In 1966 the South ground frame, in very poor condition, was spiked out of use on 3rd June and all traffic thereafter was worked into the siding via the North ground frame.

From 31st December, 1879 Welton Hill Colliery, a Duchy of Cornwall mine, had a siding from the BNSR. From its opening in January 1815 it used the Somerset Coal Canal tramway and was the furthest distance from Midford, where it joined the canal, and also had the highest toll – 8*d*. per ton to cart it to Radstock plus a haulage charge of 1*s*. 10*d*. per ton. A narrow gauge tramway

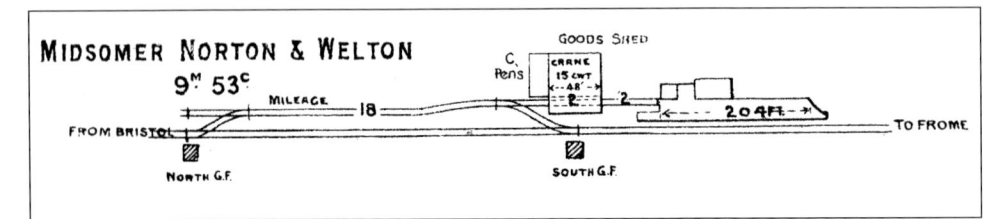

Midsomer Norton & Welton station viewed in the up direction *circa* 1912. Two large casks are on the platform in addition to the milk churns. Epps' cocoa and Hudson's soap are advertised.
Author's Collection

Midsomer Norton & Welton *circa* 1920. The 'C' marks commencement of a speed restriction. Beyond it is the South ground frame hut. Messrs C.J. Gregory sell 'K' boots 'The best for all'. *H.J. Patterson-Rutherford*

DESCRIPTION OF THE LINE 95

A BR Standard class '3' 2-6-2T No. 82044 arrives at Midsomer Norton & Welton with a 3-coach train forming the 10.50 am Frome to Temple Meads service on 24th January, 1959.
R.E. Toop/Author's Collection

Midsomer Norton & Welton view down *circa* 1960. *Lens of Sutton Collection*

Midsomer Norton & Welton *circa* 1959. A wagon and van stand in the shed siding. Rail access to the goods shed is from its far end. *Lens of Sutton Collection*

'8750' class 0-6-0PT No. 9668 leaves Midsomer Norton & Welton with the 10.17 am Temple Meads to Frome service on a cold and frosty day, 24th January, 1959. The platform face had been recently rebuilt. Railwaymen's allotments are on the left. *R.E. Toop/Author's Collection*

with a self-acting incline connected the pit with the standard gauge siding laid at a cost of £708 and completed by June 1880. Latterly the colliery was worked at a loss and so was closed towards the end of 1896.

On 10th February, 1904 Midsomer Norton station was only staffed by the station master and a porter, but by 17th January, 1921 had increased to station master, clerk and two porters. The clerk was responsible for booking passenger trains, making invoices for goods traffic, entering up the goods books, preparing the monthly accounts and statistics and assisting with the correspondence. Porter No. 1 dealt with all inwards goods traffic, entered up the carmen's sheets, booked all parcels traffic, attended to the ground frame and yard shunting. Porter No. 2 checked outward goods traffic, attended to the signal and platform lamps, made up the collected tickets and assisted with the yard shunting.

Sundays at branch stations, including Midsomer Norton, involved a '3-turn shift' consisting of three hours in the morning, going home for a couple of hours, returning after lunch, having the latter part of the afternoon off and then returning in the evening.

On one occasion industrial action was seen at Midsomer Norton. After five hours' duty, staff were entitled to a break and a porter who came on duty at 7 am lunched at noon. Unfortunately this was the time when the Standard Cheque Book Co. delivered their parcels. Staff were expected to load the train and miss part of their break. One day they refused to interrupt their break, resulting in the parcels missing the train. Following discussions, overtime was paid for this extra duty. Concurrently arrangements were made for the late turn porter to be paid for extra tasks performed after the last train had left. In addition to securing the station, he was expected to remove all Tilley lamps from their poles and book and store all parcels that arrived on the last train, which often included sides of meat for the agent supplying the local butchers. This agent was waiting immediately the station opened in the morning and was irate if he was delayed while the items were booked.

Some Saturday evenings porter Vic Oakhill brought a portable gramophone for entertainment between the departure of the 10.35 pm to Frome and the last down train which left at 12.03 am. On such occasions it was not unknown for an impromptu dance to be held in the waiting room.

The line fell at 1 in 128 and ¾ mile beyond Midsomer Norton & Welton station was Old Welton Siding serving the colliery south of the line. Its story was similar to that of Welton Hill. Prior to the opening of the BNSR it had used the Somerset Coal Canal tramway, but this had proved expensive, costing 1s. 4d. to cart coal to Radstock, plus a 5½d. toll payable to the coal canal. The private siding agreement with the BNSR was dated 16th January, 1880. The cost of building the standard gauge siding and other plant needed nearly bankrupted the colliery, which closed about August 1896. Attempts at reopening proved abortive and the private siding agreement was terminated on 28th November, 1917.

Beyond the line continued to fall at 1 in 128 and at 8 miles 59 chains passed under the Somerset & Dorset Railway (S&D) at North Somerset viaduct consisting of five masonry and brick arches, which also crossed the coal canal tramway. One day in 1881 an S&D stone mason repairing this viaduct was ordered not to work above the BNSR as he was trespassing.

98   THE BRISTOL-RADSTOCK-FROME LINE

GWR lorries at Midsomer Norton. Porter Vic Oakhill stands on the right with a grounded coach body on a brick foundation behind him. *A.G. Church Collection*

Midsomer Norton & Welton station in 1933. The porter hauls a happy band of children on a station trolley. Behind is an advertisement for Palethorpe's sausages. *Author's Collection*

The 3-coach 10.50 am Frome to Temple Meads train headed by BR Standard class '3' 2-6-2T No. 82040 approaches North Somerset viaduct on 28th February, 1959. *R.E. Toop/Author's Collection*

'4575' class 2-6-2T No. 5554 takes the 10.17 am Temple Meads to Frome service beneath North Somerset viaduct on 28th February, 1959. *R.E. Toop/Author's Collection*

A BR Standard class '4' 2-6-4T crosses North Somerset viaduct with a Bournemouth to Bath Green Park train *circa* 1966. Notice the Radstock West fixed distant signal.
Christopher Steane/Author's Collection

'8750' class 0-6-0PT No. 4647 passes beneath the North Somerset viaduct with the 1.10 pm Frome to Temple Meads service on 24th February, 1959. *R.E. Toop/Author's Collection*

DESCRIPTION OF THE LINE 101

BR Standard class '3' 2-6-2T No. 82040 with the 10.50 am Frome to Temple Meads service approaches North Somerset viaduct on 28th February, 1959. The Somerset & Dorset line can be seen beyond the train. *R.E. Toop/Author's Collection*

Diesel-hydraulic No. D7000 approaches Radstock *circa* 1965 with a down freight. Vans are at the front of the train and coal wagons at the rear. *R.E. Toop*

'8750' class 0-6-0PT No. 9612 leaves Radstock with the 1.10 pm Saturdays-only Frome to Temple Meads service on 8th August, 1959. *Michael Jenkins*

The link line between the S&D (*right*) and the BNSR (*left*) being installed on 6th March, 1966. In the distance a 'Hymek' diesel-hydraulic heads the permanent way train on the BNSR. Many cars are parked on the road to the left of the BNSR, these belong to those come to witness the S&D last day special on which the photographer is travelling. The S&D down road has already been slewed to the link line and the S&D train works 'wrong line'.

Christopher Steane/Author's Collection

In 1960 BR put forward an abortive plan for demolishing this viaduct and making an embankment to carry the S&D. Up BNSR trains would have climbed at 1 in 53½ from Radstock to the S&D down line; immediately crossed the S&D up line and descended at 1 in 87 to Midsomer Norton. This plan was rendered unnecessary by the closure of the S&D on 7th March, 1966. In order to remove coal from Writhlington Colliery, hitherto served by the S&D, a chord line was opened joining the S&D with the BNSR at 8 miles 31 chains. Track was not lifted immediately following the closure of Writhlington Colliery on 16th November, 1973 as investigations were made into the possible recovery of part of the Writhlington tip. This venture was not taken up and the track was lifted.

Just prior to Radstock level crossing was where the 272 yds-long siding from Wellsway Colliery joined the main line. This was yet another siding constructed by Saunders & Ward, this time for £2,776 7s. 6d. Lady Waldegrave, owner of the pit, paid interest of 7 per cent on the cost of making the siding. Platelayers were paid 7½d. and hour and their foreman 10½d. The siding opened on 7th January, 1875 but closed when the colliery in 1897 no longer lifted coal; its coal was still raised, but via Ludlows shaft and therefore continued to provide the GWR with traffic.

The Somerset Coal Canal, Somerset & Dorset Railway and the BNSR ran parallel to Radstock (8 miles 16 chains), renamed Radstock West from 26th September, 1949. The brick and stone Clarke building was set on the up platform, while the down platform had a small timber shelter with an angled canopy. Both platforms were 251 ft in length. A large signal box was adjacent to the level crossing. At the east end of the station, until demolished in the 1950s, was an open footbridge. The station building itself was pulled down in the week beginning 1st September, 1963.

Circa 1900 Radstock was staffed by a station master, passenger guard, two signalmen, a foreman porter, two porters, three shunters and two signal porters. By 19th March, 1921 this had been amended to station master, goods clerk, clerk, junior clerk, lady clerk, two signalmen in the North signal box, two in the South box, foreman shunter, two class '2' shunters, two class '4' shunters, a goods porter, a parcel porter, two porters and a charlady. The goods clerk was in charge of the goods office and the woman clerk entered the dispatch books and prepared ledgers and invoices. The junior clerk when on duty booked all trains and prepared the passenger accounts, assisting in the goods office between trains. The other clerk took early and late turns in the booking office.

One day G.H. Soole, assistant to the Bristol divisional superintendent, entering a doorway at the station, discovered one of the porters cutting the station master's hair. Ever discreet, Soole remarked: 'Oh, I shouldn't be here' and left. Five minutes later he returned and found everyone carrying out their authorized duties, the station master with his cap hiding a half-cut head of hair.

A review showed that coal and coke traffic for January 1921, instead of about 10,000 tons was down to 1,779 and February 3,139 tons due to a general depression in the coal trade. As parcel traffic was light, it was believed that a porter could undertake the parcel porter's duties and, thus save a post. The goods porter assisted with the first two passenger trains and when on late turn, the 5.13 pm and 6.02 pm. The two class '2' and two class '4' shunters performed

Link line at Radstock looking from Bristol & North Somerset line towards the Somerset & Dorset line (*left*), spring 1966. *Christopher Steane/Author's Collection*

'Hymek' No. D7004 crosses from the ex-S&D to the ex-BNSR west of Radstock in the spring of 1966. The shunter climbs from the cab to work the ground frame in the foreground.
Christopher Steane/Author's Collection

shunting and met early and late passenger trains. A railway lorry service, cheaper than using the local carrier, started at Radstock in 1928.

South-east of the passenger station was the goods yard. On the down side were seven roads and on the other: No. 1 up, the shed road serving a substantial goods shed, an extensive cattle dock and a large wagon works. A 6-ton crane was provided. A weighbridge was on a siding on the opposite side of the main line to the locomotive turntable, and a re-railing ramp was stored in the weighbridge house. To the north, Ludlows was the first Radstock pit to be linked to the GWR, the private siding agreement signed 17th February, 1853 and the siding opened the following year. The last coal was raised at Ludlows on 19th March, 1954. Shunting at Ludlows was performed by horses until *circa* 1947 when a road tractor was utilized. *Lord Salisbury*, Peckett 0-6-0ST Works No. 1041 of 1906, arrived from Coalpit Heath Colliery north of Bristol in May 1950, but it is believed to have of only worked for a short time before being sent to Norton Hill Colliery, two miles distant.

In 1857 the broad gauge Ludlows line was extended to also serve Tyning Colliery. This crossed the Somerset & Dorset line. One of the bridges, the 'Marble Arch' was very low and caused the S&D to use restricted height locomotives. Tyning Colliery closed on 11th November, 1909, but was still used for tipping dirt from Middle Pit and Ludlows until the latter closed.

Following closure of the S&D on 7th March, 1966, movements for Writhlington sidings were propelled towards Midsomer Norton and then drawn over a new chord line and Radstock North (the ex-S&D station) to the colliery. The maximum load was not to exceed 25 four-wheeled wagons. Movements from the colliery had to be propelled towards Radstock and then drawn over Radstock West level crossing. The maximum load was not to exceed eight bogie merry-go-round wagons or their equivalent.

Wagon works were important due to so many collieries being in the area. The wagon works between Ludlows and Tyning Collieries belonged to Wheeler & Gregory, later becoming the British Wagon Co. and finally Wagon Repairs Ltd. The works was seriously inundated by flood water in December 1939 and closed in 1972.

Another important firm was Radstock Wagon Works, later E. Marcroft & Co. At first the premises were small, but it had an iron foundry for the manufacture of such parts as axle boxes and buffers. In 1929 a new wagon shop was built which could handle five wagons on each set of four roads. Two overhead cranes obviated the need for lifting jacks. With about 50 staff on its payroll, Marcroft's maintained colliery and quarry wagons on a seven year contract, usually repairing them twice. As the business expanded, the company opened sites at Mells Road, Clutton, South Wales and other locations. An additional workshop opened at Radstock in 1951 and a further one in 1961. Wagons within the complex were shunted by manpower or tractor. It hired out about 5,500 wagons in 1948. In 1980 the firm was taken over by Storage & Transport Systems which had its own fleet of wagons and Messrs Marcroft was responsible for repairing them and storing in times of recession. At one time Marcroft's maintained Foster Yeoman stone wagons. In 1983 Marcroft's modified the springs of wagons used on the Speedlink service.

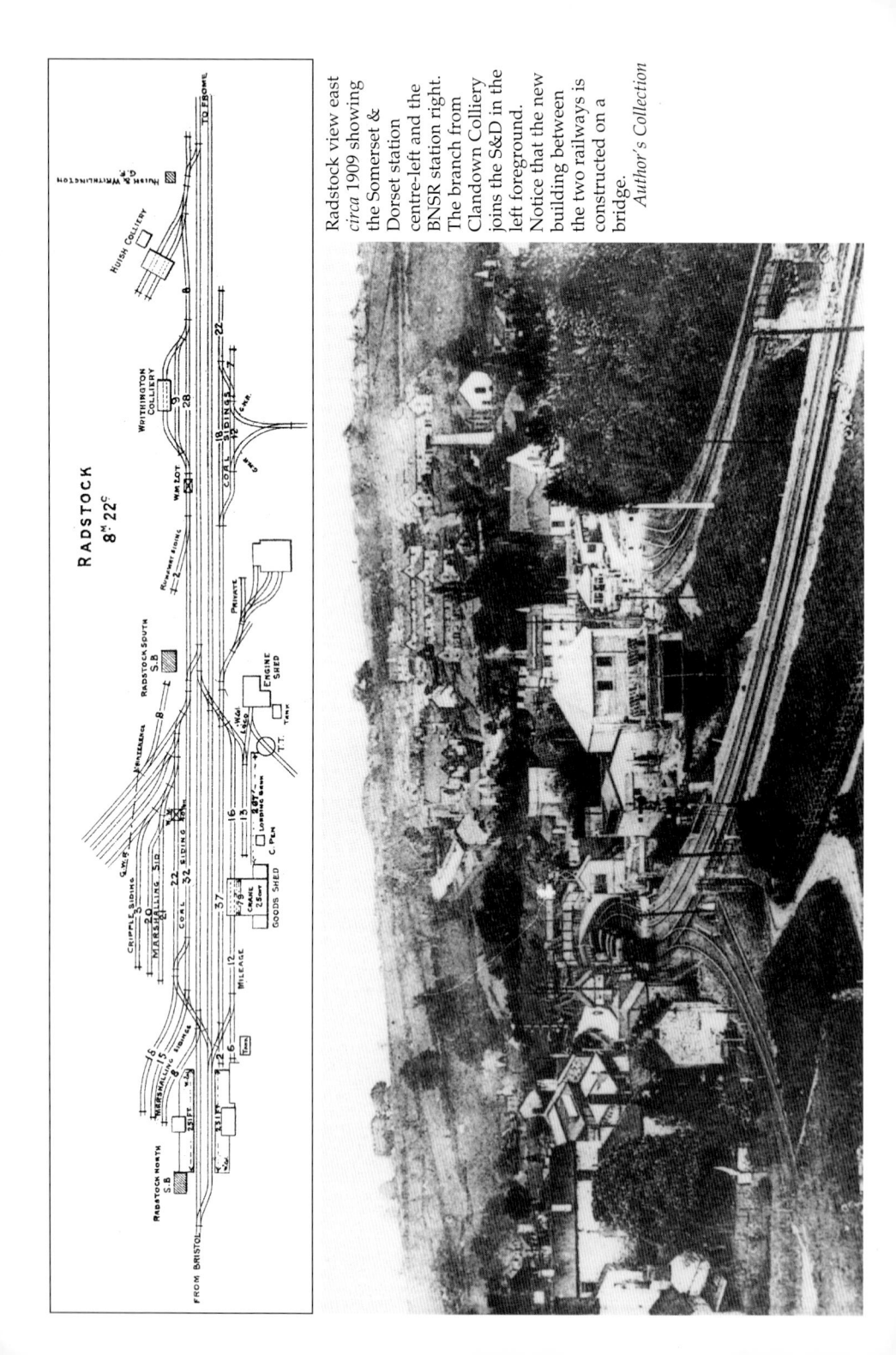

Radstock view east *circa* 1909 showing the Somerset & Dorset station centre-left and the BNSR station right. The branch from Clandown Colliery joins the S&D in the left foreground. Notice that the new building between the two railways is constructed on a bridge.
Author's Collection

A down train enters Radstock *circa* 1900 showing the original timber North signal box.
Author's Collection

A light engine, probably an outside frame 0-6-0T, stands on the up road at Radstock waiting for the signal to be pulled off. Perhaps a down train is approaching on the single line from Midsomer Norton as the crossing gates are open. The later North signal box can be seen.
Author's Collection

'8750' class 0-6-0PT No. 4636 light engine, takes on water at Radstock on 8th April, 1958.
R.E. Toop/Author's Collection

'4575' class 2-6-2T No. 5545 enters Radstock with a Temple Meads to Frome train. The signalman, right, stands ready to collect the token. Notice the ladder to maintain a gas lamp illuminating the level crossing.
M.E.J. Deane

DESCRIPTION OF THE LINE

Radstock, view down, in the 1930s. the station nameboard on the far right has a *Sunday Times* advert imediately above it.
Author's Collection

A down goods passes (the now) Radstock West on 14th August, 1959 hauled by '51XX' class 2-6-2T No. 4131. A bus for Bath stands on the station forecourt.
Author

110   THE BRISTOL-RADSTOCK-FROME LINE

Private Owners' coal wagons at Radstock *circa* 1910: Radstock Coal Co.; F. Bendle; F. Bird and Writhlington Colliery.   *M.J. Tozer Collection*

'57XX' class 0-6-0PT No. 7786 at Radstock West with a Frome to Bristol Temple Meads train, 15th August, 1959. The water tank can be seen on the right and a water crane on the left. The goods shed is behind the coach and the yard full of coal wagons. The notices on the left and right read: 'Passengers are requested to cross the line at the other end of the platform'.   *K.J. Saunders*

Left: Radstock yard, November 1966. The goods shed can be seen in the distance. Notice the pull wire to operate the gas lamp adjacent to the water column which has a make-shift brazier.
W.H. Harbor/Author's Collection

Below: '51XX' class 2-6-2T No. 4102 at Radstock with a van train on 28th February, 1959. The goods shed is on the right. The end loading dock is in the right foreground and also a re-railing ramp. *R.E. Toop/Author's Collection*

Tyning Colliery, Radstock *circa* 1900. *Author's Collection*

Platelayers at Ludlows Colliery, perhaps having carried out gauge conversion. Note the bridge rails on longitudinal sleepers. A notice on the left reads: 'Engines not to pass into the siding beyond this point'. *Author's Collection*

DESCRIPTION OF THE LINE 113

Marcroft's offices have a domestic style of architecture, 30th March, 1983. *Author*

Radstock locomotive shed, view west, 30th March, 1983. *Author*

The former Radstock engine shed used by Marcroft's for shot blasting, 30th March, 1983.
Author

Marcroft wagon repair works, Radstock on 30th March, 1983. *Author*

The shot blast bay was in the former GWR engine shed where there was also a spray paint shop. For safety, tests were made on carbon dioxide and ammonia tankers before work began on them. The testing apparatus was made by the firm which manufactured breathalyzers. Ammonia tankers had been purged with nitrogen before they arrived. Seventy to 80 men were employed by Marcroft's in 1963, but only 24 on 30th March, 1983. Latterly, if a crane was required for heavy lifts, one was hired from Messrs Sparrow. A new wheel turning lathe was purchased about 1981, capable of turning two wheels at a time. Axles were tested ultra-sonically. The Radstock works also carried out other engineering such as making hydraulic lifts for lorries. In 1983 the machine shop was little-used – just for guillotining and making pressings for local engineering companies. In former days the works had a line of blacksmiths' forges. Towards the end of the time of performing wagon repairs, sometimes two, instead of one, train was required to be run. This was because, although hitherto air- and vacuum-braked wagons could be worked in one train, any wagons not braked by the engine would be loose-coupled and braking assisted by the guard in his van. If wagons broke away, they would be stopped by the guard's brake, or catch points. When catch points and brake vans were abolished, all trains were required to have the entire train braked by air or vacuum. This meant that when both air- and vacuum-braked wagons needed repair at Radstock, two trips were required so that both types could be fully-braked. Marcroft's Radstock works closed in 1988, with a loss of three clerical and 22 engineering jobs. The last train left on 6th July, 1988.

Radstock had the only public level crossing on the branch. Road users found it particularly frustrating because as it was parallel with the Somerset & Dorset level crossing, it was quite likely that if they were not held up by one, they were by the other. Complaints were made and on 29th November, 1877 the Queen's Bench Division considered the case of the Board of Trade versus the S&D and the BNSR. The application was to force the companies to replace the two level crossings with a bridge in accordance with a Board of Trade order made in August 1875. Such a bridge would have cost £20,000 to £30,000 and the railway had no land for it. There was no case against the BNSR because that company had been leased to the GWR in perpetuity, while the Midland Railway and the London & South Western Railway, lessees of the S&D said that it did not apply to them as the S&D had carried out the requirements of its Act. Since the scheme could not be carried out by only one company, the Board of Trade was forced to drop the matter.

Complaints were resurrected periodically and a record was kept of the number of occasions on which the Great Western closed the gates across the road from 6.00 am until 10.00 pm from 5th to 8th July, 1882. The results were:

No. of mins. gates closed	1	2	3	4	5	6	7	8	9	10	11	12	Total time h. m.
5th July Wednesday	-	3	2	4	3	2	2	-	2	1	-	1	1 49
6th July Thursday	-	2	2	4	1	4	1	1	1	3	2	-	2 11
7th July Friday	1	1	2	4	3	3	1	1	2	1	-	-	1 41
8th July Saturday	-	2	1	4	2	3	1	2	3	1	-	-	1 51

116   THE BRISTOL-RADSTOCK-FROME LINE

A Ford 5000 shunting tractor at Marcroft's 3rd July, 1975.   *Author's Collection*

In the foreground a hydraulic lorry lift is placed on a temporary frame while in the background are tankers, 30th March, 1983.   *Author*

In 1931 following the death of a boy at the level crossings, Mr Gould, MP for Frome, asked Herbert Morrison, Minister of Transport, if he would state the causes of delay in carrying out proposed improvements to the crossings. No action was taken and in the 1950s increased road traffic caused problems when the signalman wished to close the gates, so, at busy times, station staff armed with red flags assisted the signalman by halting traffic so that he could swing the gates. On summer Saturdays traffic was literally held up for miles on each side of the town, the A367 in pre-motorway days being a well-used route to the south and south-west coasts. To minimize delays to road traffic, level crossing gates were required to be kept closed across the line until an electric treadle bell was rung by down trains, or, for an up passenger train, four minutes after it had left Mells Road. The gates were not opened for an up goods until the driver whistled at the fixed distant signal. At all times shunting operations were required to cease to allow the gates to be worked should a vehicle wish to cross.

The crossing was last used on 16th October, 1975 when BR diesel locomotive No. 33019 hauled preserved S&D 2-8-0 No. 88 from the former S&D line to the GWR yard before being taken to a new home at Washford on the Taunton to Minehead branch. Radstock West signal box was taken to Didcot by the Great Western Society for preservation.

Beyond Radstock engine shed were Kilmersdon Colliery sidings. The pit shaft begun in February 1874, was completed late in 1877. A private siding agreement was signed on 1st September, 1877 and the pit opened about April 1878. It was linked to the GWR by a standard gauge line about ½ mile in length. At its northern end was an inclined plane some 500 ft in length on a gradient of 1 in 8. Initially horses hauled wagons from the colliery to the head of the incline, but in 1896 these were replaced by a Kilmersdon, Hudswell, Clarke 0-4-0ST (Works No. 464 of 1896). On 10th September, 1929 Peckett 0-4-0ST (Works No. 1788) arrived new and lasted until closure. It is now preserved at Washford.

Loaded wagons were propelled to a weighbridge in order that a Bill of lading could be written out. An orange light was switched on when the next wagon was required to move to the weighbridge. The engine then pushed the train over an ungated level crossing and through fields to the head of the incline. To prevent wagons or the locomotive accidentally plunging down, a metal stop block was placed across the rails. The first wagon was uncoupled and hooked to a wire cable which passed round a braked horizontal winding drum and then led down to the foot of the incline where it was fastened to an empty wagon. A warning bell was rung, the stop block moved aside and the loaded wagon descended drawing up an empty, the two passing midway.

At the head of the incline were two levers which acted on the band brakes controlling the cable drum in the winding house. As soon as the empty wagon reached the top, a lever was pulled to place the stop block across the rails.

Meanwhile at the foot of the incline, the loaded wagon had its brake applied just before the cable stopped so that the cable was slack and made uncoupling easier. The wagon was then allowed to roll by gravity round a sharp curve to a siding parallel, but at a lower level, than the main line.

When a train of empty wagons arrived, the shunter at the foot of the incline went along the train uncoupling the wagons and recoupling with a 'D'-shaped

118 THE BRISTOL-RADSTOCK-FROME LINE

No. D3183, the Radstock diesel shunter, propels empty wagons to the foot of Kilmersdon Colliery incline, 23rd August, 1968. *Author*

Kilmersdon Colliery sidings, view towards Radstock, 6th June, 1968. The wagon on the left is probably a 'cripple'. *Author*

DESCRIPTION OF THE LINE

Ammonia tankers stand on the former down line, 30th March, 1983. Part of the former triangle at the foot of Kilmersdon Colliery incline can be seen on the left. *Author*

Ammonia tankers in the foreground stand on the former Kilmersdon Colliery siding: those on the left stand at a buffer stop on the former down line. View towards Frome, 30th March, 1983. *Author*

Empty wagons at the foot of the incline *circa* 1905: Phipps, Devizes No. 555 with dumb buffers and No. 342 Writhlington/Foxcote/Kilmersdon collieries. *Author's Collection*

Empty wagons left; a loaded wagon (*right*) has been uncoupled and is gravitating to the loaded wagon sidings on the right. The main Radstock to Mells Road line is in the background, 3rd January, 1968. The incline-keeper's white hut can be seen behind the left-hand wagon. *Author*

link joining the middle link of each 3-link wagon coupling, this giving sufficient play to avoid buffer locking on the sharp curve at the foot of the incline. The 'D' link was composed of a reverse 'C'-shape and a movable shank. As each 'D'-link came between the first and second wagon, a cord was attached by the shunter to the shank and as the first wagon went up the incline, those behind it were drawn forward and when far enough, the cord was pulled, resulting in the 'D' link and its pin falling to the ground.

In 1968 an average of about 50 wagons was taken away daily. From the 1960s, most of Radstock coal was sent to the electricity generating station at Portishead and the zinc smelting plant at Avonmouth. Kilmersdon made a profit of £131,000 1965-1966 and £150,000 1966-1967.

A small culvert below the triangular junction at the foot of the colliery incline sometimes became choked. It dammed back all the water coming down the stream until it rose to a height sufficient to flood the ground floor of houses over a mile distant. At 8.30 am on Sunday 13th May, 1906 the colliery incline embankment could no longer stand the pressure and gave way and with a thunderous roar the mass of water flowed through Radstock causing hundreds of pounds worth of damage.

If absolutely necessary, coal wagons could be carefully gravitated from Kilmersdon sidings to Radstock yard. Should an engine be standing in the siding to which they were to enter the guard or shunter in charge had to instruct the driver to move to another siding and make no further move until so informed. When it was clear, the guard or shunter then released only sufficient brakes to allow the wagons to run slowly towards the yard accompanying the movement on foot and prepared to apply the brakes to bring the wagons to a stand as necessary. Gravitation was prohibited after sunset, during fog or falling snow.

In 1972 the power station at Portishead changed to oil burning. Coal winding ceased at Kilmersdon on 31st August, 1973 and at Lower Writhlington on 28th September, 1973, the last coal leaving by rail on 16th November. Kilmersdon incline closed 7th October, but was temporarily reopened in the spring of 1974 for the removal of plant. Seven National Coal Board wagons were the last to be lowered on 9th June, 1974. Following the colliery's closure, the sidings at the foot of the incline were used for storage by Messrs Marcroft until repairs ceased at the end of June 1988.

Almost directly opposite the Kilmersdon incline, from about 1867 was a self-acting incline of 2 ft 8½ in. gauge tramway from Upper Writhlington Colliery. An earlier proposal to construct a branch to the Somerset Coal Canal tramway was probably abortive. The pit closed on 28th January, 1898, but the tramway from Foxcote and Lower Writhlington collieries to the standard gauge Upper Writhlington sidings remained. The 2 ft 8½ in. gauge line from Foxcote Colliery to Turner's Tower for land sales was worked by *Foxcote*, an 0-6-0ST, Hudswell, Clarke No. 369 of 1890. The colliery closed in February 1931. Lower Writhlington Colliery used *Enterprise* a 0-4-0ST Hunslet No. 279 of 1882 delivered new; *Writhlington* a 0-6-0ST Hudswell, Clarke No. 546 of 1900 also delivered new and 0-4-0ST Peckett No 1546 of 1920, new. It is believed that all were scrapped when the line closed in 1940. The private siding agreement

View up the incline in November 1966. An empty wagon can be seen on the right. A spring point causes a descending loaded wagon to take the left-hand road. *W.H. Harbor*

A view up the incline showing both sets of spring points, 6th June, 1968. Where the track becomes double, an empty ascending wagon is directed to the left road. 16 ton mineral wagon No. B113157 has run away and overturned. *Author*

A view down the incline in November 1966. *W.H. Harbor*

Maintenance work on the incline, 6th June, 1968. A rake of empty wagons can be seen at the foot of the incline. *Author*

The loading bays at Kilmersdon Colliery on 6th January, 1968 viewed from the cab of Peckett 0-4-0ST Works No. 1788. *Author*

Hunslet 0-4-0T Works No. 1684 of 1931 at Kilmersdon Colliery, November 1966. *W.H. Harbor*

No. 1788 at Kilmersdon Colliery, 6th June, 1968.   *Author*

No. 1788 shunting near the head of the incline, 6th June, 1968.   *Author*

No. 1788 near Kilmerson Colliery in May 1972. All the wagons on the right are National Coal Board 'for internal use only' wagons. *W.H. Harbor*

No. 1788 alongside the winding house, 6th June, 1968. *Author*

DESCRIPTION OF THE LINE

Ruston & Hornsby locomotive, Works No. 200793 of 1940, at Kilmersdon Colliery on 5th October, 1965.
Revd Alan Newman

Narrow gauge tubs at Kilmersdon Colliery, November 1966.
W.H. Harbor

Decorative underline bridge over the B3139 at 6 miles 9½ chains, close to the Ammerdown Estate, 3rd September, 1989. *John Mann*

Detail of the coat of arms on the bridge pictured above, 6th February, 2008. *Author*

terminated on 31st August, 1944, the siding was taken out of use on 31st October, 1950 and lifted the following year.

Huish Colliery, a short distance south, opened in April 1824 and its coal was dispatched by road until 1855 when a 2 ft 8½ in. gauge incline linked the pit with the GWR. The mine closed on 29th February, 1912.

Examining the coalfield's production figures for the 1890s, Down & Warrington in *The History of the Somerset Coalfield* write regarding tonnages lifted from 1888 to 1899 that only a third of the total coalfield output was carried by rail. The GWR carried about eight times as much coal as the S&D. In 1899 12 pits were on the GWR and two on the S&D. 'The six pits at Radstock and Writhlington had connections to both systems and must have made greater use of the GWR, so the construction of the S&D benefitted the coalfield little.'

From Radstock South signal box the line rose at 1 in 77/69 to Mells Road (5 miles 18 chains). This section was doubled in 1880. At first simply 'Mells', on 16th November, 1898 it was renamed Mells Road to make it less deceptive as the village was two miles distant in a bee line and three by road. The main building opened on 4th March 1887, a standard GWR station of the period in red brick relieved with white. It was almost identical to one at Marlow. West to east it contained a porters' room and store; station master's office; waiting room; ladies' room and WC; and gentlemen's WC. The up platform had a wooden waiting shelter and corrugated iron lock-up. In 1909 both platforms were extended by 90 ft at their Radstock ends to 289 ft. A Design 'D' cottage was erected c.1915. A re-railing ramp was stored at the rear of the up platform. Unusually the stop board for up goods and mineral trains was sited on the down platform. Latterly the station was used by only a few passengers as the bus was more convenient. It became a halt on 17th September, 1956. During World War II hospital trains arrived with wounded soldiers bound for Longleat House which was used as a convalescent home for United States' servicemen. Although Frome and Warminster stations were nearer, their use would have delayed wartime traffic. At one time Mells Road dealt with milk from 28 farms.

A single siding and goods shed 84 ft 6 in. x 30 ft 6 in. with a 1½ ton crane within, was situated north of the passenger station, but to the south were two looped sidings and two terminal roads. The loops were between Mells North signal box and Mells South box, but these closed on 13th March, 1910 and were replaced by a single box set midway. This opened on 13th March, 1910 and closed 15th August, 1966. Marcroft's had a wagon repair siding on the up side opposite the signal box, while a wagon examiner's hut was situated near the east end of the up platform.

Circa 1900 the station was staffed by a station master, three porter-signalmen and two signalmen. On 15th January, 1921 it employed a station master, lady clerk, two signalmen, two shunters, a parcel porter and two porters. The female clerk was engaged chiefly in the goods office preparing accounts and entering the books. The parcel porter dealt with parcels work, prepared statistics and invoiced goods outwards traffic. The porter was mainly employed in the goods shed, while the second porter attended to all passenger trains, signal, station and office lamps, and sheeted and roped wagons. The shunters between them covered 7.30 am to 11.00 pm.

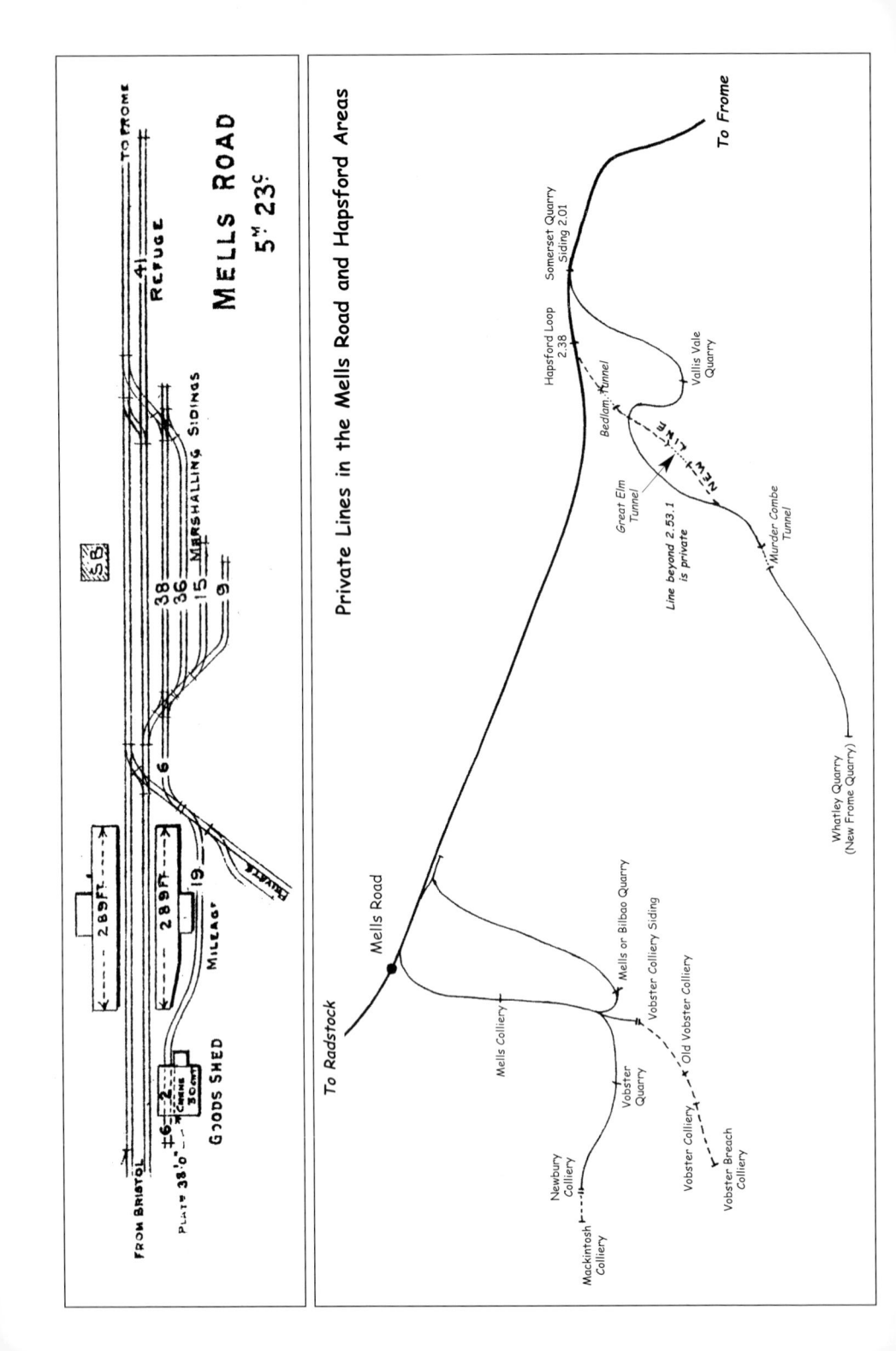

MELLS ROAD 5M 23C

Private Lines in the Mells Road and Hapsford Areas

DESCRIPTION OF THE LINE 131

'8750' class 0-6-0PT No. 9615 working the 1.30 pm Saturdays-only Temple Meads to Frome service on 8th August, 1959, climbing the 1 in 69 to Mells Road Halt. *Michael Jenkins*

Mells Road Halt on 27th March, 1959. The back of the stop board is to the right of the station nameboard. *R.E. Toop*

Mells Road, view up, 19th April, 1963. *Author*

'57XX' class 0-6-0PT No. 7784 (82D, Westbury) at Mells Road Halt with a down freight on 4th April, 1959. Three wagons carry sheeted timber and behind these is a runner wagon and a typical Great Western Railway 'Toad' brake van. *R.E. Toop*

DESCRIPTION OF THE LINE 133

BR Standard class '3' 2-6-2T No. 82040 in lined green livery arrives at Mells Road Halt on 4th April, 1959 with the 10.50 am Frome to Temple Meads service. On the left is the wagon examiner's hut. *R.E. Toop*

'8750' class 0-6-0PT No. 9668 and a B-set form the 10.17 am Temple Meads to Frome service on 4th April, 1959 and enter Mells Road Halt. The engine is commendably clean even though it has been out of shops for a few years. Notice the stop board, right, and the goods shed, left. Its siding is level, but the main line falls at 1 in 67. *R.E. Toop*

134 THE BRISTOL-RADSTOCK-FROME LINE

Mells Road looking neglected *circa* 1964. The waiting shelter on the up platform has been removed. On the far right is a Berry Wiggins tar tanker, while in the distance are wagons awaiting repair. *Lens of Sutton Collection*

The fireman of '4575' class 2-6-2T No. 5542 working the 1.10 pm Frome to Temple Meads service leans out to surrender the token to the Mells Road signalman, 4th April, 1959. *R.E. Toop*

Due to the gradient, no shunting was permitted on the down line unless the engine was leading towards Radstock, or points from the down line were set for the goods shed sidings. All wagons shunted from the down main to the goods shed siding had to remain coupled to the engine or train until they had been propelled into the siding. The station master was responsible for seeing that no less than two hand scotches and a brake stick were always ready for use at the Radstock end of the station. On 23rd September, 1927 a private siding agreement was made with S.C. Gilson & Sons for a nine-wagon siding built with a loading bank so that steam lorries could bring stone and chippings from Cooks Wood Quarry. In 1982 Messrs Weaver stored redundant sleepers at Mells Road dispatching them by road. The station closed to ordinary goods traffic on 15th June, 1964.

Immediately south of the passenger station the 2 mile 12 ch. long branch to Vobster curved from the main line to serve collieries and two quarries. It partly followed the route of the abandoned Dorset & Somerset Canal. The Newbury Railway as it was called, began when on 31st August, 1858 the Westbury Iron Co. Ltd leased Newbury Colliery to provide coal for its blast furnaces. Between 1869 and 1874 the line carried 193,000 tons of coal and coke. The broad gauge line was constructed by Rowland Brotherhood, an original Westbury company shareholder. When building the line, limestone was discovered near Vobster crossroads, so the iron company leased this land to provide limestone for its furnaces. Vobster quarry was productive and around 1900 put 36,000 tons of stone on rail annually.

Mackintosh Colliery, ½ mile west of Newbury Colliery, opened in 1867. Its coal was carried by narrow gauge tramway to the Newbury pit where it was loaded into broad gauge wagons. It closed on 5th December, 1919. Ironically, immediately prior to closure, a start had been made on building a standard gauge extension to the colliery. The last coal was wound at Newbury on 8th August, 1927, following which the track between the colliery and Vobster Quarry was lifted. In the 1950s a large proportion of Vobster Quarry's output was used by London Transport for ballast. The quarry closed on 30th June, 1966. Mells Colliery opened in the mid-1860s and closed on 30th October, 1943. In 1965 only the Mells Road end of the line was used for dealing with cement and Tarmac products.

It is believed that in broad gauge days the Newbury Railway was worked by a GWR locomotive. About 1870 the Westbury Iron Co. Ltd purchased a broad gauge convertible Henry Hughes 0-4-0ST to work the line. With conversion concurrently with the GWR line in June 1874, it was replaced by a standard gauge Hudswell, Clarke & Rodgers 0-6-0ST (Works No. 153). The convertible locomotive was regauged at Westbury Iron Works and returned to the Newbury Railway for use when No. 153 was unavailable. No. 153 worked the line until the mid-1930s when it was scrapped. *Mosscotte*, a Manning, Wardle 0-6-0ST (Works No. 1426 of 1898) ex-Stockport Corporation's Kinder Reservoir construction arrived in 1912. *Mildred*, an Avonside 0-6-0ST, No. 1763 of 1917, ex-Inland Waterways & Docks, Purfleet No. 33, arrived on the Newbury line by June 1920. Transferred to the adjacent Roads Reconstruction Ltd on 1st January, 1934, it was derelict by 1955 and scrapped in February 1959. No. 292 *Nidd*, a

136   THE BRISTOL-RADSTOCK-FROME LINE

View up at the Vobster branch junction on 26th June, 1981. Some track has been lifted, but pointwork has not been replaced by plain rail.   *John Mann*

Sentinel Works No. 9398 inside the shed at Vobster Quarry on 19th April, 1963.   *Author*

Kerr, Stuart 0-4-0ST No. 3112 of 1918, arrived about 1930. *Nidd* was able to handle 40 loaded wagons to Mells Road. It was scrapped *circa* 1955.

An 0-4-0 vertical-boilered Sentinel, No. 6219 of 1927, rebuilt from 0-4-0 petrol/paraffin Manning, Wardle No. 1954 of 1918, ran on the line. Its date of withdrawal is unknown. In May 1953 Sentinel No. 9398 of 1950 arrived, a 100 hp locomotive which had been the builder's demonstrator. It was sent to Thomas Hill (Rotherham) Ltd in January 1965 and possibly re-emerged as diesel-hydraulic No. 153c. A similar Sentinel, New Frome Quarry No. 1 (Works No. 9374 of 1947), arrived in 1963 and was returned in August 1965 following the cessation of traffic on the Newbury Railway.

Mells Colliery had a Hunslet 0-4-0ST which arrived around 1922. It was probably scrapped soon after the arrival from the GWR, Swindon, of 0-6-0T Chapman & Furneaux Works No. 1161 of 1898, in March 1931. This engine was built for the Lambourn Valley Railway (LVR) which ran from Newbury to Lambourn in Berkshire. Named *Ealhswith*, it was sold to the Cambrian Railways in June 1904 when the LVR found it more economical to use steam railmotors hired from the GWR. The Cambrian numbered it 26 and when the Cambrian was taken over by the GWR in 1922, it became No. 820. The GWR withdrew it in March 1930. In February 1945 Mells Colliery sold it for £100 to George Cohen for scrap. The Newbury line probably used a Manning, Wardle 0-6-0ST (Works No. 1426) supplied new in 1898 to contractor Abraham Kellett. Final motive power on the Newbury Railway was a buffer-fitted road vehicle which shunted the bitumen terminal close to Mells Road station. Roads Reconstruction Ltd owned rectangular tar wagons lettered 'Mells Road Tar Works'. They were painted in a livery of black with white lettering and red shading, the 'RR' symbol in yellow. Being non-pool wagons they escaped requisitioning in 1939 for common user purposes and so continued to run as private owner wagons during the BR era. This tar distillation plant ceased production in 1964. Amey Roadstone Construction (ARC), successors to Roads Reconstruction, terminated the private siding agreement on 21st May, 1968 and the Newbury Railway was lifted in July 1973.

Mells Quarry had two private sidings beside the main line near the passenger platform, each holding 12 wagons. One siding was for full wagons and the other for empties. As the connection from the refuge siding to the private line was on a falling 1 in 100, wagons were required to remain coupled to the engine until they had been propelled inside the gate. The gates were then padlocked across the line and the lever working the points to release the siding chained and padlocked. The keys of both padlocks were held in the signal box.

A new 2 ft gauge line, the Vobster Light Railway ran for a mile from near Holwell Farm Restaurant, Mells, along the Newbury Railway formation. Worked by eight 4-wheeled diesel locomotives, it opened in 1992 and closed in 1994.

East of Vobster Quarry a standard gauge line ran south-west to serve Bilboa Colliery from which a narrow gauge system linked with Old Vobster Colliery, Vobster Colliery and Vobster Breach Colliery. Near Bilboa coal depot, a line curved east to Bilboa Quarry which was also served by a direct line from south of Mells Road station. The Bilbao Railway was laid under an agreement of October 1925 and the line worked by *Nidd* and a Hudswell, Clarke 0-4-0ST (Works No. 700

0-6-0T *Ealhswith*, later used on the Somersetshire Newbury Railway, seen here at the Berkshire Newbury station with a train to Lambourn. As was contemporary practice, the engine has side chains in addition to a central coupling.
Author's Collection

Vertical-boilered Sentinel Works No. 9398 of 1950 at Vobster Quarry on 20th July, 1954.
Revd Alan Newman

of 1907). The quarry was taken over by Roads Reconstruction Ltd in 1934 and the line closed as a connection was made from the Newbury Railway.

Back on the main line, beyond Mells Road the track was single. A mile south of the station it fell at 1 in 48 and then for ¾ mile at 1 in 60. Near the foot of this incline, in 1894 two looped sidings were provided to serve the 2 ft gauge tramway from Somerset Stone Quarries. Access was via ground frames, Somerset Quarries North (2 miles 15 chains) or Somerset Quarries South (2 miles 1 chain). As the main line was on a gradient of 1 in 51, for safety the siding adjacent and parallel with the main line was always required to be kept clear for a train calling, which in all cases was required to be shunted into it and not allowed to stand on the main line without an engine being attached. The siding was normally worked by a pilot trip from Frome. The ground frames were unlocked by train staff for the section, or the Frome to Somerset Quarries shunting staff for trains from Frome not going through to Mells Road. When a steam engine experienced difficulty in lifting a train out of Hapsford siding, a quarry Sentinel would assist at the rear as far as the notice board. A guard collected consignment notes from quarry staff and gave them to the Frome station master.

Initially the quarry's internal lines were horse-worked 2 ft 3 in. gauge, but in 1907 *Midge*, a Kerr, Stuart 0-4-0ST (Works No. 1017) arrived, followed in 1910 by sister engine *Wren* No. 1188. When Roads Reconstruction (1934) Ltd took over the working, the line was replaced by one of 2 ft gauge.

The 2 ft gauge line was worked by Kerr, Stuart 0-4-2ST No. 3065 of 1918 which arrived from Tytherington Quarry about 1934; Avonside 0-4-0T No. 2072 of 1933 from Messrs Pugsley about November 1941 and ex-works Ruston & Hornsby 4-wheeled diesel-mechanical Nos. 198313 and 200507, both new in 1940.

In 1940 a new quarry opened at Whatley, a 2½ mile-long narrow gauge line passing along the extremely picturesquely wooded Vallis Vale. In 1943 this narrow gauge line was replaced by one of standard gauge, enabling larger and more economic wagons to be used. These were 10-12 ton capacity side-tippers built by Hudson. From 1946 stone was loaded into these by excavator and hauled to Hapsford in trains of approximately eight wagons. The steepest gradient an empty train had to climb was about 1 in 50 and the sharpest curve traversed had a 120 ft radius.

The line was worked by *Medway*, a Barclay 0-4-0ST (Works No. 969 of 1903) which came from George Cohen about 1943. It was dismantled in 1956 but the frame and water tank were retained as a water carrier until scrapped about November 1974. Sentinel vertical boiler No. 6090 of 1925 arrived from Road Reconstruction's Cranmore depot in September 1944. This engine was notable for having been shown at the Wembley Exhibition of 1925. It was scrapped about April 1969. *Nidd* came from Vobster Quarry and returned *circa* 1949. A Vulcan 0-4-0ST No. 798 of 1876 arrived from Sandford Quarry in 1946 and was scrapped in August 1949. In 1947 and 1948 Nos. 1, 2, and 3, vertical boiler Sentinels (Works Nos. 9374, 9386, 9387) arrived new. Locals called them 'tiffers' due to the sound of their exhaust. A Fowler 0-4-0 diesel-mechanical No. 19645 of 1932 came from Cranmore depot and after working the line was sent on to Sandford Quarry. A vertical boiler Sentinel No. 9391 of 1949 arrived from Sandford Quarry in September 1964 and was sent to Thomas Hill in January

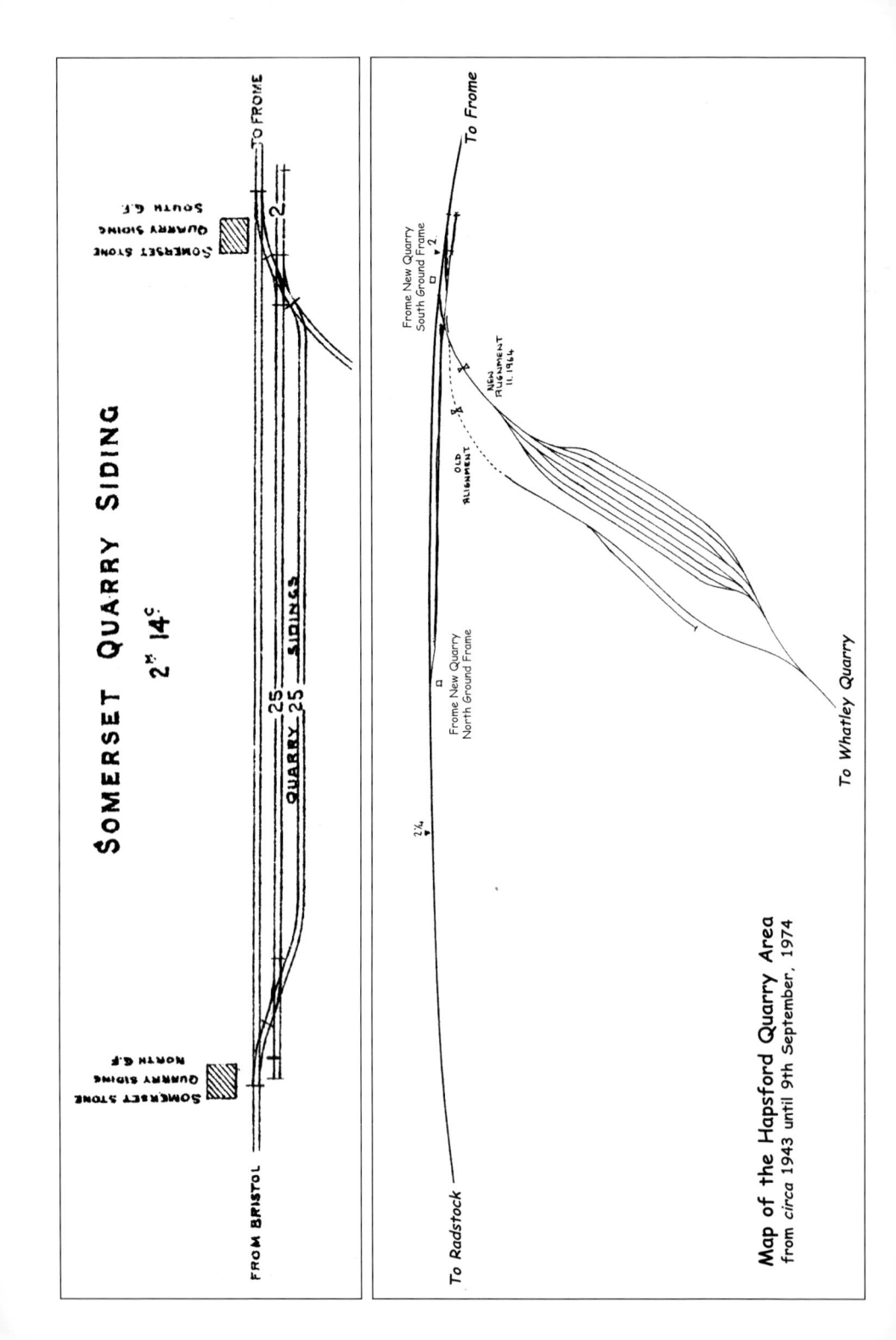

SOMERSET QUARRY SIDING
2ᴍ 14ᶜ

Map of the Hapsford Quarry Area
from *circa* 1943 until 9th September, 1974

Mells Colliery *circa* 1918. The loading plant is beneath the corrugated iron buildings. Both horse-drawn carts are being loaded from chutes. *Author's Collection*

Staff at Mells Colliery in the early 1900s. *Left to right:* Gilbert West, chief clerk, Christopher James, clerk, Herbert Withers, dispatch clerk and Mr Wyatt, secretary.

Collection Gerald Quartley

Somerset Quarries North ground frame, view west on 26th February, 1979. Notice the lighting alongside the track. *John Mann*

Somerset Quarries North ground frame in autumn 1983. Since the previous photograph was taken the track has been slewed to give a straight run to Whatley Quarry. *John Mann*

DESCRIPTION OF THE LINE 143

The sylvan entrance to Hapsford Quarry/Whatley Quarry line on 3rd April, 1956. A loaded hopper wagon awaits collection. The sign above the right-hand gate reads: 'Notice: Only engines of the 19XX class may go beyond this board'. The lower notice says that persons not fastening the gate were liable to a penalty of 40 shillings. *Author*

Medway, Andrew Barclay No. 969 of 1903 at Hapsford Quarry on 20th July, 1954. It has a wooden buffer beam and no three-link coupling at the front. It came via George Cohen, from the Associated Portland Cement Manufacturers Ltd, Burham Works, Kent. *Revd Alan Newman*

Vertical-boilered Sentinel No. 6090 of 1925 at Hapsford Quarry on 20th July, 1958.
Revd Alan Newman

Roads Reconstruction No. 3 at Hapsford on 12th October, 1967.
Revd Alan Newman

No. D6508, a Southern Region Birmingham Railway Carriage & Wagon Co. type '3', leaves the main line at Somerset Stone Quarries South ground frame with bogie wagons and descends towards the Exchange Sidings on 5th November, 1968. *Author*

A general view of Hapsford Exchange Sidings on 5th November, 1968. *Author*

The severe curve on the approach to Whatley Quarry on 3rd April, 1956. *Author*

Whatley stone terminal: Amey's locomotive shed is on the left, adjacent is a grounded van body, 31st May, 1978. *John Mann*

DESCRIPTION OF THE LINE 147

Hapsford screening plant on 24th May, 1958 with locomotives Nos. 1 and 6090 in view.
R.E. Toop

Whatley, view towards the loading plant on 6th October, 2007. *Author*

ARC Nos. 2 and 3 draw loaded bogie hopper wagons from Whatley Quarry in May 1972.
W.H. Harbor

ARC Nos. 2 and 3 near Whatley loading plant in May 1972.
W.H. Harbor

DESCRIPTION OF THE LINE 149

No. 3 at Hapsford Quarry. The engine shed is in the background, 12th October, 1967.
Revd Alan Newman

No. 3 in the locomotive shed at Hapsford on 3rd April, 1956. The right-hand track has no shed door, so is sheltered by a sheet. *Author*

Roads Reconstruction No. 1 in Whatley Quarry on 10th May, 1958. *R.E. Toop*

No. 3 at Hapsford on 9th May, 1959. These internal use wagons have brakes on one side only.
Revd Alan Newman

DESCRIPTION OF THE LINE   151

Diesel-hydraulic locomotives Nos. 3 and 2 in tandem approaching Great Elm level crossing with empty wagons to Whatley Quarry on 5th November, 1968. The line has been reconstructed with heavier rail. The sharpest curves have been eased to enable main line wagons to reach Whatley Quarry, in this case they are 21.5 tonne hoppers.   *Author*

ARC diesel-hydraulic Sentinels in tandem haul loaded bogie hoppers over Great Elm level crossing on 27th May, 1970.   *Author*

152 THE BRISTOL-RADSTOCK-FROME LINE

Somerset Quarries North Junction and the north portal of Bedlam tunnel in July 1986; line to Radstock to the right.
John Mann

The viaduct and south portal of Bedlam tunnel in autumn 1985. Cables for communication are in the channelling on the right. Notice the electric light in the tunnel.
John Mann

1965. Steam began to be ousted in earnest when a new No. 1, a four-wheeled diesel-hydraulic rebuilt Thomas Hill/Sentinel (Works No. 133V) appeared in 1963, followed by No. 2 (Works No, 136C) in 1964. In 1965 Thomas Hill four-wheeled diesel-hydraulic No. 3 (Works No. 152V) appeared and No. 4 (Works No. 200V) in 1968.

On 13th April, 1987 0-6-0 diesel-hydraulic Rolls Royce (Works No. 10220 of 1965), ex-Port of Bristol No. 41, was hired from Thomas Hill for two months in 1987 and when returned was replaced by No. 53, Thomas Hill 0-6-0 diesel-hydraulic No. 261V of 1976 which was retained until 9th July, 1988.

Pride of Whatley, a Thomas Hill six-wheeled diesel-hydraulic (Works No. 325V) of 1987, arrived new, while No. 68 was ex-BR 0-6-0 diesel-electric No. 08652 built at Horwich in 1959 which was occasionally borrowed from the Merehead stone terminal. No. 08296 built at Derby in 1957 and No. 08947 built at Darlington in 1962 also appeared. *Whatley Endeavour*, a Bo-Bo diesel-electric, General Motors (No. 37903 of 1972) originally new to the Boke Project, Guinea, arrived on 30th July, 2002 following overhaul. A 4-wheel brake tender was supplied by Thomas Hill/Sentinel in 1965, but was scrapped *circa* 1969 following collision damage. It was not replaced as the use of continuous brakes rendered it superfluous.

Until November 1964 Roads Reconstruction/Amalgamated Roadstone Construction (ARC) took wagons from the Hapsford plant to be collected from a gate near the South ground frame (*see map page 140*). To deal with the planned expansion, eight looped sidings were provided inside the gate and from 1965 BR locomotives collected and delivered from these sidings. The junction was realigned, the South ground frame moving slightly east to 1 mile 78 chains.

The line to Whatley Quarry had some of its extremely sharp curves eased so that main line 50 ton capacity hopper wagons could travel to the quarry and thus avoid transhipment at Hapsford. These track improvements were made in 1967. The Thomas Hill diesel-hydraulics usually worked in tandem worked from one cab. A stone processing plant was in use at Whatley by 1965 so that stone no longer needed processing at Hapsford.

As traffic developed economies were required. A quarry graduate trainee was asked to solve the problem of severe curves in the winding valley preventing main line locomotives reaching Whatley. His solution was to straighten the line using tunnels. Such a route meant that the quarry only had to provide locomotives for shunting and not for a trip from the quarry to the exchange sidings.

The new 2¾ mile-long line opened on 9th September, 1974 (*see map page 130*). Built at a cost of £500,000 it left the Radstock branch at the Radstock end of the Hapsford Loop (2 miles 38 chains) and passed through three tunnels; a 'Please sound your horn' notice before each. There was Bedlam tunnel, 269 yds-long (2 miles 51 chains to 2 miles 64 chains) with both portals of Bath stone. It is a shallow tunnel and supported by curved steel beams at 2 ft intervals, with concrete slabs set between. Then follows a two-span steel bridge on concrete abutments over Mells River and then Great Elm tunnel, 319 yds (2 miles 76 chains to 3 miles 11 chains), also on a curve. Its northern portal is natural rock and the tunnel is unlined. The route passes along Fordbury Bottom on the alignment of the original railway to Murder Combe tunnel, 55 yds (3 miles 56 chains to 3 miles 58 chains) before reaching Whatley Quarry.

154 THE BRISTOL-RADSTOCK-FROME LINE

The north portal of Bedlam tunnel, autumn 1983. A notice warns of the danger of entering the tunnel. *John Mann*

English Electric class '37s' Nos. 37258 and 37224 with a train of BR hoppers for Whatley Quarry cross the two-span girder bridge over the Mells River on 29th August, 1978. *Author*

DESCRIPTION OF THE LINE 155

Class '37s' Nos. 37258 and 37224 emerge from Great Elm tunnel and run light towards Westbury on 29th August, 1978. They are passing a polite notice that reads: 'Please sound your horn'.
Author

The south portal of Great Elm tunnel, 6th February, 2008. *Author*

Right: The tight curve to Murder Combe tunnel. Note the flat-bottomed track with spacers to maintain the gauge, 10th December, 1972.
John Mann

Below: The rather less sharply curved track to the entrance to Murder Combe tunnel after easing to allow access of main line locomotives. The curve is check-railed and subject to a 10 mph speed restriction, 6th October, 2007. *Author*

DESCRIPTION OF THE LINE

On the main line the ½ mile-long Hapsford Loop (replacing the former Somerset Quarry Siding) was provided between Somerset Quarry South ground frame and Somerset Quarry North ground frame (2 miles 38 chains), the lines to Whatley and Radstock dividing at the latter. Points were set for Whatley and a train for Mells Road direction faced a 'Stop and Reverse Points' board. The quarry branch curved and descended through a clay and stone cutting. Somerset Quarry North ground frame was taken out of use on 20th November, 1975 after which trains were directed to the respective routes at the South ground frame. However, to save maintenance of the loop, on 12th November, 1976 the South frame was closed and the North frame reinstated, replaced by Hapsford ground frame on 6th/8th October, 1984. The permanent way was maintained by the quarry, but inspected by BR weekly.

Aided by a £3.7m government grant, in 1987 Whatley Quarry installed an automatic loading system which put 2½ million tons of stone on rail annually and took it off the roads.

Today Whatley Quarry extends to about one square kilometre and has an annual output from its crushing and screening plant of up to 5 million tonnes of which approximately 70 per cent is dispatched by rail. Two pairs of double-ended sidings are served by a conveyor, the fifth road being a run-round loop. Each siding has a capacity of up to 30 bogie wagons. Should traffic require it, two trains may be loaded simultaneously: one by conveyor and the other from trackside mechanical grabs. Eight to ten trains leave daily. The 413 wagon fleet consists of two types: bogie hoppers for use at terminals with bottom door discharge facilities, and bogie box wagons for discharge by mechanical grab. Most destinations for the stone are in south-east England – Allington, Ardingly, Dagenham, Fareham, Exeter, Hayes, Hothfield, St Pancras and West Drayton. The scalpings (waste material) sold for infill is occasionally sent by rail to Tytherington, South Gloucestershire, for local distribution.

Beyond Somerset Quarry Sidings were a series of timber viaducts over the River Frome: Leonard's Mill 62 yds (1 mile 25 chains); Gas House 41 yds (0 miles 66 chains) with five spans on brick piers; North Row 46 yds (0 miles 51 chains) also five spans and Willow Vale 37 yds (0 miles 30 chains) with five spans. All these viaducts were replaced in iron in 1902/1903, the replacement at Gas House costing £1,959. Four chains from Frome West Junction was an occupation overbridge built with laminated beams, surprisingly still in use in 1957.

There were two looped sidings: Gas Works at 0 miles 59 chains which had a weighbridge. It opened *circa* 1895 and was removed 8th February, 1948 as gas was piped from Bath. If clearing the Gas Works siding by the Mells Road to Frome goods would delay a passenger train, a separate trip was run.

Frome Market Siding North ground frame was at 0 miles 50 chains and the South 0 miles 42 chains. The siding had a cattle pen. It opened *circa* 1888 and was taken out of use on 30th October, 1968. The Market Siding was worked from Frome without a brake van and, if propelled , a competent man was to ride on the leading vehicle, or if drawn, on the rear vehicle. Both sidings were worked by Annett's key attached to the electric train staff, or the Frome West to Somerset Quarries shunting staff.

At Frome West signal box (0 miles 15 chains) the line bifurcated: the left-hand double track ran to Frome North box and the right-hand was used by trains to

Above: The 62 yds-long Leonard's Mill viaduct on 14th April, 1991. The centre rails guard against a derailed train plunging off the viaduct.
John Mann

Right: Leonard's Mill viaduct.
John Mann

DESCRIPTION OF THE LINE 159

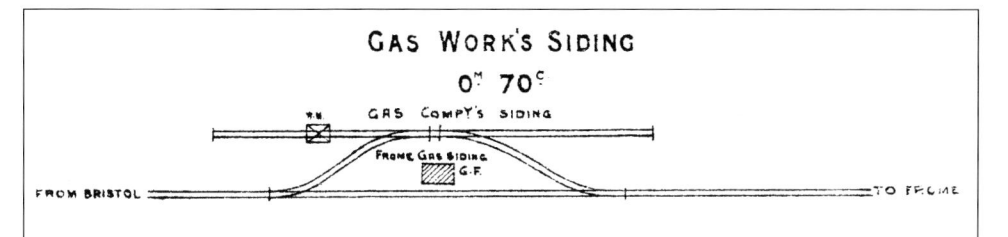

The 41 yds-long Gas House viaduct view north on 6th October, 2007. *Author*

The timber-built 46 yds-long North Row viaduct in 1902. Notice the supporting props. Work on the replacement bridge has started. *Author's Collection*

'8750' class 0-6-0PT No. 9612 with the 2.53 pm Temple Meads to Frome service on 8th August, 1959, crossing North Row viaduct. The end of Frome Market siding is on the far right.
Matthew Jenkins

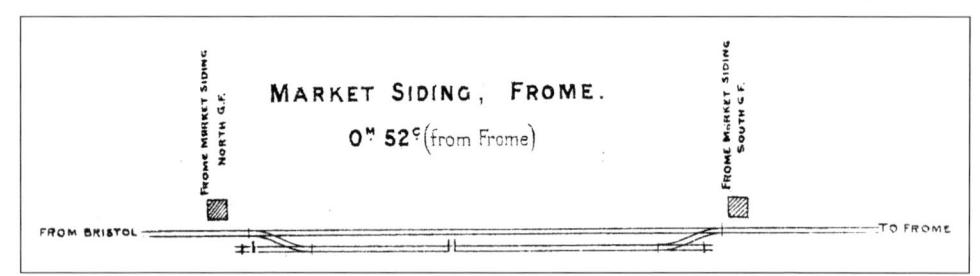

The 37 yds-long timber-built Willow Vale viaduct in 1902, just prior to its replacement. Note the props.
Author's Collection

Frome and the west. It opened with the introduction of passenger services on 5th July, 1875. With the withdrawal of passenger services on 2nd November, 1959, the line to Frome station became redundant as all trains from the branch proceeded towards Westbury. The West Junction to North Junction line (Mineral Loop) was singled 11th August, 1968 using the former down line, the up road becoming a siding. This line served Mileage Yard C, while that to Radstock Branch Junction and Frome station had Mileage Yard B. From 1921 to 1964 Edward Cockey & Sons Ltd had a private siding to serve its iron works making such products as gas holders, standards, pillars and iron roofs. Mileage Yard B had its sidings lifted on 3rd December, 1974. Frome West signal box had been reduced to a ground frame on 24th September, 1933. Frome North, or Mineral Junction, signal box closed 6th/8th October, 1984 and is now preserved at Didcot Railway Centre. Approaching Frome West signal box, a train for Frome station gave two whistles, or for Frome North, three long whistles. At Frome Middle box (north of the station and closed on 17th September, 1933 replaced by a new South box) a train to or from the branch gave two whistles.

Frome station opened on 7th October, 1850 as the temporary terminus of the Wilts, Somerset & Weymouth Railway. The Grade II station is unusual because it is almost entirely constructed of timber, whereas most other stations with train sheds had stone buildings. The station is believed to have been designed by J.R. Hannaford, one of Brunel's assistants, in the office of R.H. Brereton, Brunel's chief assistant. The roof carries a full-length glazed vent with a cut-out in the end gables. The roof truss has slender iron ties supported on the up side by the single-storey station offices, and on the other by wooden columns along the platform, cantilever-fashion, the overhang passing backwards to the rear side wall. The offices have a corrugated iron hipped roof, a small canopy and red brick chimney stacks.

The down platform had a waiting room. At the up end of the up platform was a short bay platform with umbrella canopy. Diesel railcars, auto-train trailers and vehicles over 70 ft in length were prohibited from using the bay road. Drivers were instructed that after reversing into this platform, they must not start forward until the guard had checked that the couplings were intact as the reverse curve could cause a coupling link to rise over a drawbar hook.

About 1875 a covered footbridge was situated immediately north of the train shed and before the bay platform canopy. The up platform was extended 50 ft north in 1893 and the down southwards late in 1920 or early 1921. In 1882 a station master's house was built for £260 by Frome builder John Vallis, adjacent to the end of the bay platform.

Following a decrease in passenger traffic, the down road through the station was lifted on 19th August 1970 and the up bay taken out of use on 17th May, 1971. By this time the 120-year-old structure was showing its age, the train shed being propped up with a steel post. BR proposed its demolition and replacement with a modern 'bus-stop' type platform shelter. Fortunately local opinion opposed this notion and had the building listed.

South of the up platform was a loading bank with a 3 ton crane, a goods shed with 1½ ton crane and a 6 ton crane in the yard on the down side. Further south was a single-road engine shed. The goods shed was designed by C. Hellman.

Former Frome West Junction; siding on the right is for Tarmac, 18th August, 1982. *John Mann*

Tarmac sidings, left, and the Radstock line on the right, 17th June, 1983, looking from North Junction to the former West Junction. *John Mann*

DESCRIPTION OF THE LINE 163

Frome North Junction, view looking west; main line left, Radstock line to the right, autumn 1985.
John Mann

Frome North Junction, view looking towards Radstock on 14th June, 1988. *Author*

164   THE BRISTOL-RADSTOCK-FROME LINE

A down stopping train hauled by a 'Metro' class 2-4-0T calls at Frome. The rails are set on longitudinal sleepers. *Author's Collection*

The station pilot, an 0-6-0PT, at Frome down platform on 20th May, 1922. A porter rolls a milk churn. *Lens of Sutton Collection*

DESCRIPTION OF THE LINE 165

Frome station, viewed in the up direction *circa* 1960; Frome South box is beyond the train shed.
Lens of Sutton Collection

A view in the up direction from beneath the train shed in May 1974. *S. Apperley*

166 THE BRISTOL-RADSTOCK-FROME LINE

The exterior of the timber-built station at Frome, May 1974. *S. Apperley*

Frome view in the down direction. The structure beyond the South signal box is a footbridge.
M.J. Tozer Collection

DESCRIPTION OF THE LINE

Frome station, viewed in the down direction in May 1974. The bay platform is on the right. A Swindon 3-car Cross-Country dmu is at the end of the platform. Beyond the corrugated iron shed is a large quantity of concrete ducting for use in connection with the elimination of semaphore signalling.
S. Apperley

BR Standard class '3' 2-6-2T No. 82042 (of Bristol Bath Road shed) with the 10.00 am Temple Meads to Frome service, at Frome on Sunday 13th September, 1959, the last day of Sunday working. This train carried 50 to 60 passengers whose destination was Weymouth.
Michael Jenkins

Frome station, viewed in the down direction *circa* 1935. An up stopping train hauled by a 4-6-0 approaches while at the end of the down platform an 0-6-0PT takes on water. The 3-ton yard crane can be seen by the rake of wagons at the loading bank, while E. Bailey & Son Ltd's large malthouse is on the far right. *Author's Collection*

Ex-GWR 'Hall' class 4-6-0 No. 4927 *Saint Brides Hall* (of Bristol Bath Road shed) at Frome with a down express, 13th September, 1959. On the right is a B-set below a loading gauge. The timber-built goods shed is on the left. *Michael Jenkins*

'4575' class 2-6-2T No. 5509 arrives at Frome with a train from Temple Meads on 17th August, 1958. It is painted in lined green livery and has the new style crest. The bracket signal is worth a second look. *Hugh Davies*

Cattle pens were sited on the up side. Late in 1931 a milk siding for Express Dairies was added alongside the bay platform, railway milk tankers going to London. The milk sidings were taken out of use on 15th June, 1966. From 1891 until 1967 a siding served the maltings of E. Bailey & Son Ltd. Latterly bulk grain wagons were used for transport. On the down side were the signal department's stores and workshops. From the first week of January 1974 Mobil Oil Ltd used sidings on the east side of the passenger station and by 1983 they had been placed in a secure compound.

Circa 1900 Frome was staffed by a station master, two shunters, three goods guards, two foremen, three passenger guards, four signalmen, two porters, one policeman and two lad porters. Around 1950 this had been altered to: station master, five porters, two yard foremen, eight guards, eight shunters, three booking clerks and three signalmen in the South box.

The bay platform at Frome on 15th August, 1970. On the right are the remains of the former milk siding. *John Mann*

'Dean Goods' 0-6-0 No. 2395 at Hallatrow *circa* 1910. *Gerald Quartley Collection*

'1661' class 0-6-0ST No. 1682 and '2721' 0-6-0PT No. 2783 at Radstock *circa* 1920.
Author's Collection

Chapter Four

Locomotives

It is not known what locomotives first worked the broad gauge branch, but it is assumed that they would have had to be 0-6-0s to cope with the gradients. *Whetham* and *Miles* 'Sir Watkin' class 0-6-0STs were certainly shedded at Radstock in 1873 and worked coal traffic to Salisbury. In standard gauge days, goods trains were worked by 0-6-0STs and 0-6-0 'Standard Goods' while by World War I the '2301' class had appeared.

Passenger trains were worked by 0-4-2T and 2-4-0T engines which were in due course superseded by '45XX' class 2-6-2Ts and '57XX' 0-6-0PTs. By June 1910, 59 ft steam rail motor No. 82 was allocated to Radstock shed and its principal use was over the Camerton branch. In 1927 the Radstock branch was upgraded to allow 'Blue' route-restricted locomotives and their use on heavier trains gave an estimated saving of almost £3,000 annually. From about 1935 'ROD' class 2-8-0s were popular for Bristol to Radstock workings, being suited for hauling heavy loads up steep gradients. They would happily plod up gradients with only 80 lb. of steam as opposed to a maximum of 185. Too long to turn at Radstock, they usually ran tender-first from Bristol. Engines used included Nos. 3011/4/7/32/44/46.

The *Railway Observer* for November 1955 reported No. 3017 taking 44 wagons and a brake van on the early morning freight from Bristol. This represented the maximum number of empties an ROD was permitted to take unaided over the 1 in 60 gradients, though on this occasion the first six wagons were actually loaded.

During World War II the 'RODs' were transferred for main line duties and 2-6-2Ts substituted on the branch. The 'RODs' returned *circa* 1950 when the National Coal Board complained that the Prairie tanks were unable to clear the traffic due to their lack of haulage capacity.

In January 1955 four engines worked goods trains on the branch:

Frome '57XX' class 0-6-0PT

Days	dep.	From	To	arr.	Type
Mon.-Sat.	7.00 *am*	Frome	Radstock	8.16 *am*	Freight
Mon.-Sat.	8.45	Radstock	Old Mills Siding	9.04	Freight
Mon.-Sat.	9.24	Old Mills Siding	Radstock	9.56	Freight
Mon.-Fri.	12.40 *pm*	Radstock	Hallatrow	1.25 *pm*	Freight
Mon.-Fri.	2.25	Hallatrow	Radstock	3.10	Freight
Mon.-Fri.	4.00	Radstock	Frome	4.44	Freight
Mon.-Fri.	5.06	Frome	Westbury	5.24	Freight
Mon.-Fri.	5.50	Westbury	Frome	6.00	Engine and brake van
Sat. only	12.45	Radstock	Frome	1.49	Freight
Sat. only	2.45	Frome	Westbury	3.00	Freight
Sat. only	3.05	Westbury	Frome	3.15	Engine and brake van

'ROD' class 2-8-0 No. 3034 at Radstock, 7th February, 1953. *Revd Alan Newman*

'4575' class 2-6-2T No. 4590 at Frome with a down stopping train, *circa* 1939.
P.Q. Treloar Collection

Frome '57XX' class 0-6-0PT

Days	dep.	From	To	arr.	Type
Mon.-Fri.	11.30 am	Frome	Radstock	12.26 pm	Freight
Mon.-Fri.	?.??	Radstock	Mells Road	?.??	Engine and brake van
Mon.-Fri.	4.50 pm	Mells Rd	Frome	5.14	Freight
Mon.-Fri.	5.52	Frome	Westbury	6.08	Freight
Mon.-Fri.	7.40	Westbury	Frome	7.58	Freight

Frome '57XX' class 0-6-0PT

Days	dep.	From	To	arr.	Type
Mon.-Sat.	8.10 am	Frome	Somerset Quarries	8.20 am	Engine and brake van
Mon.-Sat.	8.35	Somerset Quarries	Frome	8.45	Freight
Mon.-Sat.	9.10	Frome	Somerset Quarries	9.20	Freight
Mon.-Sat.	9.35	Somerset Quarries	Frome	9.43	Engine and brake van
Sat. only	11.30	Frome	Somerset Quarries	11.40	Freight
Mon.-Fri.	11.50	Frome	Somerset Quarries	12.00 nn	Freight
Mon.-Sat.	12.10 pm	Somerset Quarries	Frome	12.20 pm	Freight
Mon.-Sat.	2.45	Frome	Somerset Quarries	2.55	Engine and brake van
Mon.-Sat.	3.15	Somerset Quarries	Frome	3.25	Freight

Bristol St Philip's Marsh '30XX' class 2-8-0

Days	dep.	From	To	arr.	Type
Mon.-Fri.	8.32 am	Bristol E. Depot	Hallatrow	10.39 am	Freight
Mon.-Fri.	11.25	Hallatrow	Bristol E. Depot	1.34 pm	Freight
Sat. only	8.32	Bristol E. Depot	Radstock	12.17	Freight
Sat. only	12.45 pm	Radstock	Bristol E. Depot	2.59	Freight
Mon.-Fri.	2.05	Bristol E. Depot	Radstock	4.21	Freight
Mon.-Fri.	5.00	Radstock	Bristol Kingsland Rd	7.55	Freight

In 1948 and 1949 '81XX' class 2-6-2T No. 8105, a St Philip's Marsh engine, worked the daily goods to Pensford and Radstock until transferred to Bristol, Bath Road in the four weeks ending 5th November, 1949. At one time '31XX' class 2-6-2Ts No. 3114 and No. 3120 were shedded at St Philip's Marsh and were frequently used on the branch. Overflow pipes were fitted to limit the water capacity from 2,000 to 1,600 gallons and this reduced their top heaviness. Some drivers desired the extra water capacity and blanked off the overflow pipes with corks.

When the 'RODs' were withdrawn as life-expired in the 1950s, it was believed that '41XX' class 2-6-2Ts would be a suitable replacement. During the last week of September 1955, No. 4131, recently transferred to St Philip's Marsh from Neyland, was tested over the branch, but with a load of only 15-20 wagons made hard-going.

On 10th October, 1955 a '94XX' class 0-6-0PT was tried and later a '2251' class 0-6-0. They proved not overwhelmingly successful and it was decided to use a '41XX' in the autumn.

A '56XX' class 0-6-2T appeared on a ballast train on 1st March, 1956. During the summer of 1956 a '43XX' class 2-6-0 was tested and No. 5367 became the

'4575' class 2-6-2T No. 5554 allocated to Westbury, rounds the North Somerset Junction to Marsh Junction curve on 27th June, 1959 with the 10.17 am Saturdays-only Temple Meads to Frome service.
Michael Jenkins

'8750' class 0-6-0PT at Radstock, February 1961. The brake van is rather off course. It is branded: 'To work 9.15 pm (SX) Bristol TM to Acton, 8.48 pm (SO) Bristol TM to Acton, 8.5 pm (SX) Paddington to Kingsland Road, 8.40 pm (SO) Paddington to Bristol TM'.
Roger Holmes

regular engine, but was not a great success, especially when running tender-first, through lack of sanders for reverse working. Occasionally when working a down freight it would slip to a standstill by Fry's Bottom Colliery resulting in the train being divided and brought to Clutton in two portions.

On 9th August, 1956 No. 4131 returned, but stalled with 26 empties and a brake van near Marsh Junction at the foot of the 1 in 62 bank. The train was divided: the first 14 wagons being taken to Brislington and placed in a siding while No. 4131 returned for the rest of the train, Nos. 4102 and 5104 also often appeared. A correspondent to the September 1955 *Railway Observer* wrote: 'The 'ROD' 2-8-0s, for so long complete masters of the job, are sorely missed'. '42XX' class 2-8-0T No. 4231 worked goods trains over the branch regularly in the late 1950s, while 'Manor' class 4-6-0s were very rarely seen.

A Radstock to Bristol coal train double-headed by two '56XX' class 0-6-2Ts was not unknown. '28xx' class 2-8-0s were not generally allowed over the branch, but sometimes one was permitted on an engineering train. In the late 1950s goods trains were generally handled by '22XX' class 0-6-0, '57XX' or '94XX' class 0-6-0PT or a large Prairie tank. One driver of a '41XX' engine found that he had a loose tyre caused by the heat generated from braking on the long gradients. In the 1950s normally only 0-6-0PTs worked goods trains south of Radstock.

Passenger trains were usually hauled by '45XX' or '55XX' class 2-6-2Ts or '57XX' class 0-6-0PTs. On Saturday 19th May, 1956 the 5.55 pm express from Frome to Temple Meads was loaded to seven coaches - a tough proposition for the '45XX' to work over the steeply-graded line.

On 11th January, 1955 London Midland & Scottish Railway (LMS)-designed Ivatt class '2MT' 2-6-0 No. 46527 headed the 6.47 am Bristol to Frome for the first time. Subsequently No. 46507 appeared regularly on the 5.20 pm Temple Meads to Frome and Wells. On 10th March, 1955 Ivatt class '2MT' 2-6-2T No. 41202 worked over the line on the 6.47 am and continued to appear on branch trains.

The 10.50 am Frome to Temple Meads was normally worked by a Bristol, Bath Road '45XX' class 2-6-2T, but on 1st September, 1956 was headed by No. 5518 of Gloucester, Horton Road, fresh from the Swindon shops. On 15th September, 1956 the same train was hauled by Ivatt class '2' 2-6-2T No. 41294 of Ashford, which also had been through the Swindon shops, whilst the 12 noon train the following day produced No. 4584 of Truro.

In March 1958 BR Standard class '3' 2-6-2Ts displaced from the Cardiff Valleys by dmus, worked some branch trains. '43XX' class engines were used on excursion trains, such as to Weston-super-Mare, an example being No. 6368 on 3rd August, 1953. On Whit Monday, 1956 the 10.50 am Frome to Temple Meads was worked by 2-6-0 No. 6399 which, with seven corridor coaches, ran through to Weston-super-Mare. Its return working in the evening was treated as an extra train over the North Somerset branch, this allowing it to avoid Temple Meads station by traversing the Bristol Avoiding Line, but necessitating a reversal and change of engine at the East Depot Down Yard signal box. No. 6320, an oil-burner converted back to coal, took a 10-coach Bedminster to Weymouth excursion unassisted up Brislington Bank quite easily. Certainly in the latter period of passenger working, a tender engine was used on Christmas Day, because this type carried sufficient water for a return trip, so that any

BR Standard class '3' 2-6-2T No. 82042 between Whitchurch Halt and the summit near Maes Knoll. The 10.00 am Saturdays-only Temple Meads to Frome service on 2nd August, 1959 has its B-set strengthened with an ex-LNER corridor coach. *Michael Jenkins*

Ivatt class '2' 2-6-2T No. 41203 between Marsh Junction and the River Avon viaduct with the 5.20 pm Temple Meads to Frome service, 25th July, 1959. *Michael Jenkins*

interruption to a water supply would not be a problem and delay either crew or passengers. On 28th April, 1957, 4-4-0 No. 3440 *City of Truro* piloted 2-6-2T No. 5528 with an RCTS 'North Somerset Railtour' over the line.

The last passenger train from Temple Meads to Frome on 31st October, 1959, the 7.45 pm, was hauled by No. 5532 (a Frome engine) with five coaches (two non-corridor and three corridor). The last train Frome to Temple Meads, No. 41203 headed the same five coaches with 0-6-0PT No. 9612 'inside' the train engine to assist up the bank to Mells Road. From Mells Road onwards, No. 41203 was unassisted.

GWR diesel railcars often worked the 1.05 pm Temple Meads-Clevedon-Cheddar Valley-Radstock-Temple Meads. A BR diesel set appeared on 10th May, 1958 when an enthusiasts' special ran from Lyme Regis to Gloucester.

The late 1940s diagram for diesel railcars over the branch included:

6.50 am Temple Meads-Frome-Bruton (then empty coaching stock to Frome)
8.55 am Weds, Sats-only Frome-Radstock
9.37 am Weds, Sats-only Radstock-Frome-Wells
6.06 pm Frome-Temple Meads (part of Temple Meads-Clevedon-Cheddar Valley turn)

The complete diagram used the railcar for 18½ hours out of 24 during which it covered 265½ miles. In mid-August 1948 the diesel comprised No. 22 and No. 38 with third class corridor No. 1960 as intermediate trailer, but in late August, the duty was worked by No. 24 hauling a third class corridor.

Branch passenger traffic was handled by Bath Road No. 4 link with 12 turns of duty generally using '45XX' or '55XX' class tank engine or Collett 0-6-0s. One interesting pre-World War II turn for St Philip's Marsh freight men was working the 5.30 am goods to Radstock; then travelling 'on the cushions' to Frome, there relieving the 3.30 am ex-Weymouth goods crew and working the '28XX' or '43XX' back to Bristol via Westbury.

Maximum loads at April 1913 were:

Hallatrow-Brislington:	2 tender engines, 28 vehicles + van
	or 1 tender engine, 1 tank engine, 30 vehicles + van
	or 2 tank engines, 32 vehicles + van
Brislington-Bristol:	2 engines, 45 vehicles + van

In the June 1958 working timetable appendix 'Blue' engines were restricted to an overall limit of 25 mph, while engines of BR Standard class '4' 4-6-0 and 'Manor' class 4-6-0 were not to exceed 5 mph through platforms at Mells Road Halt; 'Red' '84XX' and '94XX' class 0-6-0PTs were allowed a speed not exceeding 20 mph throughout.

When double-loaded trains worked over any part of the line from Marsh Junction to Radstock, both engines were required to work at the front. Double-loaded trains Marsh Junction to Clutton, or Hallatrow to Old Mills, and double-loaded up trains Radstock to Bristol were required to have two brake vans with a guard in each. A single train was not to exceed 28 loaded wagons. Double-loaded freight trains from Radstock to Mells Road could be assisted in the rear.

In 1957 English Electric designed and built an experimental 0-6-0 shunter D226, soon renumbered D0226 to avoid confusion with type '4' locomotives. It was

'Warship' class diesel-hydraulic No. D820 *Grenville* at Radstock. It has made a trial run on 23rd August, 1968 with a train of empty wagons. Two locomotive inspectors are visible. No. D3183, the Radstock diesel shunter, stands on the right. *Author*

No. D3183 the Radstock shunter, on 23rd August, 1968. *Author*

made in order to evaluate the slightly higher power output of a 500 bhp engine compared with the earlier 350 bhp pattern. It had diesel-electric transmission and a maximum speed of 35 mph compared with 15 mph of a standard shunter. The additional speed was obtained by using a double reduction gear box for the final drive. On 13th October, 1959 it was sent from Stratford (Eastern Region) to St Philip's Marsh for two weeks testing on the Western Region. D0226 appeared one Friday tea time at Temple Meads platform 7 heading a passenger train to Frome only very shortly before the branch closed to passenger traffic. This was probably the first appearance of a diesel locomotive on the branch. It carried a black livery relieved with a broad red band on its hood coming to a 'V' at the front.

As St Philip's Marsh steam shed was to close on 13th June, 1964, on 28th April a 'Hymek' diesel-hydraulic was tested on the 8.20 am East Depot to Radstock coal empties going into all sidings en route. It returned at noon with three empty 'Vanfits' and 21 loaded 16-ton mineral wagons. The experiment proved successful so on 15th June, 1964 the Bristol to Radstock freight service was dieselized using 'Hymeks' supplied by the Bath Road depot. If one was unavailable, until it closed on 16th November, 1965, the ex-LMS Barrow Road shed supplied a steam locomotive.

From 14th June, 1964 the line was worked under 'one engine in steam' regulations causing closure of signal boxes at Pensford, Clutton and Hallatrow. Westbury and Frome continued to use '57XX' class 0-6-0PTs at the southern end of the line, but with the closure of Westbury shed in September 1965, 'Hymeks' took over at this end of the line too.

The first diesel-hydraulic 'Warship' to appear on the branch was No. D820 *Grenville* on 23rd August, 1968 and 'Western' class diesel-hydraulic No. D1053 *Western Patriarch* appeared in October 1968. Class '31s' and '33s' were fairly frequent visitors to Hapsford siding from where they were worked ballast trains to Westbury, Salisbury and the Southern Region. Coal trains from Radstock to Portishead power station via Westbury in 1968 were initially worked by 'Hymeks', but 'Warships' also took their turn. By the end of November 1969 No. 1040 *Western Queen* was in use after being fitted with an anti-slip device. A diesel shunter was based at Radstock for yard duties and working to and from Writhlington Colliery.

When the improved line to Whatley Quarry opened on 9th September, 1974, BR locomotives were able to work there including class '33s' (often in pairs), classes '37', '45', '46' (very rare), '47', '50' and '56'. In 1986 the latter class hauled trains to Southern Region terminals at Ardingly, Allington, Chislehurst, Fareham and Totton. When HRH The Princess Royal opened the automatic loading system at the quarry on 9th October, 1987 she named No. 56001 *Whatley*.

Contemporary BR locomotives had poor availability, whereas those built by General Motors had 98 per cent - one of the best in the world for a freight locomotive. The best way to get traction is to have a certain amount of slip and the General Motors design was best for this and had the ability to haul approximately 5,100 tonnes. Foster Yeoman wished to have its own fleet of General Motors locomotives and after overcoming the problem of BR drivers unwilling to drive non-BR locomotives, in 1989 purchased a fleet of class '59s'. In 1990 class '59s' built by General Motors were purchased by ARC and named appropriately:

'Hymek' class diesel-hydraulic No. D7002 having the left the train in Hapsford yard, leaves with a 'Shark' 'Return to Yate for Tytherington Quarry' 20 ton brake van. Notice its ballast ploughs. It was built in 1957 by the Birmingham Railway Carriage & Wagon Co. *Author*

Class '37' No. 37224 emerges from Bedlam tunnel with empty ARC hoppers, 29th August, 1978.
Author

Class '56' No. 56039 climbs Upton Scudamore Bank, assisted by No. 56048 at the rear, on a stone train from Whatley Quarry on 7th April, 1989. *Bob Sweet*

Class '56' 56001 *Whatley* on display at Merehead Quarry open day on 25th June, 1989. In the background is preserved BR Standard class '4' 4-6-0 No. 75029. *Bob Sweet*

Class '59' No. 59101 *Village of Whatley* displayed at Merehead Quarry open day on 28th June, 1998. The locomotive is carrying the revised ARC livery. *Bob Sweet*

Class '59' No. 59101, in Hanson livery, approaches Fairwood Road Junction, Westbury, on stone empties bound for Whatley Quarry on 11th August, 2004. *Bob Sweet*

59101	*Village of Whatley*
59102	*Village of Chantry*
59103	*Village of Mells*
59104	*Village of Great Elm*

In October 1993 ARC at Whatley and Foster Yeoman's similar activities at Merehead combined their traction resources. As Mendip Rail the joint operation offered the advantage that locomotives and rolling stock could be interchanged to match the needs of the respective quarries. This cut mileages of stock and proved economic. ARC later became Hanson Aggregates, and Foster Yeoman, Aggregate Industries, Mendip Rail continuing to run rail operations. Merger of resources enabled the combined wagon fleet to be reduced by 250 vehicles in the first five years. Both companies livery is blue and silver with the owner's logo on the body. Mendip Rail also maintains six red English, Welsh & Scottish Railway (EWS) locomotives Nos. 59201-6, now owned by DB Schenker.

Fuel tanks are usually topped up each time a locomotive returns to the quarry. An 'A' examination is carried out every seven days; 'A+' every 13 weeks; 'B' every 6 months and 'B+' annually. Every six weeks a locomotive is washed. Most of the maintenance is carried out at Merehead, Whatley just being used for fuelling and minor servicing. Tyres are re-turned at Cardiff Canton. Shunting at Whatley loading terminal is carried out by No. 120, a General Motors design, ex-BR No. 08652 and Vanguard 0-4-0 shunter No. 4. On 28th February, 1992 the Swindon & Cricklade Railway loaned its class '25' No. D5222 to ARC while its 0-6-0 diesel *Pride of Whatley* was out of service. A total of 12 fitting staff are engaged at Merehead and Whatley depots.

Locomotive Sheds

Radstock

The single-track shed 74 ft x 20 ft is a stone-walled building with a slate roof and still extant. It was lengthened at the east end partly in sandstone, the west end being limestone. The addition was very neatly carried out and is not immediately noticeable. Situated at the east end of the goods yard, the broad gauge shed opened in 1866 and was converted to standard gauge track in June 1874, offset as only one line was moved . In 1873 a pump house was erected to lift water from the adjacent brook. In 1894 a coal stage and a 41 ft 6 in. diameter turntable were installed nearby. The wall of the turntable pit formed a bank of the nearby stream, so a walkway had to be cantilevered out over the brook for enginemen pushing a locomotive round. Some tank engine drivers turned their engine so that it would face chimney-first for the return journey. Extension bars were supplied to enable longer engines to be turned. The table was removed in 1951. An inspection pit was provided both inside and outside the shed.

On 1st January, 1901 the shed was allocated 'Metro' class 2-4-0T No. 1459. The shed closed in 1929.

Latterly a class '08' diesel shunter was allocated to the ex-S&D shed at Radstock. Initially the engine was changed weekly, but later this period was

'8750' class 0-6-0PT No. 4636 (of Westbury shed) outside the timber-built Frome locomotive shed. No. 4636 was new to Westbury in December 1942 and its last GWR shed (before nationalization) was Frome. It was withdrawn in September 1965 from Westbury. Another 0-6-0PT stands behind No. 4636. On the left are two '45XX' class 2-6-2Ts. In the background is the malthouse.

Colin Roberts Collection

A '4575' class 2-6-2T outside Frome locomotive shed *circa* 1939. The barrow is to carry bundles of fire lighters and the bucket on the tank for crew washing. It is a summer view as the steam heating pipe has been removed.

P.Q. Treloar Collection

extended to six weeks, it returning to Westbury shed on a Saturday afternoon. At Radstock it was refuelled from a BP road tanker. With the closure of Writhlington Colliery on 16th November, 1973, the shunter was removed and the train engine shunted Radstock west yard.

Steam railmotors allocated to Radstock (for the Camerton branch)

No.	Month/Year
2	9/13
4	9/12
10	6/12, 8/12
11	9/12
14	7/12, 11/12
17	1/13, 3/13, 8/13, 11/13, 1/14, 5/14, 9/14
25	1/15
26	11/10
27	2/12
30	12/10, 3/11, 11/11
42	12/11, 11/12
43	7/11
44	12/12
46	10/10
48	12/11, 4/12
62	4/13, 12/13, 3/14, 10/14, 2/15
69	2/15
80	9/10
81	6/11, 1/12, 7/13, 6/14
82	6/10
86	2/13, 10/13, 11/13
87	1/14, 10/14, 11/14
89	12/14

Total 23

Frome

The 60 ft x 20 ft shed was a timber building with slated roof. Designed by Hannaford, it contained two 52 ft-long inspection pits, the inside one later filled in. The Kelbus sand drier was inside the shed. Nearby was a mess hut, enginemen's cabin, chargeman's hut - also used for storing lamps and oil, and a shunters' cabin. Originally a coal stage was provided, but by the 1950s coal was loaded directly from wagon to bunker. Near the shed entrance was a water column fed from a tank on the opposite side of the main line. There was no turntable as the shed was only allocated tank engines. Should a tender engine have needed turning this could have been carried out on the triangle. Latterly Frome was a sub-depot to Westbury and used the main depot's GWR code 'WES' or BR '82D'. Staff in the 1950s comprised: three chargemen, about eight locomotive crews, two steam fitters and nine shed hands. The time allowed to prepare a fire and raise sufficient steam to move a locomotive was 1 hour 45 minutes. The shed closed in September 1963.

Frome allocation, March 1854
Argo   'Premier' class 0-6-0
Eclipse   'Sun' class 2-2-2ST
Stromboli   'Leo' class 2-4-0
Virgo   'Leo' class 2-4-0
Morning Star   4-2-2ST

Total   5

Frome allocation, May 1922
986   'Metro' class 2-4-0T
1135   '1016' class 0-6-0ST
1180, 1228, 1598   '1076' class 0-6-0PT
1791   '1854' class 0-6-0PT
1814, 1817   '1813' class 0-6-0PT
2769   '2721' class 0-6-0PT
56, 57   Steam railmotor 70 ft 'Branch' type

Total   9 + 2 steam railmotors

Frome allocation, 1st January, 1934
2705   '655' class 0-6-0PT
2799   '2721' class 0-6-0PT
4536   '45XX' class 2-6-2T
5514, 5563   '4575' class 2-6-2T
5402   '54XX' class 0-6-0PT
8745   '57XX' class 0-6-0PT

Total   7

Frome allocation, 31st December, 1947
2023   '2021' class 0-6-0PT
3731, 3735, 3758, 4636, 9762   '8750' class 0-6-0PT
5403, 5406   '54XX' class 0-6-0PT
5718, 8744, 8745   '57XX' class 0-6-0PT

Total   11

In the 1950s about seven '57XX' class 0-6-0PTs were allocated to Frome for freight and shunting. Early in 1955 they included Nos. 3696, 3735, 4607, 4636, 4647, 5701, 5718, 5757, 5767, 5771, 7727, 7748, 7784, 8744, 9612, 9615, 9628, 9762.

Frome allocation, 30th September, 1956
3614, 3696, 4647, 5771, 7727, 7784   '57XX' class 0-6-0PT
4551, 4572   '45XX' class 2-6-2T

Total   8

Engines seen on shed in June 1959 were:

3614, 4636, 5757, 7784, 9668   '57XX' class 0-6-0PT
4555   '45XX' class 2-6-2T
5508, 5542   '4575' class 2-6-2T

Chapter Five

Timetables and Train Working

Passenger

On 3rd September, 1873 four trains ran each way on weekdays only, most taking 50 minutes each way between Temple Meads and Radstock. Single fares for first, second, third and Parliamentary class trains were 3s. 9d., 2s. 6d., 1s. 9d. and 1s. 4d. respectively with first class returns at 6s. 3d. and second at 4s. 3d. All trains carried three classes and one each way carried passengers at Parliamentary fares. The service was capable of being worked by one set of coaches. On weekdays the last down train left Bristol at 6.15 pm, but on Saturdays an extra train left Temple Meads at 8.30 pm.

Through working of standard gauge passenger trains from Temple Meads to Frome began on 5th July, 1875. Five trains ran each way, all classes were carried. On weekdays trains crossed at Radstock. Two trains ran each way on Sundays. Trains took 1 hour 15 mins each way for the 24¼ miles, but the 12.30 pm ex-Temple Meads omitted Brislington and arrived at Frome at 1.40 pm.

By February 1888 the first train left Radstock at 7.25 am for Temple Meads, but all the others, five each way, ran to or from Frome except the 8.22 pm from Bristol which terminated at Radstock. The time taken varied between 1 hour 10 minutes and 1 hour 15 minutes. On Sundays two each way worked throughout. In 1889 five down passenger trains were run plus the 6.30 pm Bristol to Radstock, the down trains taking 1 hour 5 minutes to 1 hour 8 minutes, and five up trains 1 hour 3 minutes to 1 hour 13 minutes. Two ran on Sundays.

The 1895 timetable showed six down, and additionally, one Bristol to Radstock Thursdays- and Saturdays-only and a mid-evening train Bristol to Radstock. There were six up plus the first train, the 7.42 am Radstock to Bristol. Two ran on Sundays. The similar service in 1903 showed one down train which originated from Wells and another which ran through from Taunton. The six up trains included one from Wells, one from Yatton, one Weymouth to Portishead and one from Bath. On Sundays two trains ran each way. The 16th January, 1913 saw a new steam railmotor service introduced to cater for miners. It left Clutton at 5.50 am and ran to Mells Road before returning from there to Radstock. There was one train running on Thursdays- and Saturdays-only from Bristol to Radstock, and another just to Hallatrow. One of the through trains was from Weston-super-Mare and another from Portishead. The 6.26 pm motor train from the Cam Valley ran from Hallatrow to Radstock. In the up direction, of the six through trains, one went to Wells and another to Portishead. Trains not originating and terminating at Temple Meads reduced platform time at this very busy station.

In July 1925 eight ran each way plus a Saturdays-only Bristol to Radstock and return, trains taking about 1 hour 10 minutes. Two ran on Sundays. The summer of 1932 had eight each way plus two Saturdays-only each way plus a non-stop Saturdays-only Bristol to Frome taking 1 hour 8 minutes. Four trains ran on Sunday.

In November 1944 five ran each way plus a Saturdays-only and two each way on Sundays. Down trains took four minutes or so over the hour, but one up

Above: 'Metro' and pannier tank engines heading passenger trains at Hallatrow, looking towards Radstock *circa* 1910. Porters are in the correct position on the platform with barrows ready to offload any incoming parcels traffic.
Author's Collection

Right: Handbill advertising a half-day excursion to London on 2nd October, 1926 from stations between Whitchurch Halt and Frome.

Great Western Railway.

On SATURDAY, OCTOBER 2nd
A HALF-DAY EXPRESS EXCURSION will run to

LONDON

Leaving	At	Return Fares, Third Class.
	p.m.	
Whitchurch Halt	12 22	
Pensford	12 33	
Clutton	12 43	**6/-**
Hallatrow	12 48	
Midsomer Norton & Welton	12 56	
Radstock	1 3	
Mells Road	1 13	**5/6**
Frome	1 35	
Paddington arr.	3 40	

The Return Train will leave Paddington Station at 12.20 a.m. (early Sunday morning).

TAKE YOUR TICKET IN ADVANCE.

Children under three years of age, FREE; three and under twelve, HALF-PRICE. NO LUGGAGE ALLOWED.

FELIX J. C. POLE, General Manager.
PADDINGTON STATION, Sept., 1926.

Bristol, 3,000   Burleigh Ltd., Printers, Bristol.   B7/1091

train not calling at Whitchurch Halt and only setting down at Brislington, ran from Frome to Bristol in 58 minutes, while the first up train calling at all stations took 1 hour 1 minute.

Eight down trains were run in the summer of 1948, the first being a diesel railcar to Bruton. This car ran a 9.40 am Wednesdays- and Saturdays-only Radstock to Frome and Wells service. Eight up trains were run (one diesel) plus the Wednesdays- and Saturdays-only diesel Frome to Radstock. The 10.50 am Frome to Bristol did not call at Whitchurch and Brislington (except on Saturdays when it set down at Brislington) and made the journey in 58 minutes. The 5.55 pm ex-Frome which only called at Radstock and Pensford took the same time. It was a connection off the 3.40 pm Weymouth Quay boat train, for expresses for the North: the 7.15 pm to Manchester and Glasgow or the 7.25 pm to Newcastle.

The 5.55 pm branch train carried express passenger code 'A' headlamps, but was often a 0-6-0PT hauling a two-coach non-corridor 'B-set'. In the event of the 5.55 pm running late, Frome advised Bristol to hold the connections to the North. No corresponding down express was run over the North Somerset as passengers from Bristol and beyond travelled via Westbury on the 8.30 am Weston-super-Mare to Weymouth which connected with the down boat train.

As the 5.55 pm only served two stations, all branch stations were served by a train which left Frome at 6.05 pm and arrived at Temple Meads at 7.21 pm, taking 1 hour 16 minutes. This was often worked by a GWR railcar which left Bristol at 1.15 pm to Clevedon, giving the auto-engine working most of the branch trains an opportunity to have its fire cleaned at Yatton shed. The diesel went round the Cheddar Valley line to Frome.

When an auto-trailer was returned from Swindon to Yatton after overhaul, it nearly always seemed to arrive the wrong way round and had to be sent back to Bristol to be turned by being run round the avoiding line. One not-too-bright shunter at Yatton thought he could overcome the problem by coupling it to the rear of the 6.10 pm round the Cheddar Valley line and back to Bristol via Radstock. All it achieved was to describe a circle and arrive back at Yatton the same way round!

In accordance with the agreement between the British Transport Commission and the Government, from 30th June, 1958 the Western Region withdrew lightly-loaded and unremunerative workings generally caused by bus competition which served village centres. The branch timetable was roughly halved to a mere three workings from Bristol, with a gap from 6.47 am to 5.20 pm! Four trains ran from Frome, all but one retained largely for ease of crew rostering and evening season ticket holders. Four extra trains ran each way on Saturdays, but the Sunday service of three each way remained unaltered. All but one train, apart from the Channel Islands express, called at every station. On Saturdays-only the 5.55 pm ex-Frome called only at Radstock and Pensford as it used to do on other weekdays, but the economy cuts introduced three more stops to compensate for the Monday to Friday cancellation of the 6.06 pm from Frome which had hitherto dealt with passengers at stations not served by the express. The fastest down train took 1 hour 4 minutes and the fastest up 58 minutes.

Pre-World War I the whole of the Somerset coalfield closed on a mid-July Saturday and railway companies ran trips. It was not only the mines, the

Radstock Co-operative Society's works and shops closed as did the British Wagon Co., Radstock Coal & Wagon Co. and two breweries. In 1911 one such excursion to Weston-super-Mare consisted of four long (at least one had 18 'large' coaches) double-headed trains run from Radstock picking up at stations to Pensford.

In total about 3,000 passengers were carried.

Depart	Radstock	5.30 *am*	6.09 *am*	6.38 *am*	
	Welton	5.38	6.10	6.48	
	Camerton	–	–	–	6.40 *am*
	Hallatrow	5.50	6.31	7.03	7.18
	Clutton	5.56	6.41	–	7.33
	Pensford	6.05	6.52	–	–
Arrive	Weston-super-Mare	7.24	8.09	8.41	8.49

The return trains left Weston-super-Mare at 7.05, 7.53, 8.25 and 8.35 pm.

This was by no means the only destination. Four hundred passengers travelled from branch stations to Paddington, 200 of these originating from Radstock including a party of 80 employees, friends and relatives of the British Wagon Works, two coaches being reserved for them. The train was of corridor stock and called at all stations Brislington to Frome, engines being changed at the latter station. The return train left Paddington at 11.55 pm and reached Radstock at 3.30 am. The excursion to Weymouth carried 200 passengers from Radstock including 60 friends and employees of the Radstock Coal & Wagon Co., Camerton Parish Church choir, Kilmersdon Wesley Sunday School and the local Pearl Insurance Co staff. It left Radstock at 8.00 am and the return left Weymouth at 8.10 pm arriving about 10.30 pm. Two specials were also run to Weymouth via the Somerset & Dorset Railway.

On August Bank Holiday Monday, 1925, 185 passengers booked to Weston-super-Mare for a fare of 3s. 0d., while 76 travelled to Weymouth for 4s. 6d. The 1926 Strike affected excursion traffic as that year little cash was available for such luxuries, excursionists numbering only 50 and 25 respectively.

In the 1930s cheap evening trips were available from Radstock to Temple Meads on the 5.16 pm and 6.16 pm trains, a third class return costing 1s. 0d. Passengers could return by the 9.53 pm, or on Saturdays the 11.20 pm.

On 27th August, 1938 excursions from the branch were available on the 7.48 am from Radstock to Bridport 6s. 3d., Weymouth 6s. 9d., Lulworth Cove 8s. 3d. or Paddington 12s. 6d. On Sunday 28th August the 10.26 am from Radstock carried passengers to Yeovil for 3s. 2d., Weymouth 4s. 9d., Lulworth Cove 6s. 3d. Railway day return fares to Weymouth undercut coach companies which charged 6s. 6d. On Saturday 3rd September the 7.48 am carried passengers to Paddington for 12s. 0d. while the following day the 9.59 am offered a special 'half day' trip to Taunton for 4s. 2d., Exeter 5s. 3d., Dawlish/Teignmouth/ Newton Abbot 5s. 9d., Torquay and Paignton 6s. 3d., or a rail and River Dart trip for 8s. 6d. On Sunday 18th September the 10.26 am offered Radstock to Portsmouth & Southsea for 5s. 3d.

In post-World War II years, usually excursions were run on three Sundays each summer from Frome to Newport, Cardiff, Barry Island and Porthcawl, picking up at all branch stations. These trips proved very popular, attracting particularly heavy patronage from Radstock and Midsomer Norton. The eight or ten corridor coaches were hauled by a Westbury '43XX' class 2-6-0. In 1959, the last year of passenger traffic, two Sunday excursions worked from the branch to Barry Island. On Bank Holidays the 10.50 am from Frome worked through to Weston-super-Mare and, lengthened to six or seven coaches, was hauled by a Westbury '43XX'.

In 1932 a Saturdays-only luncheon car express ran in the summer from Birmingham to Weymouth, and used the branch running non-stop from Bristol Stapleton Road to Frome. The return train travelled via Westbury.

Inherited from the GWR which certainly advertised them in 1932, in January 1953 the Western Region supplied walking tour tickets from Bristol stations to various places to which one could hike, usually less than 10 miles, and return from another station. On the Bristol to Frome line rambles were suggested from Hallatrow or Farrington Gurney to Wells (or reverse) 9½ miles. There was also:

Keynsham & Somerdale to Pensford, 5 to 9 miles depending on choice of route
Whitchurch Halt to Flax Bourton, 9 miles
Whitchurch Halt to Keynsham & Somerdale, 4 miles

These walks, too, could be taken in the reverse direction. Fares varied: for instance Hallatrow to Wells fare was 6s. 9d. from Temple Meads third class, or 10s. 0d. first, or 7s. 6d. and 11s. 3d. respectively from Clifton Down. The ticket for Keynsham to Pensford walk cost a mere 1s. 8d. from Temple Meads or 2s. 3d. from Clifton Down, with first class fares 2s. 6d. and 3s. 6d. In 1959 special cheap day return fares were available any day, by any train after 9.30 am, a return from Brislington to Clevedon being 3s. 2d. or to Weston-super-Mare 4s. 0d.

The branch carried a significant quantity of milk traffic:

1911 Station	No. of churns	Income £	s.	d.
Brislington	–	–	–	–
Pensford	11,919	471	8	0
Clutton	18,701	935	0	0
Hallatrow	34,423	1,942	9	1
Midsomer Norton & Welton	12,498	744	5	4
Radstock	7,814	492	2	7
Mells Road	32,539	2,028	0	4
Frome	68,541	4,719	0	6

1925 Station	No. of churns	Income £	s.	d.
Brislington	–	–	–	–
Pensford	3,474	332	13	10
Clutton	8,993	732	17	0
Hallatrow	7,198	774	19	9
Midsomer Norton & Welton	6,395	738	11	3
Radstock	4,682	441	15	0
Mells Road	12,641	1,340	16	5
Frome	54,231	5,694	15	9

In the early 1880s the branch coaching set generally comprised of 4-wheelers: a first and a second class coach sandwiched between a pair of brake thirds. From the 1930s a two-coach 'B' set was used.

"Point to Point" Running Times—continued.

9.—cont.—Between Reading and Wootton Bassett—cont.

WATER COLUMNS.
Reading, Didcot, Wantage Road, Uffington, Swindon.

RUNAWAY CATCH POINTS.
Swindon East (Down Middle Line), 150 feet in advance of East Box.
Swindon West (Up Middle Line), 125 feet in advance of West Box.

TROUGHS.
Between Pangbourne and Goring.

10.—Between Bristol and Frome or Westbury via Radstock.

Between	Passenger Trains Down	Passenger Trains Up	Express Freight Trains Down	Express Freight Trains Up
	Minutes	Minutes	Minutes	Minutes
North Somerset Junction and Marsh Junction	2	2	3	3
Marsh Junction and Pensford	12	11	25	22
Pensford and Clutton	8	6	15	14
Clutton and Hallatrow	3	3	9	6
Hallatrow and Midsomer Norton	7	6	15	15
Midsomer Norton and Radstock	3	3	4	3
Radstock and Mells Road	7	7	15	12
Mells Road and Frome	10	12	22	20
At Frome Station	5	5	10	10
Frome West Ground Frame and Frome North Junction	—	—	5	5
At Frome North Junction (Salisbury Line Trains)	—	—	10	10
Frome North Junction and Westbury	—	—	13	13
Frome Station and Westbury	9	9	15	15
At Westbury (Salisbury Line Trains)	5	5	15	15

WATER COLUMNS.
Hallatrow, Radstock and Frome.

RUNAWAY CATCH POINTS.
Marsh Junction (Down Branch), 113 feet in rear of Single Line Junction.
Radstock (Down Line), 151 feet on Mells Road side of South Box.
N.B.—The points leading to Down Goods Yard Sidings at Radstock are normally self-acting catch points but are controlled from Radstock South Box.
Mells Road (Down Line), 875 feet in rear of Down Home Signal.

SINGLE LINE LOOPS AT STATIONS.

	Down	Up
Pensford	737	737
Pensford and Bromley Collieries	446‡	446‡
Clutton	786	771
Hallatrow	990	1013

‡—Siding available for Down or Up Freight Train. Two Passenger Trains cannot be crossed at these places.

STOP BOARDS.

For Down Trains.
At 19m. 8ch. between Brislington and Pensford.
At 14m. 57ch. between Clutton and Pensford.
At 13m. 51ch. between Clutton and Hallatrow.
Near 11m. 60ch. between Hallatrow and Midsomer Norton.
At 3m. 74ch. between Mells Road and Frome North Junction.

For Up Trains.
At 5m. 19ch. between Mells Road and Radstock.
Near 11m. 60ch. between Old Mills and Hallatrow.
At 19m. 20ch. between Pensford and Brislington.
Near 22 m.p., Brislington Station.

Extract from a booklet, *Arrangements for the Diversion of Through Trains to Alternative Routes in cases of Emergency*, published in June 1940.

Diversion of Trains to Alternative Routes in cases of Emergency—*continued*.

Obstruction between Bathampton Inclusive and East Depot Inclusive.   CODE **B.D. 5**

ALTERNATIVE ROUTES.
BETWEEN READING OR SWINDON AND BRISTOL } (a) Via Swindon and Badminton.
BETWEEN HOLT JUNCTION AND BRISTOL   (b) Via Trowbridge, Frome and Radstock.
BETWEEN SOUTH WALES AND SALISBURY AND WEYMOUTH LINES } (c) Via Badminton, Wootton Bassett and Melksham.
BETWEEN WEYMOUTH AND SALISBURY LINES AND BRISTOL   (d) Via Radstock.

MAIN LINE TRAINS.

Trains from Swindon or East thereof to Bristol or beyond and vice versa usually running via Box to run via Badminton and Filton Junction.

BRADFORD-ON-AVON LINE TRAINS.

Passenger trains from Bristol or beyond to Reading and London usually running via Bradford-on-Avon to be suspended between Bristol and Bradford-on-Avon. In each case where such a train is booked to call at Bradford-on-Avon, a train must start from Bradford-on-Avon at the booked time. Westbury to provide engine and coaches.

Passenger trains from London, Reading, etc., to Bristol or beyond usually running via Bradford-on-Avon must run via Trowbridge, Frome and Radstock, calling at Trowbridge. To be reversed at Frome and engines to be changed there.

Trains usually running via Bradford-on-Avon and Bath, from or to the Salisbury or Weymouth lines or beyond (except South Wales freight trains) must run via Radstock. Salisbury line trains to be reversed at Frome Passenger Station and Westbury, and Locomotive Department to arrange as far as practicable for engines to be changed at Frome and at Westbury.

Freight trains to work as arranged by Control staff.

Special trains between the North of England, Midlands, and Salisbury and Weymouth lines must not be run via Severn Tunnel, nor Standish Junction and Yate, but must run via Oxford and Swindon, or Stratford-on-Avon, Gloucester and Swindon, or Hereford, Gloucester and Swindon, according to circumstances.

Bath passenger train traffic can, if convenient, be conveyed via Bristol over L M S Railway between Bath and Bristol (Temple Meads), or via Radstock (over S. & D. Railway between Bath and Radstock).

ENGINE RESTRICTIONS.

See Code B.D.1, page 9.

Between BRISTOL and FROME via RADSTOCK. The heaviest engines permitted to run AT NORMAL SPEEDS are the following :

Class	Type	Engine Numbers
4-4-0	——	{ 3200 to 3228. { 3252 to 3291.
2-4-0	——	}
0-4-2 (tank)	——	} All engines of these classes.
2-4-0 (tank)	——	}
2-6-2 (tank)	——	4400 to 4410, 45XX and 55XX classes.
0-6-0	——	2251, 23XX, 24XX and 25XX classes.
0-6-0 (tank)	——	Various classes.

The following classes are permitted AT SPEED NOT EXCEEDING 25 M.P.H. :

*4-6-0   78XX (Manor)
4-4-0   33XX, 34XX.
2-6-0   26XX, 43XX, 53XX, 63XX and 73XX.
2-8-0   28XX and 30XX.
2-6-2 (tank) 41XX, 51XX and 61XX, 81XX.
0-6-0 (tank) 17XX, 18XX, 27XX, 36XX, 37XX, 57XX, 67XX, 77XX, 87XX, 97XX

(*—5 m.p.h. Mells Road Up and Down Platforms).

Double Heading between Bristol and Frome via Radstock is permitted only under following conditions :

(1) Any permitted tender engine may run coupled to another permitted tender engine always provided the chimneys of each engine are facing in the same direction, i.e. "chimney towards tender".

(2) Tank engines may be run coupled together as follows : subject to maximum speed of 15 m.p.h. over the River Avon Bridge at 22m. 70chs. between Marsh Junction and Brislington :

  (a) Two "Yellow" group engines.
  (b) A "Yellow" group and uncoloured engine.
  (c) Two uncoloured group engines.

Note. The running of two "Blue" group tank engines, or a "Blue" and "Yellow" group tank engine coupled together over this section is prohibited.

For Running Times, see pages 56 to 80.

Extract from a booklet, *Arrangements for the Diversion of Through Trains to Alternative Routes in cases of Emergency*, published in June 1940.

RADSTOCK BRANCH.—(Single Line.)

Down. **Chippenham to Radstock.** ***Week Days.***

Dist	STATIONS.	1	2	3	4	5	6					
		a.m.	a.m.	a.m.	p.m.	p.m.	p.m.					
	Chip'nham dp.	.	.	..	.	.	When required only.	.	.	.	.	.
8¾	Holt	..	..	.	..	..		..	..	..	..	..
11¾	Trowbridge	...	...	9 30	...	...		...	...	...	...	...
15¾	Westbury arr.	.		9 45	..	.		.	.	.	.	.
	Westbury dep.	..	..	10 0	...	..		..	..	..	..	..
21¼	Frome ...... arr.	...	...	10 20	.	...		...	...	...	...	...
	Frome ...... dep.	6 0	10 15	11 15	2 15	2 45	5 45	.	.	.	.	.
26½	Mells	6 30	10 45	11 45	2 45	3 15	6 15	..	..	..	..	..
	Mells	—	—	—	—	—	..	...	...	...	...	...
	Vobster	—	—	—	—	—	..	.	.	.	.	.
	Newbury ..	—	—	—	—	—	...	..	..	..	..	..
19½	Radstock .. arr.	6 45	11 0	12 0	3 0	3 30	6 30	...	...	...	...	...

Radstock to Chippenham. ***Up.***

Dist	STATIONS.	7	8	9	10	11	12	
		a.m.	a.m.	p.m.	p.m.	p.m.	p.m.	
	Radstock . dep.	7 15	8 45	12 45	.	4 15	7 0	...
...	Newbury ...	—	—	—	..	—	—	...
...	Vobster	—	—	—	...	—	—	...
...	Mells	—	—	—	.	—	—	...
3	Mells	7 40	9 10	1 10	1 40	4 40	7 25	..
8½	Frome ...... arr.	8 0	9 45	1 30	2 0	5 0	7 45	.
	Frome ...... dep.	8 15						..
13¾	Westbury	8 35	..	...	..	..	When required only.	..
17¾	Trowbridge...arr.	8 50	...	...	...	...		...
13¾	Holt	..	..	..	.	..		..
29½	Chip'nham arr.	...	...	...	...	...		...

This is a Single Line. worked by a Pilotman.

GWR working timetable, Frome to Radstock, August 1871.

Freight

When the mineral branch opened to Radstock on 14th November, 1854 there was no fixed timetable, trains running as required. In 1871 five trains ran from Frome to Radstock plus one if required (one through Trowbridge), four Radstock to Frome and one if required and one Mells to Frome – 45 minutes was allowed each way between Frome and Radstock. With the opening of the BNSR from Bristol to Radstock and the conversion to standard gauge of the former mineral line, for freight purposes the branch continued to be worked in two halves. In 1876 two 'goods and coal' trains ran each way between Bristol and Radstock worked by a Bristol engine; six return trips Radstock to Mells ('Road' was not added until 16th November, 1898) by the Radstock engine and four Frome to Mells by the Frome engine.

In 1877 this was amended to six up coal trains Radstock to Mells taking 20 minutes; four coal trains Mells to Frome taking 25 minutes and two goods and coal trains Bristol to Radstock taking respectively 2 hours 25 minutes and 2 hours 55 minutes. Six coal trains ran from Mells to Radstock in 15 minutes; four coal trains Frome to Mells in 25 minutes and two coal and goods trains Radstock to Bristol taking 1 hour 45 minutes and 2 hours.

In 1882 one goods was run from Bristol to Hallatrow; six coal trains Radstock to Mells; four coal trains Mells to Frome; two goods and coal Bristol to Radstock; six coal Mells to Radstock; four coal Frome to Mells and three goods and coal Radstock to Bristol.

The 1889 time table showed two goods and coal trains Bristol to Hallatrow and one extra if required; one Bristol to Frome goods and coal; two Radstock to Frome goods and coal running if required and a Radstock to Yeovil coal train. Two goods and coal trains ran from Frome to Bristol; two Frome to Radstock and a goods from Old Mills to Bristol and one goods and coal Mells to Bristol plus several short workings to run if required.

In the down direction in 1895 one goods and coal ran from Bristol to Hallatrow; two goods and coal Bristol to Frome; one goods Bristol to Radstock; while up trains consisted of two coal from Clutton to Bristol and two goods and coal Frome to Bristol.

In 1922 one goods and coal ran from Bristol to Mells Road, one goods and coal Bristol to Hallatrow; one goods Bristol to Radstock; one coal empties Bristol to Pensford & Bromley Siding; two coal Radstock to Frome; one goods and coal Bristol to Old Mills; one goods Radstock to Westbury; one goods Bristol to Frome and one coal Mells Road to Patney & Chirton. In the up direction were: one goods from Hallatrow to Bristol; one coal empties Frome to Radstock; one Frome to Somerset Quarries Siding; one goods and coal Mells Road to Bristol; one goods Frome to Hallatrow, goods Westbury to Radstock, Holt to Mells Road coal empties, one goods Frome to Radstock and one goods Radstock to Bristol.

In 1934 Bristol engines worked return trains from East Depot to Mells Road; East Depot to Pensford; East Depot to Radstock returning to Kingsland Road. The Frome engine worked from Frome to Radstock and back and a Westbury engine made return trips Westbury to Mells Road and Westbury to Radstock.

BRISTOL, RADSTOCK AND FROME.

DOWN TRAINS.—WEEK DAYS.

Distance from Bristol F.N.	Ruling Gradient 1 in	STATIONS.	Time Allow. for Point to Point Times. Mins	Allow for Stop. Mins	Allow for Ordinary Freight Trains See page 2 Mins	1 Goods and Coal A.M.	2 Goods and Coal A.M.	3 Passenger A.M.	4 Stone A.M.	5 Coal Empties A.M.	6 Goods A.M.	7 Passenger A.M.	8 Passenger P.M.	9 Coal P.M.	10 Goods P.M.	11 Passenger P.M.	12 Passenger P.M.	13 Goods P.M.	14	15 Westbury Goods P.M.	16 Coal P.M.	17 Goods P.M.	18 Passenger P.M.	19 Putney & C. Coal P.M.
—	—	Bristol (Tmpl. Mds) dep.																						
—	—	East Depot "													1 56		2 5	2 50	3 35			4 25		5 10
2 7	—	Marsh Junction "	4		1	5 30	7 20	6 57		MSX	9 40	10 35	1 12		CxS	CS	CS	CS			C4 3C8	CS	5 18
4 20	62 R	Bridlington "	5		1	CS	CS	CS		CS	CS	CS	CS			2 9	2 58						5 25
5 0	—	Whitchurch Halt "						7 12			9 55	10 43	1 20			2 20	3 11	4 P 0			4 P 52	5 31	
6 68	60	Stop Board { arr. dep.	14	2	1	5P68 6 6	7P47	7 17		RR	10P13 10 22	10 56 10 57	1 33 1x35		2P28 2x37	2 26 2 28	3 12	4 10 4x48		4P52 5P2	5 32	
7 34	60 R	Pensford { arr. dep.	6		1	6 15	7P58	7 20			10•37 11P25	CxS			2x39	CxS	CxS				SX		
9 74	60 R	Pensford and Bromley Siding	3		2	CS	CR		9 40	CS	11•11	11 5	1x43		CS	2•16	3 20	5 4		5•11	5P22	CS	5 40 5 42
11 37	71 F	Clutton { arr. dep.	12		1	6ST33 61 43	8 15 8x30	7 28 7 30		9P 59 12P17	12•10 12P28	11x 8	1 44		3P 0	2•20 2 42	3 22 3 25	5P 8 5 13			5P22 5 27	5P59	5 45
11 33	58 F	Stop Board { arr. dep.	2		2	6P49 6ST55	8P36 8 41	7 33 7 35		10 5	12 28 12 43	1x11 1x13	1x47 1x48		3 6 3 9	2 44	3 27	5x10 6P59			5x50	5P59	5 47
12 36	65 R	Hallatrow	4			7 5																		
13 37	73 F	Old Mills Siding	4			7P14				Suspended.	12P52 2 5				3P17 3x35							CS	CxS	
14 11	177 F	Midsomer Norton & Welton	4		1	CS		7 42 7 44			2 11 2 20	11 20 11 21	1 56 1 56			2 51 2 53	3 34 3 36						5 54 5 56	
15 72	—	Radstock { arr. dep.	4		1	7 24 7 30		7x50 7 58	9 30		2 26	11x 23 11 27	2 2 2 10	12 45 1x 3	4 5	2 57	3 40 3 42	6 11 6x45		4 45 CR	5 20	8x13 6 45	6 0 6 2	
18 71	128 F	Mells Road	15		2	7x35 8 5		8 1	9 40			11 35 11 36	2x11	1x 8 2P29		SO	3 50 3x51	8 4		5x10 5P17	5 28	8 4 8P10	6 10 6x12	6 48 6P57
20 14 21 79	204 F 48 F	Stop Board Somerset Quar. Sdg	3 7	1 2		8 25												8P10						
23 24	51 F	Gas Works Siding	4	1														SO	5 33					
23 41	276 R	Market Siding { arr. dep.		1																				
23 73	76 R	Frome Mineral Junc. { arr. dep.	3												2 40				8 29			8 29	CS 6 23	7 13
24 14	76 R	Frome	5					8 12	9 40			11 47	2 23										6 40	

Radstock and Mells Road, RR Trip. In addition to the trips shewn in the Tables, a trip from Radstock to Mells Road and back will be run daily, worked by Train Engine available at most convenient time.

Suspended on Saturdays.

Working timetable for down trains, 13th July to 20th September, 1925.

BRISTOL, RADSTOCK AND FROME.

DOWN TRAINS.—WEEK DAYS.

STATIONS.		20 M Goods P.M.	21 M Passenger P.M.	22 Passenger P.M.	23 M Coal P.M.	24 M Coal P.M.	25 M Passenger P.M.	26 Passenger P.M.
Bristol (Temple Meade)	dep.	..	6 17	7 50	..	..	9 40	..
East Depot	,,	..	CS	CS			CS	..
Marsh Junction	,,	..	6 25	7 58			9 48	..
Brislington	,,	..	6 32	8 5			9 55	..
Whitchurch Halt	,,	..	..	..	SUSPENDED.		..	..
Stop Board	arr.	..	6×37	8×10			10× 0	..
Pensford	dep.	..	6 39	8 11			10 2	..
Pensford & Bromley Sdg.	arr.	..	C×S	..			..	..
	dep.	..	6×46	8 18			10×10	..
Clutton	arr.	..	6 47	8 19			10 11	..
Stop Board	dep.	..	6 50	8×22	8 20		10 14	..
Hallatrow	arr.	..	6×56	8 24	8 38		10 15	..
Stop Board	dep.	..	..	..	8 37		..	..
Old Mills Siding	arr.	RR	CS	..	8 45	9 52	..	..
Midsomer Norton & Welton	dep.	6 50	7 2	8 30	8 46	9P25 9P59	10 21	..
Radstock	arr.	7 8	7 5	8 31	..	..	10 23	..
	dep.	..	7×9	8 35	..	..	10 27	..
Mells Road	arr.	..	7 11	8 37	..	..	10 29	..
Stop Board	dep.	..	7 19	8 45	9 20	..	Y	..
Somerset Quarries Siding	,,	..	7 20	8 46	9P28	..	..	..
Gas Works Siding	,,	..	..	..	..	..	..	..
Market Siding	,,	..	..	9 45	..	..	..	..
Frome Mineral Junction	arr.	..	CS	CS	CS	CS	CS	..
Frome	dep.	..	7 31	8 57	9 58	10 18	10 43	..

SUNDAYS.

		1 B Passenger A.M.	2	8 B Passenger P.M.	4
Bristol (Temple Meade)	dep.	9 25	..	4 50	..
East Depot	,,	CS	..	CS	..
Marsh Junction	,,	9 33	..	4 58	..
Brislington	,,	9 40	..	5 5	..
Whitchurch Halt	,,	..	..	..	..
Stop Board	arr.	9 45	..	5 10	..
Pensford	dep.	9 47	..	5 11	..
Pensford & Bromley Sdg.	arr.	..	..	..	..
	dep.	..	..	..	..
Clutton	arr.	9 54	..	5 18	..
Stop Board	dep.	9 58	..	5 21	..
Hallatrow	arr.	10 1	..	5 24	..
Stop Board	dep.	10 8	..	5 26	..
Old Mills Siding	arr.	..	..	..	..
Midsomer Norton & Welton	dep.	10 14	..	5 32	..
Radstock	arr.	10 21	..	5 34	..
	dep.	10 26	..	5 38	..
Mells Road	arr.	10 28	..	5 41	..
Stop Board	dep.	10 36	..	5 49	..
Somerset Quarries Siding	,,	10 42	..	5 52	..
Frome Mineral Junction	arr.	CS	..	CS	..
Frome	dep.	10 53	..	6 3	..

Single Line, Marsh Junction to Radstock Station worked by Electric Train Staff, the Staff Stations and crossing places being Marsh June., Pensford, Pensford and Bromley Siding‡, Clutton, Hallatrow, Old Mills‡, and Radstock Station.

Electric Train Tablet worked between Clutton and Pensford when Pensford and Bromley Colliery is out of circuit.

‡Pensford and Bromley Siding and Old Mills are only available for shunting a light Engine, or Goods Train (at Old Mills short Goods Train only can be shunted), for a Train to pass in the same or opposite direction.

Double Line, Radstock Station to Mells Road South End.

Single Line, Mells Road South End to Frome Mineral Junction, worked by Electric Train Staff, Mells Road and Frome West Box being the Staff Stations.

Y calls at Mells Road to set down only. Running time Radstock to Frome, when not required to call, 17 minutes.

Special Trains to clear North Somerset Line of Surplus Coal Traffic.

Radstock must advise Control Office, Bristol, when specials are required to any point on North Somerset Line to clear traffic, and arrangements will be made accordingly.

Working timetable for down trains (continued), 13th July to 20th September, 1925.

FROME, RADSTOCK AND BRISTOL.

UP TRAINS. WEEK DAYS.

Distances From Frome	Station No.	Ruling Gradient 1 in	Point to 1 point T Mins.	Allow for Stop. Mins.	Allow for Ordinary Freight Trains. Step at 2 Mins.	STATIONS.	1 M Passenger A.M.	2 B Passenger A.M.	3 M Goods A.M.	4 M Coal Empties A.M.	5 M Goods A.M.	6 M Coal A.M.	7 B Passenger A.M.	8	9 M Goods and Coal A.M.	10 K	11 11.30 a.m. Westbury Goods P.M.	12 B Passenger P.M.	13 M Goods P.M.	14 M Holt Coal Empties P.M.	15 Weston-s-M Passenger P.M.	16 B Passenger P.M.	17 B Portishead Passenger P.M.	18 Goods and Coal P.M.	19 Goods and Coal P.M.
M. C.																									
—	585	—	—	—	—	Frome arr.	7 37						10 35					12 42	2 40		3 25		4 55	Suspended	
— 21	582	76 F	—	—	—	Frome Mini. Junc. dep.	CS	8 25		8 40	9 V 5	Suspended.	CS		8 45		12 20	CS	CS	3 40	CS		CS		SX
— 53	1193	76 F	—	—	1	Market Sdg. "		CS							8P50			12K54	3x 0	4 0			5x 7		
— 70	1192	276 F	4	—	—	Gas W'ks Sdg. "									9 0			12 55	3 20		3 37	SO			5 0
2 15	1191	51 F	3	2	2	Somerset Qrs. Sdg. "				9 15					11K30		12 10	1X 1	8P 25		3 38		5 8		
5 23	1190	48 R	11	—	1	Mells Rd. arr.	7 49	8 37		9 30		MSX10 54	10 47		11 35		1X10	1 2	3 35		3 44		5 14	Sats. only.	
5 26						" dep.	7 50	8 38		9P 85		10 56	10 48		11 50		1P 15	1 6			3 46	4 20	5 16		
8 22	1187	69 F	8	1	1	Radstock arr.	7X 56	8X 44		9 45		11 0	11 0		11 56		1 25	1 8			3 50	4 24	5 20		5 • 8
						" dep.	7X 57	8X 43			V Mineral Loop.	11 3	10 56		12 15					4 0	3 51	4 25	5 22	4P 38	5X50
9 53	1184	128 R	3	—	1	M.Nort.& Welton dep.	8 1	8 49				RR	11 10		12P23								CS	4 30	6 3
10 57	1188	177 R	4	—	1	Old Mills Sg. am. dep.	8 2	8 50					11 11		12X20			1 15			CS	CS	5 29	7 43	6 X 5
11 66	1182	73 R	4	—	1	Stop Board " dep.	CS	CS			Does not run when No. 3 is running.		11 14		1 0			1 17			3 58	4 32	5 31	6 12	6 X 5
12 61	1181	58 R	6	2	2	Hallatrow arr. dep.	8 9 8 10	8 57 8 59					11 18		1X 45			1 21			3 59 4 3	4 33	5X35	6 X 12	7 12
14 20						Clutton arr.	8X14	9 3	10 28			10 X 48	11X21		1P53			1X22			4 5	4 39	5 41	7 • 12	7X12
14 63	1241	71 R	3	—	—	Stop Board & "	8 16	9 6	10 36			10X 36									CS	CS	CS	7P 20	7P 20
16 60	1180	60 F	6	—	1	Penaford Sid arr. Bromley Sid " dep.	8 24	9 13	11X42			11 42	11 28		2 2			1 29			4 12	4 46	5 48	CR	
17 36			2	—	1	Pensford dep.	8 25	9 14	11P50			11P53	11 29		2 28						4 14	4 50	5 50		
19 26	1179	66 R	8	—	1	Stop Board " dep.			11 59			11 59			2X32			1K34						7 30	7 30
19 74						Whitch'rch H. dep.	8 32	9 21	12 10				11 36		2 57			1 41			4 21	4 55	5 57	8 8	8 18
22 7	1069	60 F	8	3	1	Brislington arr. dep.	8 36 8 39	9 25 9 28	12 20 12P39				11 40 11 43		3P 9			1 46 1 49			4 25 4 28	4 59 5 2	6 1 6 5	8P 20 8 30	8P 20 8 30
23 16	1067	62 F	3	—	1	Marsh Junction "			12 49						3P19									8P35	8P 35
23 61	1073	500 R	1	—	—	East Depot arr.		CS	12P55				CS		3 35						CS	CS	CS	8 35	CS
23 32	1079	—	—	—	—	N.Som.Jun. arr.	CS	:	1 6						3 44									8 44	8 44
24 14						Bristol (Tm.Ms.)	8 46	9 35					11 50					1 56			4 35	5	9 6 12		

Frome Shunting Engine.—**U** Worked by Frome Engine, Shunter and Porter

U Worked by Frome Engine, Shunter and Porter No. 3 is running.—Must assist Goods Trains as required from Frome to Mells Road.

Working timetable for up trains, 13th July to 20th September, 1925.

FROME, RADSTOCK AND BRISTOL.

UP TRAINS—WEEK DAYS.

STATIONS.		20 A Pass. P.M.	21 Coal. P.M.	22 B Pass. P.M.	23 Goods. P.M.	24 K Goods. P.M.	25 B Pass. P.M.	26 K Goods and Coal. P.M.
Frome	arr.	5 57	...	6 22	...	...	7 55	...
	dep.	CS	...	CS	...	...	8 35	...
Frome Mineral Junction	,,	...	...	...	...	...	CS	...
Market Siding	,,	...	...	...	...	...	...	...
Gas Works Siding	,,	...	...	...	RR	SO	...	...
Somerset Quarries Siding	,,	C×S	RR	6×34	...	...	8×47	...
Mells Road	arr.	...	6 15	6 35	7×30	...	8 48	...
	dep.	...	6P20	...	7P25	RR	...	...
Stop Board	,,	6 15	6 30	6×41	7 35	...	8 54	9 0
Radstock	arr.	6 17	...	6 42	...	7 55	8 56	9 8
	dep.	...	TSO	6 46	...	...	9 0	9 10
Midsomer Norton and Welton.	,,	...	...	6 47	...	7 45	9 2	9 15
Old Mills Siding	,,	C×S	...	CS	...	7 52	...	...
Stop Board	,,	...	...	...	...	8P0	...	9P23
Hallatrow	arr.	CS	...	6×44	...	8 5	9 9	9 29
	dep.	...	...	6 55	...	8×25	9 14	9 50
Clutton	,,	C×S	...	6 59	...	8 33	9 15	9 58
Stop Board	,,	...	...	7×2	...	9×18	...	10×16
Pensford & Bromley Siding	,,	...	...	...	...	9P26	...	10P23
Pensford	arr.	6 36	...	7 9	...	9 36	9 22	10 32
	dep.	6×38	...	7 11	...	9×55	9 23	10 45
Stop Board	,,	...	...	...	...	10P8	...	10P07
Whitchurch Halt	,,	...	...	7 18	...	...	9 30	11 7
Brislington	,,	...	...	7 22	...	10 18	9 34	11P12
Marsh Junction	arr.	...	...	7 27	...	10P23	9 37	CS
East Depot	,,	C8	...	...	...	...	CS	...
North Somerset Junction	,,	...	...	...	...	10 32	...	11V21
Bristol (Temple Meads)	arr.	6 55	...	7 34	...	...	9 44	...

SUNDAYS.

	1 B Pass. NOON.	2 P.M.	3 B Pass. P.M.	4
	12 0	...	6 45	...
	CS	...	CS	...
	...	...	...	...
	...	...	...	...
	...	...	...	...
	12 12	...	6 57	...
	12 19	...	7 0	...
	...	...	...	...
	12 25	...	7 6	...
	012 27	...	7 9	...
	12 31	...	7 13	...
	12 34	...	7 16	...
	...	...	...	...
	...	...	...	...
	12 40	...	7 22	...
	12 46	...	7 27	...
	12 50	...	7 31	...
	12 56	...	7 35	...
	...	...	...	...
	...	...	...	...
	1 3	...	7 42	...
	1 4	...	7 45	...
	...	...	...	...
	1 11	...	7 52	...
	1 15	...	7 56	...
	1 18	...	8 2	...
	CS	...	CS	...
	...	...	...	...
	1 25	...	8 9	...

Working of Engines—Bristol, Radstock, Frome and Camerton.

1.—5.30 a.m. East Depot to Mells Road 8.45 a.m. Mells Road to East Depôt.
2.—7.20 a.m. East Depot to Hallatrow. 10.28 a.m. Hallatrow to Bristol. 4.30 (SX) p.m. East Depot to Mells Road. 8.4 p.m. (SX) Mells Road to East Depot.
3.—9.40 a.m. East Depot to Radstock, assist 4.45 p.m. Radstock to Mells Road if required. 0.0 p.m. Radstock to Bristol.
4.—1.55 p.m. East Depôt to Radstock, 5.0 p.m. Radstock to Bristol (SX), 4.30 p.m. ex Old Mills (SO).
5.—8.40 a.m. Frome to Radstock, 12.45 p.m. Radstock to Frome.
6.—11.48 a.m. Frome to Freshford and Frome. Suspended.
7.—(Trowbridge Engine) 12.55 a.m. Frome to Mells Road, 6.43 p.m. Mells Road to Patney.
8.—2.40 p.m. Frome to Radstock, RR trips to Mells Road if required, 8.20 p.m. Radstock to Frome.
9.—11.30 a.m. Westbury to Radstock, 4.45 p.m. Radstock to Westbury.
10.—If 7.35 p.m. (SO) Radstock to Bristol is required to run engine van and guard to leave East Depot attached to 1.55 p.m. goods.

V Kingsland Road.

Working timetable for up trains (continued), 13th July to 20th September, 1925.

WEEKDAYS — BRISTOL, RADSTOCK AND FROME

SINGLE LINE—Marsh Junction to Radstock West Station, worked by Electric Train Token. Crossing places are: Marsh Junction, Pensford, Pensford and Bromley Siding, Clutton, Hallatrow and Radstock West Station.

‡—Pensford and Bromley Siding is only available for shunting a light Engine, or Freight Train (at Old Mills short Freight Train only can be shunted), for a train to pass in the same or opposite direction.

DOUBLE LINE, Radstock Station to Mells Road South End.

SINGLE LINE, Mells Road South End to Frome worked by Electric Train Token, Mells Road and Frome South Box being the Token Stations.

DOWN

Mile Post Mileage (M C)	Mileage from Bristol (T.M.) (M C)	Station	Ruling Gradient 1 in	EBV			Stone	To Westbury		To Westbury	To Westbury
				K	G	K	K	K	K	K	K
				am	am	am	SX am	SO am	PM	SX PM	SX PM	SX PM
— —	0 78	BRISTOL (East Depot) dep	—	..	..	..	8 32	8 32	..	2 5	..	..
23 10	2 7	Marsh Junction	62 R	..	..	..	..	..	..	..	..	..
22 1	5 0	Brislington	60 R	..	..	..	..	..	..	..	..	..
19 7	6 57	Stop Board	66 F	..	..	..	9‡16	9‡16	..	2‡33	..	..
17 31		Pensford arr		..	..	..	9 25	9 25	..	..	..	..
		dep		..	..	..	9 35	9 35	..	..	..	..
16 52	7 36	Pensford and Bromley arr	60 R	..	..	..	9 40	9 40	..	..	..	..
		Siding dep		..	..	..	10 0	10 0	..	..	..	..
14 13	9 75	Clutton arr	60 R	..	..	..	10 16	10 16	..	2 57	..	..
		dep		..	..	..	10 26	10 26	..	3 7	..	..
13 51	10 37	Stop Board	71 F	..	..	..	10‡33	10‡33	..	3‡14	..	..
12 57	11 31	Hallatrow arr	58 F	..	..	..	10 39	10 39	..	3 20	..	..
		dep		..	..	..	11 20	..	..	3*45	2‡25	..
11 52	12 36	Stop Board	65 R	..	..	..	11‡30	..	..	3‡55	2‡35	..
10 50	13 37	Old Mills Siding arr	73 F	..	..	..	11 36	..	..	4 0 1	2 41	..
		dep		..	..	..	11 55	..	..	4‡0 11	3 0	..
9 47	14 41	Midsomer Norton and W. arr	177 F	..	..	9 24	12 1	..	..	R	..	..
		dep		..	..	9 30	12 11	..	..	..	..	..
8 16	15 72	RADSTOCK WEST... arr	128 F	..	..	9 56	12 17	..	..	4 21	3 10	..
		dep		..	..	..	..	..	12 45	..	4 0	..
5 18	18 70	Mells Road arr	69 R	..	..	..	..	..	1 3	..	4 18	..
		dep		..	..	..	..	..	1 25	..	4 20	4 50
3 74	20 14	Stop Board	204 F	..	..	..	..	..	1‡33	..	4‡28	4‡58
2 8	21 79	Somerset Quarry Siding	48 F	8 35	9‡35	..	..	12 15	..	3 15	..	..
0 0	23 73	FROME MINERAL arr JUNCTION	76 R	8 45	9‡43	..	..	12 25	1 49	3 25	4 44	5 14

If necessary Engine, Van and Guard to return to Hallatrow and work traffic from there to Old Mills

WEEKDAYS — FROME, RADSTOCK AND BRISTOL

UP

Station	Ruling Gradient 1 in	EBV			Empties		Empties		EBV	
		K	G	K	K	K	K	K	K	G	K
		SX am	SO am	SX am	SX am	SX am	SX am	SX am	SO PM	PM	SX PM
FROME MINERAL JUNCTION dep	76 F	7 0	8†10	9 10	11 30	11 50	..	2†45	..	..	..
Somerset Quarry Siding	51 R	..	8†20	9 20	11 40	12 0	..	2†55	..	..	..
Mells Road arr	48 F	7 20	..	..	11 50	..	..	..	Kingsland Road	..	..
dep		8 0	..	..	12 10	..	..	..	..	..	..
Stop Board	69 F	8P 6	..	..	12P16	..	..	..	Z	..	..
RADSTOCK WEST... arr	69 F	8 16	..	..	12 26	..	..	..	..	..	..
dep		8 45	..	..	..	..	12 40	12 45	5 0	..	..
Midsomer Norton and W. arr	128 R	8 50	..	..	..	..	R	R	..	..	..
dep		8 58	..	..	..	..	12 44	..	..	..	..
Old Mills Siding arr	177 R	9 4	..	..	..	..	12 49	R	..	..	..
dep		..	..	..	..	..	1 10	..	..	..	..
Stop Board	73 R	..	..	..	..	..	1P19	1P 7	5P16	..	..
Hallatrow arr	65 R	..	..	..	..	..	1 25	1 7	5 22	..	..
dep		..	..	..	..	11 25	..	1 20	5 32	..	..
Clutton arr	58 R	..	..	..	..	11 33	..	1 28	5 40	..	..
dep		..	..	..	..	12* 5	..	2‡ 5	7‡ 0	..	..
Stop Board	71 R	..	..	..	..	12‡15	..	2‡14	7P 6	..	..
Pensford and Bromley arr	60 F	..	..	..	..	12 24	..	..	..	..	..
Siding dep		..	..	..	..	12 41	..	2 21	..	..	..
Pensford arr	60 F	..	..	..	..	12 45	..	..	..	..	..
dep		..	..	..	..	12 53	..	2‡23	7 17	..	..
Stop Board	66 R	..	..	..	..	1P 7	..	2‡35	7‡29	..	..
Brislington	60 F	..	..	..	..	1 17	..	2 45	7 39	..	..
dep		..	..	..	..	1 25	..	2 50	7‡41	..	..
Marsh Junction	62 F	..	..	..	..	..	..	..	7*50	..	..
BRISTOL (East Depot) arr	—	..	..	..	..	1 34	..	2 59	7 55	..	..

Freight working timetable, 10th September to 10th June, 1956.

Bristol to Radstock trains were goods, goods and coal, or coal, but south of Radstock usually either coal or empties.

The year 1948 saw two stone trains from Somerset Quarries Siding to Frome; one freight and coal Bristol to Clutton; one freight Midsomer Norton to Radstock; one freight Bristol to Radstock; one freight Bristol to Frome; one freight Clutton to Frome, and one freight Mells Road to Westbury. In the up direction were one freight and empties Frome to Midsomer Norton; two empties Frome to Somerset Quarries Siding; one freight Clutton to Bristol, one freight Radstock to Clutton; one freight Frome to Radstock and one freight Radstock to Bristol.

The 1955 timetable offered four trains from Somerset Quarries Siding to Frome; one Old Mills to Radstock; one Bristol to Hallatrow, one Bristol to Radstock, one Hallatrow to Frome and one Mells Road to Frome. Up trains were: one Frome to Old Mills; two Frome to Somerset Quarries and one from Frome to Radstock West. In 1962 there were two trips from East Depot to Radstock in the morning and one to Old Mills. In the afternoon one was run to Radstock. From Frome two ran to Radstock and one to Old Mills.

Other Freight Matters

In 1907 the Radstock to Bristol line had to be kept open at night to cope with the volume of coal traffic originating from Dunkerton Colliery and the generally increased traffic on other sections of the BNSR.

In the mid-1930s small consignments were conveyed to Radstock on the 5.30 am ex-East Depot in a station truck where they were transferred to the 12.45 pm to Frome. In the opposite direction a station truck left Frome at 8.40 am and at Radstock the 8.45 am Mells Road to East Depot took it on to Bristol. The 8.40 and the 8.45 also carried a station truck which departed from Paddington at 10.50 pm the previous evening on the Weymouth train.

The GWR country lorry service operated vehicles from Frome, Radstock, Midsomer Norton and Hallatrow. From the late 1940s, small consignments hitherto carried in a station truck, came under the zonal system. The Frome lorry covered the district to Midsomer Norton while the Hallatrow lorry covered the remainder. From the introduction of this system, only full wagon loads were carried to or from other stations.

Air raids on 25th and 26th April, 1942 severed the up main line at Bath. Until two-line working was restored on 15th May, some trains were diverted via Radstock, one such being the 1.20 am Bristol to Weymouth goods. Locomotives used on diverted workings included 'Manors', 'Halls', '28XX', 'RODs', '26XX', '43XX' and 'Bulldogs'.

In 1967 13,000 wagons of coal were worked between Radstock and Portishead via Pensford. In 1968 the combined total lifted from Writhlington and Kilmersdon pits amounted to 150,000 tons, most of which was rail borne. In the early 1970s 'merry-go-round' trains of 'HAA' (32½ ton four-wheeled air-braked hopper) wagons carried coal from Radstock to Didcot power station, 34 wagons behind a 'Western' class diesel-hydraulic and 36 for a Brush class '47'. 'Warship' class diesel-hydraulics were limited to thirty 16-ton wagons.

Some Private Owner Wagon Liveries

Name of Company	Body Colour	Lettering colour
Braysdown Colliery	Black	White
Foxcote Colliery	Bauxite	White
S.C. Gilson & Sons	Red	White
Kilmersdon Colliery	Bauxite	White
Ludlows Colliery	Black	White
Mells Colliery	Lead	White shaded black
Mells Road Tar Works	Black	White
Mells Stone Quarry	Red	White
Newbury Colliery	Lead	White
Radstock Coal Co.	Black	White
Roads Reconstruction (1934) Ltd	Grey	White

In daylight and clear weather, up to 12 wagons could be propelled from East Depot to Brislington. The leading vehicle was required to carry a headlamp and a guard had to ride on, or near the leading vehicle to obtain a clear view and signal to the driver. Speed was limited to 10 mph and 4 mph over the facing points at Brislington. Only the North ground frame could be used. Similar instructions were issued for propelling a train from Radstock West to Midsomer Norton.

In 1930 traffic between North Somerset Junction and Radstock passing to South Wales, stations below Keynsham and to the Cheddar Valley line, except Wells, was required to work via Bristol. Traffic from Old Mills to Mells Road to Taunton and the West, Melksham, Holt Junction, the Devizes line, Trowbridge, Bradford-on-Avon, Salisbury and Weymouth lines had to work via Frome.

The 5.30 am Bristol to Mells Road goods was worked in turn by three guards. Enterprisingly, from the GWR they rented shooting and trapping rights on the company's land at Mells Road. The timetable required the Radstock signal boxes opened at 7.30 am to enable the 5.30 am goods to be shunted into a siding to allow the 7.00 am passenger train ex-Temple Meads and the 7.25 am from Frome to pass. For a consideration, the signalmen agreed to come on duty early to allow the guard to reach Mells Road ahead of the 7.00 am from Bristol which arrived there at 8.03 am. This gave the guard time to remove rabbits from snares and set traps before commencing shunting. The goods driver was also suitably rewarded.

Chapter Six

Signalling and Permanent Way

Signalling

In broad gauge days, certainly by 1871, the single track Radstock mineral branch was worked by a pilotman. The BNSR used absolute block working and the train staff and ticket. All its signal boxes were built by Saxby & Farmer. Following the broad gauge conversion and opening from Bristol to Frome throughout to passenger traffic, the single line was worked in four lengths:

	Shape of staff	*Colour of ticket*
North Somerset Junction-Pensford	Square	Red
Pensford-Radstock	Triangular	Blue
Radstock-Mells	Square	White
Mells-Frome	Round	White

Developments at Hallatrow for the opening of the Camerton branch on 1st March, 1882 enabled Hallatrow to cross two goods trains, or a goods and a passenger train. The above was modified to:

	Shape of staff	*Colour of ticket*
Pensford-Hallatrow	Round	White
Hallatrow-Radstock	Triangular	Blue
(Radstock-Mells double track from 1880)		
Mells-Frome Junction	Round	White

Further modifications were needed due to the insertion of the Contractor's Crossing signal box worked under special instruction dated 17th June, 1889. This temporary box was installed to deal with the construction of the Bristol Avoiding Line which opened on 10th April, 1892. On this date Marsh Junction replaced the temporary signal box.

	Shape of staff	*Colour of ticket*
North Somerset Junction-Contractor's Crossing	Round	Blue
Contractor's Crossing-Pensford	Square	Red

Between 1895 and 1898 the electric train staff was installed on all single line sections. An electric train tablet was used between Clutton and Pensford when Pensford & Bromley box was switched out of circuit.

At Hallatrow there was a rare example of a 32 in. elevated disc signal, colloquially a 'banjo', used as a running signal. Most, if not all, distant signals on the branch were fixed.

In the severe winter of 1940, due to telegraph lines being brought down by the weight of snow and ice, the time interval system was used on the double track between Radstock and Mells Road.

On 14th June, 1964 signal boxes at Pensford, Clutton and Hallatrow were closed, Bristol to Radstock being worked under 'one engine in steam'

Frome Mineral Junction signal box as rebuilt at Didcot Railway Centre, 19th August, 1992.
Author

regulations, this coinciding with the advent of dieselization. On that same date, Old Mills Siding was worked by the train staff instead of the electric train token. By 1978 the 'No signalman token' was in use from Frome North to Whatley Quarry or Mells Road, and 'One train only' from Mells Road to Radstock. The 'One train only' staff, applicable to trains over the Mells Road-Radstock section, was required to be held by the guard of such a train when proceeding between Frome North and Mells Road. The guard had to obtain it from, and return it to, the Frome North signalman. To ensure safety, no train could pass the stop board indicating the end of the 'One train only' section without the permission of the Radstock shunter.

No movement of BR locomotives to, or within, Whatley exchange sidings could take place until authorized by the BR shunter responsible for ensuring that all points were correctly set and that no conflicting movement would be made by an ARC locomotive. BR engines were not to be detached, or the continuous brake released, until the guard had adequately secured the train by applying the hand brakes at the Frome end.

Prior to 13th May, 1984 when Westbury panel box opened, as the points at Hapsford Loop were set for Whatley Quarry, the guard of a train to Radstock telephoned Frome North box asking for a 'release' for the Radstock line token instrument. When this was given, he removed a key token from the machine and unlocked the frame in order to set the road to Radstock, resetting it to Whatley immediately the train had crossed the junction. After 13th May, 1984 he obtained the release from Westbury panel and removed the token, this action electrically unlocking circuits of a mini panel. When given a release, he pressed a button to set the motor-worked points for Radstock, the train passed to the Radstock branch, the guard reset the points for the Whatley Quarry line and checked with Westbury that all was in order.

Today signalling through to Whatley Quarry is controlled by Network Rail. Beyond Great Elm Tunnel, the driver of a down train receives a siren from the Automatic Warning System (AWS) inductor of a permanent yellow aspect, and

SIGNALLING AND PERMANENT WAY

another from a permanent red aspect at the mouth of Murder Combe tunnel. When the line is clear into the reception sidings, a position light signal displays two white lights to allow the train to draw ahead.

Two of the branch signal boxes are preserved at Didcot Railway Centre. Radstock North (later renamed 'West') signal box was rebuilt *circa* 1908 and 6 ft of the brick base of the original structure re-used. Following closure on 17th January, 1973 this signal box, and one crossing gate was purchased by the Great Western Society. An interesting feature of this box was that in order to ensure that the signalman did not unduly delay road traffic at this busy box by closing the gates too early, a Siemen's mercury treadle was situated at North Somerset viaduct to sound a warning bell. The other preserved signal box is Frome Mineral Junction opened in 1875 and closed on 6th October, 1984.

Marsh Junction and Pensford & Bromley signal boxes were the only ones on the branch which had picking up and setting down posts for the train staff. The speed limit was 15 mph if using the post, but 10 mph if the exchange was by hand. Diesel railcars were required to stop because missed tokens caused broken windows.

Many boxes on the branch had a garden and so a few lumps of coal to augment the supply in the signalman's coal bunker, resulted in vegetables for footplate crews at very reasonable price. One signalman on the line made cast lead soldiers and an employee at St Philip's Marsh shed collected old mudhole door gaskets to supply his need for basic material.

The guard of a down train receives from the signalman what is probably a token with an Annett's key at the end for working a siding within a block at Mells Road, February 1961.
Roger Holmes

Clutton signal box. Notice the vestibule at the top of the steps to avoid draughts in the box. Below the man standing at the head of the stairs is a two-handled saw. *Clutton History Group*

The single line Pensford to Clutton token preserved in Kidderminster Railway Museum.
Author

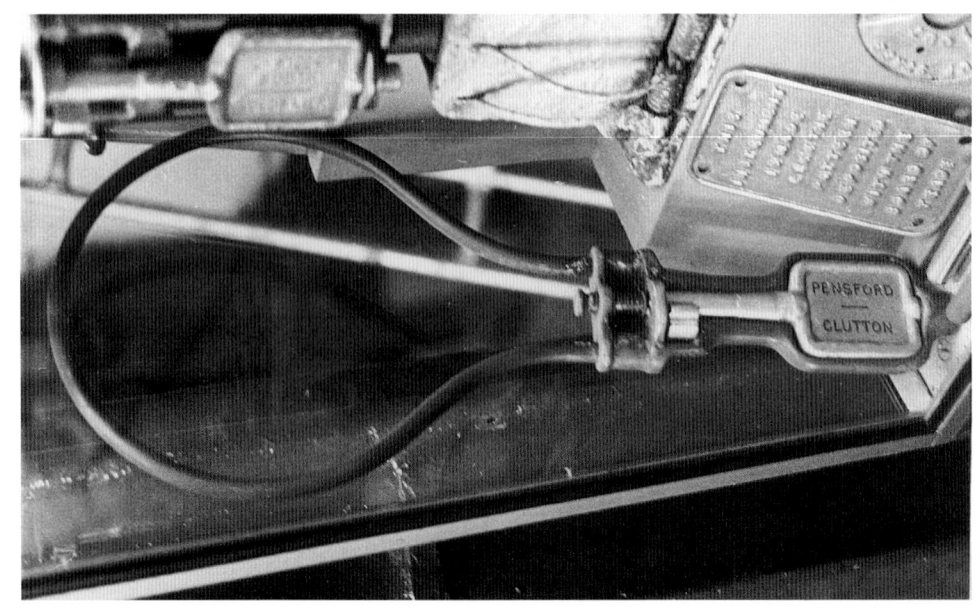

SIGNALLING AND PERMANENT WAY 207

Hallatrow viewed in the down direction *circa* 1910. The rodding to 18 sets of points is impressive. *Author's Collection*

Hallatrow signal box and interesting point work *circa* 1960. Notice that the timber crossing is staggered. *Lens of Sutton Collection*

BR Standard class '3' 2-6-2T No. 82042 working the 10.00 am Temple Meads to Frome service on 13th September, 1959, the last day of Sunday service on the branch, approaches Radstock. Notice the permanent way hut and rails for parking a permanent way trolley off the main line.

Michael Jenkins

Above: Motor trolley and trailer parked at right-angles to the main line at Chelwood Bridge, 21st February, 1950.

Author

Right: The Clutton permanent way gang on a motor trolley, back row: J. Gatehouse, G. Tiley, T, Bourton and Dan Perry. Front row: T. Owen and J. Brain. Bill Pooley is on the left-hand trolley.

Clutton History Group

Permanent Way

The broad gauge Frome to Radstock mineral branch was maintained by Messrs Brotherhood of Chippenham until June 1861 when the work was taken over by the GWR. In the 1930s the motor trolley system of permanent way maintenance was adopted between Marsh Junction and Radstock West signal box. The home stations for the engineering gangs responsible for the section were at Pensford and Clutton, the former maintaining Marsh Junction to Clutton, and the latter the remainder of the route to Radstock.

Telephones and occupation key boxes were provided every mile. When a motor trolley was removed from the track, the ganger inserted the key into the nearest key box to enable the signalman to open the section to a train, because the withdrawal of that occupation key had locked the normal token for the relevant section. When a key was removed it disconnected the instruments by a slide being withdrawn and until a key was placed in a lineside box, or signal box, the instrument was inoperable. During World War II one of the two signalwomen at Clutton hung her handbag on the slide; its weight drew it out fractionally and disconnected her instruments. She panicked and instituted pilot working. The signal lineman quickly spotted the fault.

Working on the permanent way could be fraught with danger. Shortly after the BNSR opened, on 20th March, 1874, two Chelwood men, John Bates aged 29 and Albert Stock, 42, permanent way packers, proceeded to Clutton on a permanent way trolley and before arriving, the 3.40 pm down train approached from behind round a sharp curve. The men attempted to remove the trolley from the line, but before they could do so, the locomotive's stone guard struck the trolley, shattering it and knocking the men over. Bates had his ribs smashed, while Stock received similar injuries, plus a serious head wound. They were taken by train to Bristol General Hospital where Bates died the same evening.

The Frome to Old Mills length came within the Yeovil permanent way inspector's district while the rest of the branch was under Bristol.

The permanent way gang and porters at Clutton. The ganger is holding a track gauge.
Clutton History Group

NORTH SOMERSET BRANCH.
MARSH JUNCTION TO FROME.
OCCUPATION OF LINE BETWEEN BRISTOL (MARSH JUNCTION) AND RADSTOCK WEST SIGNAL BOX BY THE ENGINEERING DEPARTMENT.

The Motor Trolley System of maintenance operates from 22m. 76ch. near Marsh Junction to 8m. 23ch. near Radstock West Signal Box.

The home stations of the engineering gangs responsible for the Section of Line are Pensford and Clutton.

The Pensford gang maintain the line between 22m. 76ch. and 14m. 20ch., and the Clutton gang maintain the line between 14m. 20ch. and 8m. 23ch.

The Instructions for the Motor Trolley System of Maintenance on Single Lines worked by Electric Token apply.

Places where Telephones and Occupation Key Boxes are fixed, giving the mileage and number of hut.

Section—Marsh Junction to Pensford (One Key).
    Gang No. 126 .. .. 22m. 76ch. to 17m. 30ch

    Marsh Junction Signal Box.   M. CH
        Box No. 1 .. .. 22 10
        Box No. 2 .. .. 21 11
        Box No. 3 .. .. 20 16
        Box No. 4 .. .. 19 32
        Box No. 5 .. .. 18 26
    Pensford Signal Box.

The Telephones communicate with the Signalman at Pensford.

Section—Pensford to Clutton (One Key).
    Gang. No. 126 .. .. .. 17m. 30ch. to 14m. 20ch

    Pensford Signal Box.
    Pensford & Bromley Old Signal Box
    (In box outside).   M. CH
        Box No. 6 .. .. 15 65
        Box No. 7 .. .. 14 78
    Clutton Signal Box.

The Telephones communicate with the Signalman at Clutton.

Section—Clutton to Hallatrow (One Key).
    Gang No. 125 .. .. .. 14m. 20ch. to 12m. 58ch

    Clutton Signal Box.   M. CH.
        Box No. 8 .. .. 13 34
    Hallatrow Signal Box.

The Telephones communicate with the Signalman at Clutton.

Section—Hallatrow to Radstock (One Key).
    Gang No. 125 .. .. .. 12m. 58ch. to 8m. 23ch.
    Hallatrow Signal Box.   M. CH.
        Box No. 9 .. .. 11 54
        Box No. 10 .. .. 10 50
        Box No. 11 .. .. 9 66
        Box No. 12 .. .. 9 2
    Radstock West Signal Box.

The Telephones communicate with the Signalman at Radstock West.

For the section Clutton—Pensford a control instrument with three Slides, (1) Control (2) Occupation Key, Clutton—Pensford & Bromley (3) Occupation Key, Pensford & Bromley—Pensford, is provided at Clutton. The instrument should be operated in the same manner as described in the Standard Instructions, with the addition that it will be necessary for the Signalman at Clutton to ask the Ganger to press the plunger provided in connection with Occupation Key Box to enable the Signalman to withdraw the Occupation Slide applicable, i.e., 2 or 3.

It is possible to have occupation of the Clutton—Pensford & Bromley and Pensford & Bromley—Pensford Sections simultaneously, but both occupation Keys must be restored before the token working can be resumed.

The Signal Box at Pensford & Bromley is now closed.

Instructions for the motor trolley system of maintenance from the
Sectional Appendix to the Working Time Table, Bristol Traffic District, October 1960.

Chapter Seven

Regeneration?

In the autumn of 1988 Dennis Haines, manager of a construction materials company, was behind the idea for regenerating the Radstock to Frome line. He believed that £200,000 could put the line in a safe condition to carry passenger traffic. The local authority supported the idea in principle, but not with finance and no large business group was interested. In February 1989 the Somerset & Avon Railway Company (SARA) was formed.

In 1990 the Wansdyke District Council approved a multi-million pound plan for redeveloping the railway land at Radstock, building about 120 flats and houses, plus offices and a car park. SARA hoped to build a station, obtain a lease from BR of six miles of disused track and start operating trains in 1991. SARA had two of ARC's diesel-hydraulics from Whatley Quarry, one almost in running condition.

Perhaps significantly on All Fools' Day, 1996 the local authority changed from Wansdyke to Bath & North East Somerset (BANES), the latter set up when the county of Avon was abolished. This had serious implications for SARA as the new authority was not so keen on a railway and wanted to use all the land for building. To gain the support of the local authority, in 1998 the preservationists changed their ideals and name to the North Somerset Railway Co. Ltd. They hoped to be granted a TOC to run one diesel commuter train each way daily Radstock to Frome, Melksham and Chippenham and run steam trains on the branch at weekends. It was also expected that 150,000 tonnes of animal foodstuffs would travel on the line annually. A new station would be built just west of the former wagon works as BANES wished to demolish the remains of the down platform and erect a non-railway building.

Some floors in the former wagon works were made from wagon headstocks. Preservationists found that had they laid bullhead rail in the shops, there would have been insufficient head clearance for their stock. Quite a quantity of bridge rail was found in the sheds and the use of this allowed the necessary height.

At the time of writing, efforts to re-open the line are on 'hold'. The weakness of the scheme is that most commuters from Norton-Radstock need to travel to Bristol or Bath, rather than Frome. The nearby Somerset & Dorset Railway Heritage Trust's line at Midsomer Norton is extending southwards, but perhaps in future may wish to link with a re-opened Radstock to Frome line. Through passenger trains could then be run from Bristol to Bournemouth, reversing at Radstock an easy procedure with dmus.

In 1998 Sustrans acquired the route beside the moribund line from Radstock to near Great Elm and in 2004 created a foot and cycle path beside the disused railway track, still *in situ*, but mostly overgrown with weeds and shrubs. Although the path is generally alongside the track, it sometimes follows the top of a cutting, or the foot of an embankment. Seats and picnic tables are provided and the route is well-used by cyclists and walkers. Bridge rail can be seen in use as fence or straining posts. The path terminates about 500 yds west of Hapsford ground frame.

Right: The GWR engine shed at Radstock on 6th March, 1999. The track is offset as it was originally broad gauge. The ash pit is in the foreground.
Author

Below: SARA's stock in the former wagon works, 17th August, 1989: a Sentinel diesel-hydraulic; LMS goods brake van and a London & North Western Railway passenger brake van.
Author

'8750' class 0-6-0PT No. 9681 on loan from the Dean Forest Railway and ex-London & North Western Railway brake van built in 1916, running at Radstock on 6th March, 1999.
Author

In November 2009 the Radstock Action Group supported the Great Western Rail Utilisation Strategy to reinstate the rail link between Radstock and Frome. This would encourage more businesses in the area including the adjacent settlements of Midsomer Norton and Paulton, by linking with London to Plymouth services without the need of having to travel by road to Bath Spa station which can take up to 45 minutes.

An early commuter train currently originating at Frome could be changed to start at Radstock and call at a new Frome market station before continuing to Paddington. Although a restored passenger service would greatly assist passengers from the Radstock area travelling to London, Trowbridge and Swindon, unfortunately it would involve a very circuitous route to reach Bath or Bristol - the main destinations of much of the present road traffic. Due to distance, the time penalty would be severe and fares high. A further drawback is that Frome station would not be served unless a chord line was built into the present Frome station.

Kevin Boak, a friend of the author, envisages the solution in a tramway system with on-street running from the centre of Bath and then utilizing the former Somerset & Dorset Railway's trackbed to Radstock, with Park & Ride facilities being offered at Midford. From Radstock the route would follow the BNSR trackbed through Midsomer Norton, Hallatrow, Clutton and Pensford to Brislington, linking there into a Bristol tram network serving the city centre.

'Dean Goods' No. 2415 at Clutton. *Clutton History Group*

'61XX' class 2-6-2T No. 6148 derailed at Hallatrow, 15th August, 1963. *Author's Collection*

Chapter Eight

Mishaps

Mercifully the line was free from serious accidents and even mishaps have been few. The most serious occurred on Saturday 15th July, 1911.

The Somerset Miners' Association had organized a day trip to Weston-super-Mare. Three long double-headed trains left Radstock picking up at Midsomer Norton, Hallatrow, Clutton and Pensford, while one double-header left from Camerton.

Four return trains were scheduled: 7.05, 7.53, 8.25 and 8.35 pm. Due to the very fine weather, an unusually large number delayed their return until the last train. Accommodation was taxed to the limit and many trippers had to be content to make the journey in the guard's van. The 18 coaches were drawn by two engines. It is recorded that the train had 118 wheels, which meant that most of the coaches were 6-wheelers. En route the train lost ½ hour on its schedule.

At Pensford, front guard Parsons was left behind on the platform, his absence not noticed by the rear guard until the train reached Clutton. 'Here he inquired of the passengers who were in the van as to the whereabouts of the guard in charge of it, and they informed him he was last seen at Pensford' – *Somerset Guardian* 21st July, 1911.

Railway officials at Clutton conferred and decided that the best policy was to uncouple the leading engine and return it to Pensford to fetch the guard.

He was duly collected, but approaching Clutton station at 11.20 pm, instead of setting the 'wrong road' in order that the locomotive could pass the coaches standing at the down platform, the signalman directed it to the down line as normal. Unfortunately the driver failed to notice this error and his engine struck the rear of the long passenger train, the end of which was standing close to the points.

The last two coaches, 6-wheel brake-third No. 1130 and 6-wheel third No. 547 were damaged and the third from last, 8-wheel third No. 2164 slightly damaged. 'After the collision all was confusion for a time, and the screams of women could be heard by others who were on the train.'

Passengers at the front of the train only felt a slight jarring, but passengers in the last three coaches were,

> … thrown violently against each other or against the opposite side of the coach. In one or two cases passengers who were seated or standing near the open doorways were thrown out on to the platform. Very fortunately, at the moment the impact took place, many of the passengers who had been riding in the rear coaches, were standing or strolling about the platform and thus escaped injury.

Dr Martin was summoned from the nearby village of Temple Cloud and attended to the worst cases, most of the 25 persons injured suffering from cuts and bruises to the face or hands, but some had loosened teeth. All except one were able to continue travelling to their home station. The exception was young Jack Ruddick of Meadgate, Camerton, who suffered a severe scalp wound. Dr Martin ordered him to stay at Clutton station until morning when he was taken home by cab. The other injured passengers were either met at Midsomer Norton by Dr Scales, or at Radstock by Dr Pollard and Dr Costabarrie and sent home in cabs provided by the GWR. The guard travelling on the light engine received slight injuries to his arm, but the driver and fireman were unhurt. The damaged last three coaches were detached at Clutton, shunted into a siding and covered with tarpaulins to prevent the public from seeing the extent of the damage. The rest of the train arrived at Radstock about midnight. There had been no spectators at Clutton that evening, as those on the train destined for Clutton had left the station a considerable time before the collision. The following day railway officials prevented sightseers from going to the siding where the damaged coaches had been placed.

Charles Kislingbury, divisional superintendent, arrived by special train at 1.00 am on Sunday to inspect the scene of the accident and the three damaged coaches. He then proceeded to Radstock and then returned to Bristol. No interruption was caused to the returning London excursion which arrived at 4.00 am en route to Bristol.

About 11.00 am on Monday 17th, Jack Ruddick regained consciousness and spoke to his family. He was seen by a GWR representative on Wednesday evening 19th July. The GWR made efforts to compensate all those injured in the accident and whose injuries had been noted at the time, the majority being seen by a company representative in conjunction with Mr Thick, the GWR station master at Radstock. Various sums of money were paid in full discharge of the company's liabilities. No time was lost – most were paid on 18th and 19th, only the most seriously injured paid later.

The official inquiry said that the front guard had been left behind at Pensford due to the fireman of the leading engine not properly observing Rule 150a. When there were two or more guards, the signal to the driver (or his representative the fireman if he had a better view), to start had to be given by the guard nearest the front of the train after exchanging signals with the guard, or guards in the rear.

The inquiry also criticized the judgement of the Clutton station master in sending an engine back for the guard and not taking account of the heavy train 'and troublesome passengers'. It added that to replace the missing guard he should have used the goods guard at Clutton, or a porter, especially in view of the fact that to return the front engine to Pensford involved using the unauthorized 'warning' signal (3-5-5 bell code) to accept it from Pensford at Clutton. (However, the BoT inspector said it was 'right' to use the signal in these emergency conditions.)

Blame also rested on signalman Gibbs of Clutton for conveying the impression to the driver of the light engine that it would be all right to run 'wrong line' at Clutton on his return from Pensford, and after telling him this, failing to set the road so that he could do so. The driver of the light engine was also held at fault for, notwithstanding the information given him by signalman Gibbs, passing the Clutton home signal at danger, especially after receiving a 'warning' signal (a verbal warning) at Pensford which only authorized him to proceed to the Clutton home signal.

On 24th July, 1911 an extensive subsidence took place in one of the sidings at Clutton giving rise to the rumour that the station had fallen in. Luckily the Greyfield Colliery 0-4-0ST *Daisy* had just passed the spot. Rails were left hanging across the hole wide enough to contain an engine. *Daisy* was unable to return to her shed at the colliery.

At 6.00 pm on Thursday 18th August, 1938 at Thicket Mead railway bridge which spanned the B3355 about ½ mile west of Midsomer Norton station, a 3-ton GPO Telephones lorry returning to Bristol loaded with a 1-ton crane fouled the bridge, the crane striking the Midsomer Norton side of the structure, displacing an iron plate forming the side of the bridge and throwing a piece of iron on the track.

On seeing this, two men who lived near the bridge, knowing that the 5.20 pm Temple Meads to Frome was shortly due, ran along the line to stop it. They failed, the train passing them unheeding their gestures.

A third man, Albert N. Dark, a GWR carman living at Midsomer Norton but employed at Radstock, ran a long the line to the fourth telegraph pole from the bridge and waved a red handkerchief. Although the driver noticed him and applied the brakes, the engine and two coaches passed Dark before they stopped.

Passengers were asked to alight and walk across in case the bridge had been weakened. To allow the engine to pass the obstruction, the injector overflow pipe had to be temporarily removed. The empty train then drew across, fortunately without mishap, and came to a halt 30 yds beyond where passengers were able to rejoin it. The delay caused the train to arrive at Radstock at 6.58 pm instead of 6.08.

All subsequent engines crossing the bridge had to have their injector pipes removed. Such was the interest, that hundreds of people visited the site during the evening. Road traffic was also affected, the bus service to Bristol having to be diverted.

In April 1944 this bridge was struck again, this time by a Sherman tank carried on a transporter. As the bridge was considered unsafe to carry passenger trains, buses were substituted for three or four days.

In 1943 a loaded United States' tank transporter racing a train, failed to negotiate Chelwood overbridge, crashed into the parapet, dislodging a coping stone which fell on the locomotive hauling an up goods train and causing steam to escape. The scalded crew was unable to control the train. The alert Pensford signalwoman, Mary Jewell, saw the escaping steam, guessed something was amiss and gave it a through road. Gravity brought it to a halt. A relief engine was sent from Bristol to rescue the train. Mary lived in Bath and reached Pensford by train to Keynsham and then cycling five miles to Pensford.

A smart St Philip's Marsh driver averted an accident at Pensford & Bromley Colliery sidings. His '31XX' class 2-6-2T was entering the sidings; the guard cut off his van so it could gravitate to the bottom of the sidings. When the driver applied his steam brake, the rigging snapped. He sounded his alarm with the brake whistle, placed the engine in back gear, opened regulator and sand valve, successfully bringing it to a halt only yards from the stop blocks.

At level crossings there was always the risk of a train running through the gates. On 7th January, 1971 thirty-two wagons arrived at Radstock, eight for repair. While these were being shunted to Marcroft's, the 24 coal wagons ran through the crossing gates.

On 5th November, 1976 the last vehicle of a loaded 41-wagon train to Theale, derailed in Hapsford Loop, breaking sleepers and misaligning the track. On 12th September, 2000 No. 59103 *Village of Mells* hauling forty-two 102-tonne 'LTF' hopper wagons, derailed by a broken rail joint, tipped over on its side and would have fallen down the embankment had not the buffer beam been supported by a bridge girder. Due to its location between Great Elm tunnel and the river bridge, no lifting gear could reach the spot. No. 59005 *Kenneth J. Painter* was brought by road from Merehead to Whatley to draw the train from the tunnel. On 19th September No. 59103 was jacked and winched upright, hauled to Whatley and taken away by road for repair. No. 59103's driver suffered broken ribs. Customers were largely unaffected as some of the 10 scheduled daily trains from Whatley were switched to Hanson's Tytherington Quarry in South Gloucestershire, while others were covered by Foster Yeoman's Torr Works on the other side of the Mendips.

A general view of Camerton New Pit in its rural setting. Lower right are coal wagons belonging to Camerton Collieries and others. *Author's Collection*

The loading screens at Camerton New Pit. *Left to right are*: Camerton Collieries 5 ton 15 cwt tare Nos. 329, 361 and 315. Wooden pit props are in the foreground. *Author's Collection*

Chapter Nine

The Camerton Branch

Although initially the Camerton branch was expected to be built at the same time as the main line, the great financial problems prevented this. As completion of the Radstock to Bristol line drew near, the Directors at their meeting on 31st December, 1872 approved a Bill for the branch's construction. The Act of 36 & 37 Vict. cap. 168 passed on 21st July, 1873 authorized the raising of £40,000 with additional borrowing powers of £13,300. Any profit from the line was to be paid only to the Camerton branch shareholders. The Great Western could subscribe any amount of capital, and in the event, provided it all.

William Clarke was appointed Engineer and on 5th August, 1873 was instructed to prepare a detailed estimate for the GWR Board. The BNSR's parlous financial situation worried the GWR and postponed further work. Confidence eventually restored, on 14th February, 1878 the GWR accepted T. Mousely's tender of £19,000 for building the 3½ mile line. For its last 1½ miles the line ran parallel with the Somerset Coal Canal and this length was purchased from the canal company. Construction proceeded and the branch was finished in early autumn 1880.

The Board of Trade report stated:

Railway Department,
Board of Trade,
5 New Street, London S.W.
15th October 1880

Sir,

I have the honor [sic] to report for the information of the Board of Trade that in compliance with the instructions contained in your Minute of the 8th inst, I have inspected the Camerton Branch of the Bristol and North Somerset Section of the Great Western Railway.

This Branch, which joins the Bristol and North Somerset line at Hallatrow station and thence runs to Camerton its present terminus, is a single line 3½ miles long on the 4 ft 8½ ins gauge. Land has been purchased for a double line and some of the overbridges constructed. The steepest gradient has an inclination of 1 in 47 and the sharpest curve a radius of 11¼ chains.

The permanent way for about a mile consists of flat bottomed steel rails weighing 72 lbs per yd, secured to each sleeper by a fang bolt and dog spike. On the remaining 2½ miles double headed steel rails have been used weighing 82 lbs per yd, fixed by inside keys in cast iron chairs weighing 30 lbs each and the sleeper by 2 iron spikes. The sleepers are creosoted and measure 8 ft 11 ins by 10 ins by 5 ins. The ballast consists of furnace slag, ashes and broken stone.

There are 4 bridges over the line constructed with brick on masonry abutments, spanned by cast iron or wrought iron girders with arches turned between them, largest span 30½ ft. Under the line there are 11 bridges, all constructed with brick or masonry abutments, 2 having brick arches and the others wrought iron girder tops, the largest span being 26½ ft. There are also 5 large culverts, of which one (6 ft span) has a timber top.

The bridges appear to have been all substantially constructed and to be standing well; the wrought and cast iron girders have sufficient theoretical strength and those under the line gave moderate deflections under test.

There are no tunnels and no public road level crossings.

The fencing is of post and rail.

'Dean Goods' 0-6-0 No. 2395 shunts wagons at Camerton *circa* 1905. The wagons behind the engine are Camerton Collieries No. 169, A.H. & S. Bird, Trowbridge and Alfred J. Smith, Bradford-on-Avon. On the lower road is Timsbury Collieries No. 115. The locomotive is on a flat-bottomed track, but the lower siding has chaired and keyed track. *Author's Collection*

The balanced incline to Lower Congyre Colliery, Timsbury *circa* 1910. Empty wagons on the left gravitate to the foot of the incline ready to be raised to the colliery, while the loaded dumb-buffered wagon, right, will gravitate to the siding for full wagons behind the photographer.
Paul Barnard Collection

Hallatrow station has been remodelled, so as to adapt it for the reception of the branch trains, and a new station has been erected at the terminus at Camerton, there being no intermediate stations. The signalling arrangements at these two have been properly carried out in a raised cabin and ground frame at Hallatrow and a raised cabin at Camerton.

I observed the following requirements:

1. At Hallatrow station the fencing near the termination of the new platform should be removed and the platform should end in a ramp. The distant signals from Bristol and Radstock require electrical repeaters, and the former should be moved further back. An additional safety point worked from the ground frame is required on the goods loop.

2. Camerton station. The cross over road at the platform should be moved further back, so that a train should not stand on the facing point. The up home signal should be moved foward and made a starting signal. The signalman's view of the distant signal requires improving by removing the branch of a tree. Clocks are required in the station and signal cabin.

3. Some additional fencing is required at several places as pointed out and a handrail on the underbridge close to Camerton station.

4. The land close to Hallatrow station has settled during the late rains and will require careful watching and treatment.

The line is to be worked with one engine at a time under steam and the train staff, and an undertaking of this at first should be sent in both by the Great Western and North Somerset companies.

Subject to this undertaking being duly received and the above requirements being promptly completed and an intimation of their completion sent to the Board of Trade, and to the line being inspected on the first convenient opportunity, the opening of the Camerton Branch for passenger traffic need not be objected to.

      I have the etc.
      C.L. Hutchinson
      Major General RE

Hutchinson's requirements were met and he reinspected and passed the line on 31st May, 1881.

There was now the curious situation where Camerton had a railway but no trains. The colliery failed to apply for a rail link and passenger and general goods traffic alone would not have been economic. Clarke told the GWR Directors on 20th July, 1881 that sidings had been laid to the colliery and the line was to be open only for goods and mineral traffic. In actual fact the line opened on 1st March, 1882 to both passenger and goods traffic.

Hallatrow, the junction station, had been modified, a short bay platform established at the Bristol end of the single main line platform. The track layout was suitably enlarged and adapted being signalled by McKenzie & Holland, the new timber signal box having a frame with 24 working levers and six spares. The branch diverged from the main line at the north end of the goods yard and curved sharply downwards at 1 in 47 setting a severe limit to loaded coal trains climbing the gradient.

Camerton station had a typical Clarke brick building. The single track layout was a run-round loop, a siding and a headshunt forming the siding to New Pit. The yard had a 2 ton crane in 1904.

In September 1898 Lower Conygre Colliery set below Timsbury and hitherto linked to the Somerset Coal Canal by narrow gauge tramway, had a standard gauge siding laid which was linked to the pit by a cable-worked incline. The Radford siding was not opened until 19th July, 1900.

An 0-6-0ST heads a goods train principally composed of coal wagons, near Paulton *circa* 1905. Behind the goods brake van is the branch passenger coach. Notice the pointed ends of the fence to deter trespassers.
Chapman & Son

A steam excavator at work in a cutting west of Midford *circa* 1909. The Somerset & Dorset Railway viaduct carrying the Bath to Evercreeech Junction line can be seen in the background.
Author's Collection

The first timetable offered in the down direction (from Hallatrow) five passenger trains, one mixed and one goods, with an up service of three passengers, one mixed and three goods trains. Goods and passenger trains alike were allowed 10 minutes in either direction for the 3½ miles. Most of the down goods consisted of empty wagons. By July 1885 the generous down service had been reduced to two passengers, one mixed and a goods, the latter 'as required'. The up service offered two passengers, one mixed and a goods 'as required'. Traffic increased and the 1900 timetable showed three down passenger trains, one mixed and four goods. In the reverse direction was one passenger, one mixed, four goods and a coal train. One goods each way called at Radford. Running times were amended to 15 minutes for goods, 13 minutes for mixed trains while passenger times remained at 10 minutes.

With an unbalanced passenger service the single 4-wheeled brake composite was returned to Hallatrow in a goods train. If there were no passengers in a down train which had no booked loaded return working, the coach was left at Hallatrow.

By 1900 the branch was worked by '1854' or '2721' class 0-6-0STs. 'Dean Goods' 0-6-0s also appeared.

Dunkerton Colliery opened in 1905 and on 4th April, 1907 the line was opened to serve it and then through to Limpley Stoke on the Bath to Westbury line on 9th May, 1910. Halts were opened at Paulton (1 miles 49 chains) on 5th January, 1914 and Timsbury & Radford (2 miles 68 chains) on 9th May, 1910.

Initially passenger trains were worked by '517' class 0-4-2Ts and an auto-coach, but within a few weeks this formation was replaced by a steam rail motor.

As a wartime economy measure the passenger service was withdrawn on 22nd March, 1915. Services were restored on 9th July, 1923, but buses proved more convenient and the service was withdrawn on 21st September, 1925.

Paulton Halt, looking towards Camerton *circa* 1930. Notice the flat-bottomed track, probably disused. *Author's Collection*

Radford & Timsbury Halt in the summer of 1910. '517' class 0-4-2T No. 562 and an auto-trailer head for Hallatrow. The Camerton fixed distant signal is on the left and at the very edge of the picture can be seen a dumb-buffered wagon in the siding laid with bridge rail on longitudinal baulks. *Author's Collection*

The small goods yard at Camerton with a 2-ton crane on the left which came in December 1900 second-hand from Stourbridge. The view is towards Hallatrow in the summer of 1910. Beyond the buffer stop was an overbridge so low that brewery drays could not access the 'Jolly Collier' on the right and barrels had to be unloaded and rolled beneath the railway. *Author's Collection*

A '517' class 0-4-2T and auto-trailer at Camerton. A raft of empty coal wagons is in the distance. This signal box opened on 3rd May, 1910 replacing an earlier one on the far side of the road bridge.
M.J. Tozer Collection

An 0-6-0ST runs round the 4-wheel coach at Camerton following its arrival from Hallatrow. Two open wagons are behind the coach. Between the locomotive and coach is a steam roller covered by a tarpaulin. On the far right is a wheelbarrow. The card was postmarked 2nd December, 1907.
Author's Collection

A '517' class 0-4-2T and auto-trailer No. 54 at Camerton in the summer of 1910 following the line's extension to Limpley Stoke. The second man on the left is the conductor with money bag and ticket punch. Camerton Old Pit can be seen in the background. *M.J. Tozer Collection*

Camerton station platform becomes the film set for *The Ghost Train* in 1931.

Author's Collection

As gradients on the Camerton to Limpley Stoke section were easier than the climb to Hallatrow, and Conygre Colliery had closed in July 1916, the section from Hallatrow to Camerton closed on 8th February, 1932. Camerton Colliery closed on 14th April, 1950 and the daily train from Limpley Stoke ceased.

The lightly-used branch was ideal for filming. Gainsborough Pictures filmed *The Ghost Train*, written by Bath author Arnold Ridley, at Camerton in 1931. It starred Jack Hulbert and Cicely Courtneidge. Jack also had a local connection having been educated at Bath College. The 'Ghost Train' itself was hauled by 'Dean Goods' class 0-6-0 No. 2381, while the train representing the 'Cornish Riviera Express' was hauled by a '43XX' class 2-6-0. Filming also took place on the double track between Radstock and Mells Road.

The GWR utilized the film for publicity and at most of the London cinemas where it was shown, the picture house vestibules were converted into replicas of GWR booking halls and folders *See The Ghost Train Country* distributed.

In November 1937 Dunkerton Colliery Sidings were used to film night scenes of the Edgar Wallace thriller *Kate Plus Ten* and again a '43XX' class locomotive was used.

In 1952 the branch provided the setting for the Ealing Studio's comedy *The Titfield Thunderbolt*. The Liverpool & Manchester Railway 0-4-2 *Lion* built in 1838 and believed to be the oldest working locomotive in the world, was the star. '14XX' class 0-4-2Ts Nos. 1401 and 1456 also appeared, as did ex-Wisbech & Upwell Tramway coach No. 7. Monkton Combe station was re-named 'Titfield'.

The Liverpool & Manchester Railway locomotive *Lion* at Monkton Combe on 23rd June, 1952, prior to being temporarily renamed 'Thunderbolt' for filming purposes.   *Author*

The entrance to Monkton Combe station, renamed as 'Titfield', on 23rd June, 1952. *Author*

'14XX' class 0-4-2T No. 1401 at Monkton Combe station on 23rd June, 1952 with ex-Wisbech & Upwell Railway coach No. 7. *Author*

Appendix One

Footplate trip from Bristol East Depot to Radstock, 12th April, 1961

Early one morning, with my footplate pass safely in my pocket, I made my way to St Philip's Marsh locomotive depot, Bristol. Enquiring at the office, I was told that No. 7772, a '57XX' class 0-6-0PT would be the engine for the 8.20 am Bristol to Radstock goods that day, though usually it was worked by a '41XX' class 2-6-2T.

No. 7772 had been built by the North British Locomotive Co. Ltd for the GWR in February 1931. After spending most of its life in South Wales, it transferred to St Philip's Marsh during the four weeks ending 16th July, 1960. It spent just over a year at Bristol before being transferred to Stourbridge, during the four weeks ending 12th August, 1961. It was withdrawn from service in November 1961.

Wending my way between the engines in the murky gloom of the shed, I spotted No. 7772 just on its way out. Much to my relief it stopped outside and I made myself known to driver Stan Denman and fireman I.R. Hathaway. We joined the queue for water and I was told there was more congestion at the shed since the Bath Road shed had been closed to steam. I noticed the pressure of 175 psi had risen to 190, only 10 short of the maximum, by the time our tanks were full.

After a short wait at St Philip's Marsh signal box we travelled along the relief line to Marsh Junction, passing No. D93, a 'Peak' class diesel-electric soon to be used on the Bristol to York run and on that day used for training enginemen.

Arriving at the down yard, Bristol East Depot, we found two wagons in the siding for us. The crew was rather surprised at this light load as the day before there had been 14 - a full load for the engine. After coupling up, Hathaway placed about a dozen shovelfuls of brickettes in the firebox as we left the yard. He told me that they produced steam well but were dusty and so the footplate needed to be kept wet for fear of a blowback singeing the crew's eyebrows.

As the branch to Radstock was single, the staff was duly collected at Marsh Junction. Soon after passing to the single line, we crossed a new concrete bridge over the Avon and climbed the 1 in 62 to Brislington past the factory where 'Bristol' bus and lorry chassis were made. The regulator was opened on the first valve and the cut-off 45 per cent.

Considering that the passenger service had been withdrawn about 18 months previously, I was agreeably surprised at the excellent condition of Brislington station, and indeed of all the stations on the branch.

The line was level through the station giving the engine a breather, though with such a light load this was not really needed. I noticed a scrap merchant's premises in the yard. The injector was opened to fill the boiler and to prevent the safety valves from blowing off.

In slight drizzle our climb continued through the suburbs. Speed was 17 mph and pressure had dropped to 180. More coal was put on and the injector opened again. We passed Whitchurch Halt and beyond could see Dundry Hill, a local landmark, enshrouded in mist. The injector was turned on again. The regulator was on the first valve and the cut-off 41 per cent.

At the summit of the 4½ mile climb was a notice: 'All down goods and mineral trains must stop dead at this board'. After making a momentary stop, for no brakes needed pinning down on such a light load, the regulator was placed in the drifting position and we descended the 1 in 66 to Pensford at 28 mph, while Hathaway washed the floor. Primroses carpeted the banks.

Immediately prior to Pensford station speed was reduced to 5 mph as heavy rain had caused the embankment to slip and tons of ashes had been tipped to fill the gap. At Pensford we stopped to change the staff. Beyond we crossed the lofty viaduct high above

230 THE BRISTOL-RADSTOCK-FROME LINE

'57XX' class 0-6-0PT No. 7772 at Bristol St Philip's Marsh shed on 12th April, 1961. *Author*

No. 7772 is filled with water. Fireman Hathaway stands on the boiler, 12th April, 1961.
Author

APPENDIX

No. 7772 at Hallatrow on 12th April, 1961. *Author*

'51XX' class 2-6-2T No. 4102 passes through Hallatrow with an up freight on 12th April, 1961.
Author

No. 7772 is filled with water at Radstock ready for the return trip on 12th April, 1961.

Author

Driver Denman and fireman Hathaway on No. 7772 at Radstock on 12th April, 1961. *Author*

the roofs of cottages. The line was very scenic and voted by Bristol footplatemen the prettiest of the branches they worked over. In the cutting on the far side of the viaduct the banks were ablaze with gorse.

We climbed the 1 in 69 at 17 mph. Again the regulator was on the first valve and cut-off 45 per cent. The injector was opened at Chelwood bridge and then we dropped down into Clutton, still at 17 mph. The garden on the platform was still lovingly tended and stones spelt out the name of the station. An empty wagon was shunted into a siding and with another change of staff we continued towards Hallatrow. At the head of 1 in 58 we obeyed another stop board.

At Hallatrow, after getting out a wagon of scrap metal and a bogie 'Macaw' to add to our train, we waited in the station for the up goods, one of three daily, to cross us. The train crew took the opportunity the stay gave them to eat their breakfast while I studied the fire. Hathaway had expected a heavy load like the previous day so in preparation had heaped the fire up at the back to produce a lot of steam. Had he known it was going to be a light train he would have used a saucer fire – throwing the coal to the sides of the box, leaving the centre hollow. The injector was opened and the fire made up before leaving.

Again we observed and obeyed a stop board and passed Farrington Gurney Halt. We raced down to Midsomer Norton at 30 mph and stopped to pick up more wagons. In the absence of a signal box, points were controlled from two ground frames. The key was detached from the staff to unlock these frames. Two wagons and a van were collected and after locking the frames and returning the key to the staff, we continued to Radstock.

We passed below the Somerset & Dorset Railway's viaduct. I was told that the National Coal Board was contemplating substituting an embankment for the viaduct as miners at Norton Hill Colliery were working towards the area (*see page 103*). The replacement of the viaduct by an embankment would have meant it would be less easily damaged by a subsidence and would therefore free coal for Norton Hill Colliery. It was believed miners would reach the area that June.

We were welcomed to Radstock by the din of riveters in the wagon works. Our average speed for the 15 miles had been 17 mph.

After uncoupling we left our train to be shunted by another Pannier and proceeded to the platform where Hathaway replenished the tanks. Returning to the goods yard we coupled to eight wagons and vans for the return trip.

As we started up the 1 in 128 bank, water flowed from one of the filler caps. Steam pressure was at the maximum of 200, the regulator on the first valve and cut-off 55 per cent. I noticed that the cab was a lot cooler than that of a BR Standard class '9F' 2-10-0 I had travelled on a few months before. At Midsomer Norton the injector was opened and we continued to climb at 15 mph. For most of the trip I sat on the fireman's wooden tip up seat and found the riding most comfortable. The injector was opened again at Farrington Gurney and just beyond we stopped to obey another stop board.

We drifted down the gradient of 1 in 65 to Hallatrow with the regulator off and the hand brake screwed down to assist the steam brake.

Pressure had dropped to 130 when we left Hallatrow, so Hathaway threw on 12 more shovelfuls. We crept up the 1 in 58 at 10 mph, but despite the effort No. 7772 was making, pressure rose to 150 and had reached 175 by the time the final climb to the summit began after Clutton. We stormed up the 1 in 71 at 12 mph and reaching the top, the safety valve blew off as we stopped at another board, so the injector was opened, for the 1 in 61 descent.

After picking up two wagons at Pensford we climbed the 1 in 65 at 10 mph with the regulator on the first valve and cut-off at 55 per cent. Pressure remained at 200 and 12 more shovels of coal were put on. The injector was opened just before the summit.

We stopped at the board, the guard climbed out and pinned down some wagon brakes. The hand brake on the engine was screwed down and Whitchurch Halt was passed at 23 mph. One empty wagon was shunted off at Brislington to be loaded with scrap metal and in exchange we collected two full ones. Now we had 11 on for East Depot.

The bank below Brislington was taken very carefully at 6 mph and we found the signal on at Marsh Junction. After a wait of six minutes we crossed the Avon and entered East Depot, five minutes late. Our average speed from Radstock had been 11 mph. After uncoupling the engine from the train we proceeded back to St Philip's Marsh where I bade the crew farewell.

12th April, 1961
Load: varied between two to six wagons
Engine: No. 7772
Average speed; 16.6 mph
Running time: 54 minutes 47 seconds

Time		Distance	Station	Actual arr.			Actual dep.			Scheduled dep.		Notes
m.	s.	miles		h.	m.	s.	h.	m.	s.	h.	m.	
–	–	–	Bristol East Depot	–	–	–	8	24	15	8	20	5 mph slack before Pensford
23	45	6	Pensford	8	48	0	8	49	0			
12	15	9¼	Clutton	9	1	15	9	7	0			
6	0	10¾	Hallatrow	9	13	0	11	5	30			
5	47	13¾	Midsomer Norton	11	11	17	11	28	0			
7	0	15¼	Radstock West	11	35	0						

Load: varied between eight to eleven wagons
Engine: No. 7772
Average speed; 11 mph
Running time: 86 minutes

Time		Distance	Station	Actual arr.			Scheduled arr.			Actual dep.		Notes
m.	s.	miles		h.	m.	s.	h.	m.	s.	h.	m.	
–	–	–	Radstock West	–	–	–	–	–	–	12	18	
21		4½	Hallatrow	12	39					12	42	
22		9¼	Pensford	1	4					1	19	5 mph slack beyond Pensford
28		14	Brislington	1	47					1	54	
10		15	Marsh Junction	2	4					2	10	
5		15¼	Bristol East Depot	2	15		2	10		–		

View of Pensford station from the cab of No. 7772 when passing over the viaduct on 12th April, 1961. *Author*

Appendix Two

Traffic dealt with at branch stations 1903 to 1933

Station	Year	Tickets issued	Season tickets	Passengers incl. season tickets	Parcels	Misc.	FORWARDED Coal, coke 'charged'	Other minerals	General merchandise	RECEIVED Coal, coke 'charged'	Other minerals	General merchandise	Coal, coke 'not charged' (forwarded & received)	Total receipts excl. 'not charged'	Livestock (forwarded & received)	Total carted tonnage
		No.	No.	£	£	£	tons	tons	tons	tons	tons	tons	tons	£	wagons	tons
Brislington	1903	8,316	?	427	84	95	9	–	36	933	2,405	440	803	771	–	108
	1913	11,576	?	665	43	1	–	–	73	688	2,740	789	2,238	890	–	235
	1923	7,492	16	580	196	14	38	–	485	1,063	65	1,125	4,222	2,835	–	544
	1924	7,461	24	652	207	14	10	–	475	1,246	165	1,879	4,408	3,549	–	464
	1925	9,233	25	646	205	12	10	6	600	676	201	2,134	4,459	3,938	–	573
	1926	7,630	22	552	221	15	18	8	442	397	203	2,308	3,174	4,004	–	556
	1927	8,143	27	578	187	14	21	–	570	473	467	3,252	4,410	5,775	–	659
	1928	9,241	21	552	194	21	9	–	246	302	285	1,472	4,220	2,391	–	225
	1929	9,323	10	571	183	26	–	–	42	277	216	820	4,219	1,060	–	77
	1930	7,685	21	502	114	13	10	–	13	296	35	289	4,487	484	–	80
	1931	7,878	25	595	101	12	–	–	40	228	54	314	4,513	569	–	78
	1932	7,956	18	653	100	4	16	–	24	191	77	600	5,360	845	–	51
	1933	8,509	19	625	88	6	–	–	10	246	6	215	4,090	344	–	63
Whitchurch Halt	1925															
	1926									Whitchurch Halt opened January 1925, receipts for 1925/26 included with Bristol Temple Meads.						
	1927	2,842	27	141	–	–										
	1928	2,091	40	109	–	–										
	1929	1,935	25	106	–	–										
	1930	1,300	24	96	–	–										
	1931	1,185	21	87	–	–										
	1932	804	8	53	–	–				Whitchurch Halt receipts included with Bristol Temple Meads from September 1932 onwards.						
Pensford	1903	27,468	?	1,097	136	412	2,553	29	82	910	1,948	237	244	936	5	209
	1913	28,730	?	1,250	127	608	26,656	–	204	889	3,049	1,642	26,193	4,463	2	336
	1923	16,521	258	1,178	225	771	46,104	5	201	129	1,085	1,582	51,318	11,757	12	320
	1924	16,453	268	1,211	218	537	48,841	34	80	164	499	1,624	74,971	10,994	17	294
	1925	18,402	283	1,300	233	393	53,519	17	334	122	399	2,615	58,522	13,692	10	273
	1926	13,204	235	973	197	397	28,513	15	149	133	134	1,750	27,993	7,645	7	250
	1927	13,628	160	932	209	71	60,493	35	112	127	143	2,328	54,686	14,625	12	278
	1928	11,956	136	875	204	55	48,352	16	84	197	88	2,094	46,991	11,879	6	150
	1929	10,676	169	762	233	284	67,977	33	56	164	169	2,268	43,926	16,593	17	141
	1930	8,347	146	626	171	120	47,907	15	57	178	29	1,156	41,238	11,659	11	152
	1931	7,742	146	665	153	24	40,591	7	66	128	142	1,694	40,761	10,311	6	212
	1932	6,023	141	514	126	206	35,883	15	65	224	40	980	37,518	8,126	5	157
	1933	7,198	134	559	119	39	31,061	20	88	154	162	868	29,318	7,170	6	161

Station	Year	Tickets issued No.	Season tickets No.	Passengers incl. season tickets £	Parcels £	Misc. £	FORWARDED Coal, coke 'charged' tons	FORWARDED Other minerals tons	FORWARDED General merchandise tons	RECEIVED Coal, coke 'charged' tons	RECEIVED Other minerals tons	RECEIVED General merchandise tons	Coal, coke 'not charged' (forwarded & received) tons	Total receipts excl. 'not charged' £	Livestock (forwarded & received) wagons	Total carted tonnage tons
Clutton	1903	24,468	?	1,654	201	555	98,092	4,331	235	84	4,784	2,983	—	21,662	37	501
	1913	23,643	?	1,501	127	920	51,090	18	319	36	1,076	4,364	3,533	6,124	11	435
	1923	20,823	395	2,073	147	787	85	17	282	1,372	376	1,528	581	1,486	13	252
	1924	19,967	364	1,946	140	710	249	61	175	1,406	241	1,462	350	1,330	30	236
	1925	18,472	375	1,832	142	767	720	41	179	1,190	142	1,025	480	1,100	10	241
	1926	16,381	406	1,588	137	510	18	20	386	733	148	1,186	235	1,258	5	201
	1927	20,192	412	1,786	131	448	196	673	243	1,616	353	772	335	1,504	1	279
	1928	17,381	400	1,564	125	196	36	129	193	1,363	135	585	279	953	10	178
	1929	17,155	375	1,501	122	331	—	162	194	2,078	62	370	263	943	11	179
	1930	14,599	373	1,334	157	318	—	118	116	988	66	278	320	720	13	142
	1931	12,780	367	1,181	134	246	—	35	76	1,392	46	329	330	715	15	150
	1932	12,017	345	1,140	121	175	—	235	216	1,021	27	210	246	852	15	141
	1933	13,530	284	1,090	133	11	—	411	37	1,118	—	186	196	762	5	126
Hallatrow	1903	21,682	?	1,611	275	1,254	111,474	1,581	747	123	1,388	3,161	275	16,237	311	1,904
	1913	49,741	?	2,517	294	1,835	81,753	856	910	128	1,344	4,418	26,656	12,482	438	2,402
	1923	26,160	196	2,604	715	1,226	62,260	1,021	647	239	670	2,986	9,989	18,013	288	1,474
	1924	25,438	168	2,554	815	950	68,260	1,086	666	289	395	3,417	4,750	18,682	219	1,497
	1925	21,420	172	2,247	834	978	53,523	3,048	336	230	221	3,025	18,445	14,639	233	1,244
	1926	16,243	163	1,709	707	631	23,355	4,779	572	81	147	2,926	4,130	10,034	175	1,228
	1927	17,875	161	1,738	756	580	48,624	2,117	442	146	159	2,758	11,340	14,089	166	1,451
	1928	12,392	90	1,114	789	458	41,899	2,300	391	212	338	1,726	9,881	11,829	183	1,202
	1929	12,458	91	1,088	912	419	42,437	1,300	385	252	214	1,591	14,134	12,179	182	1,225
	1930	9,252	102	841	857	326	44,567	666	409	255	72	1,599	5,260	13,392	138	1,439
	1931	7,311	114	685	746	323	42,254	762	341	285	230	1,853	5,019	11,836	155	1,299
	1932	6,559	84	597	1,022	124	41,375	1,097	467	79	25	2,136	5,252	12,921	127	2,054
	1933	6,056	86	685	718	146	40,878	1,216	625	5	21	2,449	3,943	14,873	110	2,526
Farrington Gurney Halt	1927	5,382	14	353	—	—	*Farrington Gurney Halt opened in July 1927.*									
	1928	9,128	20	546	—	—										
	1929	9,596	32	553	—	—										
	1930	7,670	15	417	—	—										
	1931	7,398	20	379	—	—										
	1932	6,214	27	337	—	—										
	1933	5,954	32	352	—	—										
Midsomer Norton & Welton	1903	32,667	?	1,718	200	908	—	89	1,491	208	91	1,935	7	1,461	20	713
	1913	42,872	?	2,531	272	446	—	4	1,639	86	362	3,629	320	2,868	44	1,916
	1923	41,916	157	3,778	447	1,139	13	6	1,325	96	247	2,895	4	4,433	10	1,513
	1924	40,443	125	3,928	358	780	—	45	1,414	87	265	3,102	16	4,419	9	1,697
	1925	36,990	162	3,861	359	786	—	19	1,377	27	428	3,328	12	4,412	24	1,645
	1926	30,286	150	3,138	279	647	43	66	1,130	620	353	3,212	96	4,353	16	1,457
	1927	35,050	176	3,516	278	767	—	20	1,390	87	620	3,413	34	4,897	11	1,590
	1928	35,569	191	3,573	310	407	—	40	1,605	92	149	3,785	54	5,080	10	1,472

Radstock

Year																
1930	30,666	201	3,020	406	330	21	96	2,102	108	232	5,071	35	6,663	13	2,034
1931	30,061	154	2,771	322	313	–	386	2,475	74	120	5,306	76	7,075	2	2,247
1932	26,751	160	2,641	334	358	–	358	1,997	49	41	4,772	47	5,853	4	2,903
1933	24,524	156	2,489	329	239	–	817	1,526	58	43	4,383	58	5,393	2	3,243
1903	47,277	?	2,341	339	302	129,125	1,909	1,377	468	3,184	4,599	747	21,683	44	1,450
1913	43,890	?	3,286	357	707	146,079	4,984	1,112	469	4,040	5,974	9,122	27,262	33	1,945
1923	43,854	168	4,405	373	588	118,863	349	921	233	1,085	3,913	16,448	29,270	27	1,665
1924	44,819	170	4,827	394	539	115,152	200	1,041	278	508	4,702	15,886	27,695	43	1,903
1925	42,675	203	4,801	418	603	99,681	788	1,121	121	789	4,023	21,049	24,360	56	1,782
1926	29,093	163	3,463	296	598	45,994	4,378	939	159	606	3,531	10,092	14,334	34	1,475
1927	34,039	190	4,160	361	264	88,821	2,471	804	112	1,026	3,483	23,200	24,119	29	1,574
1928	31,865	169	3,955	417	241	76,430	345	814	187	1,063	3,242	20,462	19,227	40	1,566
1929	29,493	154	3,715	414	270	89,176	465	882	150	1,302	3,399	20,922	22,666	50	1,660
1930	25,132	179	3,482	355	267	81,944	123	1,090	102	1,170	3,759	23,659	21,672	40	1,744
1931	22,779	162	2,908	325	196	78,069	76	676	70	1,233	3,743	22,008	18,787	39	1,416
1932	19,524	179	2,559	262	29	63,193	454	708	52	738	3,068	12,881	15,933	27	1,244
1933	17,881	137	2,470	244	19	64,026	273	648	21	693	2,526	4,488	15,495	25	1,254

Mells Road

Year																
1903	8,864	?	597	173	1,703	33,494	28,551	280	–	367	3,864	–	11,944	43	439
1913	10,307	?	1,021	159	1,887	60,817	44,592	661	408	3,705	6,187	39,681	21,054	14	885
1923	8,981	7	887	217	1,896	61,598	42,489	520	272	2,596	3,267	14,722	31,449	15	679
1924	8,814	16	907	213	1,765	65,458	48,694	1,037	286	1,791	3,981	21,659	31,212	16	705
1925	7,077	11	783	231	1,490	58,402	52,671	748	301	1,516	4,931	17,806	31,194	10	666
1926	5,685	24	673	179	1,342	28,162	51,688	859	385	1,653	3,577	8,279	26,330	22	608
1927	6,512	30	656	182	1,204	49,809	71,549	490	816	2,991	3,342	11,809	39,330	28	723
1928	6,548	37	626	164	1,141	36,849	88,923	759	1,305	4,367	2,910	9,184	40,515	30	536
1929	6,244	32	526	177	1,191	39,982	95,377	870	1,964	7,012	2,004	4,708	44,553	58	481
1930	5,606	26	552	198	772	34,409	113,408	636	1,701	5,563	1,547	2,348	51,021	23	519
1931	5,284	20	507	200	1,221	32,022	121,170	525	1,809	5,117	1,748	879	53,149	7	460
1932	4,874	18	455	178	589	31,091	77,397	246	1,242	2,016	1,002	755	35,891	4	558
1933	4,750	20	434	177	406	32,204	94,773	213	869	2,376	996	1,888	42,443	4	635

Brislington-Frome Line Totals

Year																
1903	170,742	?	9,445	1,408	5,229	374,747	36,490	4,248	2,726	14,167	17,219	2,076	74,694	460	5,324
1913	210,759	?	12,771	1,379	6,404	366,395	50,454	4,918	2,704	16,316	27,003	107,743	75,143	542	8,154
1923	165,747	1,197	15,505	2,320	6,421	288,903	43,887	4,381	3,404	6,124	17,296	97,284	99,243	365	6,447
1924	163,395	1,135	16,025	2,345	5,295	297,970	50,120	4,888	3,756	3,864	20,167	122,040	97,881	334	6,796
1925	154,269	1,231	15,470	2,412	5,029	265,855	56,590	4,695	2,667	3,696	21,081	120,773	93,335	343	6,424
1926	118,522	1,163	12,096	2,016	4,140	126,103	60,954	4,477	2,508	3,244	18,490	53,999	67,958	259	5,775
1927	143,753	1,197	13,860	2,104	3,348	247,964	76,865	4,092	3,377	5,759	19,348	105,814	104,339	247	6,554
1928	136,171	1,104	12,914	2,203	2,519	203,575	91,753	4,051	4,158	6,425	15,814	91,071	91,874	279	5,330
1929	130,802	1,082	12,411	2,360	2,880	239,572	97,607	4,373	4,935	9,238	14,367	88,242	103,667	334	5,426
1930	110,257	1,087	10,870	2,258	2,146	208,858	114,426	4,423	3,628	7,167	13,699	77,347	105,611	238	6,110
1931	102,418	1,029	9,778	1,981	2,372	192,936	122,436	4,199	3,986	6,942	14,987	73,586	102,442	224	5,862
1932	90,722	980	8,949	2,143	1,760	171,558	79,556	3,709	2,858	2,964	12,768	62,059	80,421	182	7,108
1933	88,402	868	8,704	1,808	1,066	168,179	97,510	3,181	2,462	3,301	11,623	43,981	86,480	152	8,008

Bibliography, Sources & Acknowledgements

Bradshaw's Railway Guides (various dates)
Bradshaw's Railway Manual, Shareholders' Guide & Directory (various dates)
British Railways Sectional Appendix to the Working Time Table and Book of Rules and Regulations, Bristol Traffic District, October 1960
High Littleton & Hallatrow by M. Browning & K. Trivett (High Littleton Parish Council, 1999)
An Historical Survey of Selected Great Western Stations Vols. 1 & 2 by R.H. Clark (OPC, 1976/1981)
The Dorset & Somerset Canal by K.R. Clew (David & Charles, 1971)
The Somerset Coal Canal and Railways by K.R. Clew (David & Charles, 1970)
Clinker's Register of Closed Passenger Stations & Goods Depots by C.R. Clinker (Avon-Anglia, 1988)
Train on Line, Vic Oakhill, A biography by R. Edwardes (Author, 1988)
Track Layout Diagrams of the GWR and BR WR Sections 19A & 21 by R.A. Cooke (Author, 1992/1988)
The History of the Somerset Coalfield by C.G. Down & A.J. Warrington (David & Charles, 1974)
The Newbury Railway by C.G. Down & A.J. Warrington (Industrial Railway Society, 1979)
St Philip's Marsh by D.J. Fleming (Bradford Barton, c.1981)
Industrial Railways and Locomotives of South Western England by R. Hateley (Industrial Railway Society, 2012)
Somerset Coal Mining Life by F. Flower (Millstream Books, 1990)
The Abbotsbury Branch by B.L. Jackson (Wild Swan, 1989)
Great Western Steam Rail Motors by J. Lewis (Wild Swan, 2004)
Brunel's Timber Bridges & Viaducts by B. Lewis (Ian Allan, 2007)
An Historical Survey of Great Western Engine Sheds 1947 by E. Lyons (OPC, 1974)
The Bath to Weymouth Line by C.G. Maggs (The Oakwood Press, 1982)
The Camerton Branch by C.G. Maggs & G. Beale (Wild Swan, 1985)
Branch Lines of Somerset by C.G. Maggs (Amberley, 2011)
Somerset Railways by C.G. Maggs (Halsgrove, 2007)
Bristol Railway Panorama by C.G. Maggs (Millstream Books, 1990)
Rail Centres: Bristol by C.G. Maggs (Ian Allan, 1981)
Foster Yeoman, The Rail Story by C.J. Marsden (Channel AV Publishing, 1998)
History of the Great Western Railway Vols. 1 & 2 by E.T. MacDermot (Ian Allan, 1964)
Frome to Bristol by V. Mitchell & K. Smith (Middleton Press, 1986)
Somerset Railway Stations by M. Oakley (The Dorset Press, 2002)
Locomotives of the Great Western Railway (various volumes) (RCTS 1952-1993)
The Story of the Westbury to Weymouth Line by D. Phillips (OPC 1994)
A Gazetteer of the Railway Contractors & Engineers of the West Country 1830-1914 by L. Popplewell (Melledgen Press, 1983)
Great Western Railway Halts Vol. 1 by K. Robertson (Irwell, 1990)
Great Western Railway Halts Vol. 2 by K. Robertson (KRB Publications, 2002)
Rails Around Frome by S. McNicol (Railmac Publications, 1984)
The West of England Resignalling by A. Vaughan (Ian Allan, 1987)
Through Countryside & Coalfield by M. Vincent (OPC, 1990)
The Bristol & North Somerset Railway 1863-1884 by D. Warnock (Temple Cloud Publications, 1978)
The Bristol & North Somerset Railway since 1884 by D.W. Warnock & R.S. Parsons (Avon-Anglia 1979)
GWR Service Time Table Appendix No. 4, 1945
Radstock Coal & Steam Vols. 1 & 2 by C. Handley (Millstream Books, 1991 & 1992)

BIBLIOGRAPHY, DOURCES & ACKNOWLEDGEMENTS

Magazines

British Railway Journal No. 8 p.266 ff 'The Standard Buildings of William Clarke'
British Railway Journal No. 9 pp346/7 'Camerton Branch Addendum'
British Railway Journal 1985 Special GWR Edition p.61 ff 'A GWR Signalwoman'
Back Track May, July & September 2004 'Railway Damage And Disruption in World War Two'
Railway Bylines Vol. 7, Issue 4 p. 164 ff 'The North Somerset Line in BR Days'
Railway Magazine September 2007 p.22 ff 'Mendip Stone'
Railway Observer - various dates
The South Western Circular Vol. 9 No. 6 pp 133/4 'Roads Reconstruction tar tank wagon, Mells'
Trains Illustrated October 1959 p.472 ff 'The Bristol-Frome Branch of the WR'
Trains Illustrated February 1960 p.127 Letter

Newspapers

Bath & Cheltenham Gazette
Bath Chronicle
Bath Herald
Bath Journal
Evening Chronicle
Somerset & Wilts Journal
Somerset Guardian
Somerset Standard

Sources

The National Archives, Kew
BNSR Directors' Minute Books 1863-1866 (RAIL 77.1)
BNSR Directors' Minute Books 1870-1881 (RAIL 77.2)
GWR Staffing c.1900 (RAIL 264.421)
GWR Staffing c.1921 (RAIL 264.453)

Acknowledgements

I would like to thank G.T. Bryant, R. Dagger, P. Edwards, G. Dawes, J. Mann, A. Dickens, T. McGill (Clutton History Group), F.W. Smith, Martin Symons (Whatley Quarry), J.L. Watts and M. Zuckerman (*Bath Chronicle*) for their help.

Especial thanks are due to Colin Roberts for checking and improving the text.

Index

Accidents 24, 26, 29, 41, 45, 61, 69, 92, 121, 209, 215 et seq.
Acts of Parliament 8, 11, 12, 16, 19, 22, 219
Amey Roadstone Construction 137, 146 et seq., 153, 179, 180, 183, 211
Avon viaduct, 45, 48
Bailey, E., 168 et seq.
Bath, 7 et seq., 17, 29 et seq. 39, 81
Bedlam tunnel 153, 180
Bethell & Walton 12, 17 et seq.
Bilboa colliery 137, 139
Bingham, J., 12 et seq., 26
Bishop Sutton, 15
Blanning, Messrs 77
Bradford-on-Avon, 8
Brassey, T., 18
Braysdown, 15, 17, 202
Brislington 23, 27, 39, 41, 49, 57, 61, 175, 177, 189, 191, 202, 229, 233, 235
Bristol 5, 7, 11, 12, 15, 23 et seq., 30, 35, 45, 81, 171 et seq., 187 et seq.
Bristol & Exeter Railway 11, 17
Bristol & North Somerset Railway 8, 11 et seq. 93, 97, 115, 209, 219
Bristol & South Western Junction Railway, 35
Bristol Commercial Vehicles, 49
Bristol Dock tramway 13
Bristol Tramways & Carriage Co., 39, 87
British Wagon Co., 105, 190
Brotherhood, R., 135
Brunel, I.K., 8
Bruton, 12, 22
Burchells, 69, 73
Camerton, 12 et seq., 29, 35, 87, 171, 215, 219 et seq., 224 et seq.
Cam Valley 7, 187
Chew Magna, 12, 15
Chippenham, 8
Clandown, 6, 7, 15
Clarke, W., 22 et seq., 49, 57, 69, 77, 93, 103, 219, 221
Closure, 5, 39, 41, 44 et seq., 179, 189
Cloud Hill, 23 et seq.
Clutton, 13 et seq., 27, 39, 41, 69, 105, 175, 179, 191 et seq., 209, 215 et seq., 233, 236
Colthurst, J., 12 et seq.
Cooks Wood Quarry, 135
Denman S., 229 et seq., 232
Dorset & Somerset Canal, 8, 135
Dunkerton, 223, 227
East Somerset Railway, 11
Evercreech, 8, 13, 17, 29

Farrington Gurney 13, 15, 19, 23, 39, 77, 81, 87, 91 et seq., 191, 233, 236
Foster Yeoman, 105, 179, 183, 217
Fowler, Messrs, 9
Foxcote, 15, 121, 202
Franco British Glass, 73
Fraser, J.G., 12 et seq., 23
Frome, 5, 8, 11, 27, 31 et seq., 39, 41, 81, 129, 139, 157, 161, 177, 179
Fry's Bottom, 15, 69, 73, 77, 175
Gas House viaduct, 157
Gauge, 5, 28 et seq., 209
Gradient, 5
Great Elm tunnel 153, 204, 217
Great Western Railway 8, 9, 11, 12, 17, 20 et seq., 77, 103, 115, 129, 219
Greyfield, 15, 69, 73, 76, 216
Grierson, J., 33
Hallatrow, 5, 12, 23, 26 et seq., 39, 77, 78 et seq., 81, 87, 91 et seq., 177, 179, 187, 191, 195, 221 et seq., 233, 236
Hannaford, J.R., 161, 185
Hapsford, 5, 44, 139, 140, 153, 157, 179, 211, 217
Hare, Mrs, 13, 15, 17
Hathaway, I.R., 229 et seq., 232
High Littleton, 15
Hinton Bluett, 15
Huish, 15, 32, 39, 129
Hutchinson, Maj. Gen., 221
Imperial Mercantile Credit Association, 21
Jewell, M. & D., 61, 217
Kennet & Avon Canal, 7
Kilmersdon, 5, 39, 41 ,44, 117, 121, 201 et seq.
Kislingbury, C., 216
Lawrence & Fry, 17
Leonards Mill viaduct, 157
Liddiard, Mr 33
Limpley Stoke, 7, 77, 87, 223
Locomotives, 7, 25 et seq., 41, 73, 91 et seq., 139, 153, 171 et seq.
London & South Western Railway 9, 12, 35
Ludlows colliery 9, 103, 105, 112, 202
Mackintosh colliery, 135
Mackay, J., 25 et seq.
Mappin Bros, 15
Marcroft 5, 44, 77, 105, 115, 121, 129, 211, 217
Marsh Jn, 39, 41, 44 et seq., 175, 205, 209, 229
Mckenzie & Holland, 79, 221
Mcmurtrie, J., 7, 18
Mells Road 5, 32 et seq., 41, 44, 61, 105, 129 et seq., 135, 137, 139, 147, 177, 187, 191 et seq., 202 et seq., 237

Mendip Rail, 183
Merehead, 153, 183, 217
Middle Pit, 39, 105
Midford, 6, 7, 93, 222
Midsomer Norton, 12, 15, 22, 39, 41, 61, 91 et seq., 97, 103, 191, 202, 215, 233, 236
Mobil Oil, 169
Monkton Combe, 227
Montague Baillie, 20
Murder Combe tunnel, 153, 205
Naish, W., 6, 22
Nettlebridge, 17
Newbury Railway & colliery, 135, 137, 139, 202
New Rock, 15
North Row viaduct, 157
North Somerset Brick & Tile, 93
North Somerset Jn, 24 et seq., 45, 202 et seq.
North Somerset viaduct, 97, 103
Oakhill viaduct, 97, 98
Old Mills, 29, 41, 67, 87, 90 et seq., 171, 177, 195 et seq., 204, 209
Opening, 9, 29, 33, 41, 221
Overend & Gurney, 12, 19
Parnall Aircraft, 87
Paulton, 12, 15, 18, 77, 81, 222 et seq.
Pensford, 5, 17 et seq., 39, 41, 57 et seq., 173, 179, 189 et seq., 209, 215 et seq., 229, 233, 235
Pensford & Bromley colliery 57, 61, 65, 67, 69, 195, 205, 217
Permanent way 7, 9, 27 et seq., 32, 103, 209 et seq., 219
Perry, J., 23, 25 et seq.
Piercy, B., 13, 19, 22
Purnell, Messrs, 77, 81
Radford, 221, 223
Radstock, 5, 7 et seq., 12, 15, 19 et seq., 31 et seq., 39, 92, 103, 105, 115, 117, 129, 171, 175, 177,179, 183, 185, 187 et seq., 209, 215 et seq., 233, 237
Radstock Coal Co., 110, 202
Radstock wagon works, 105, 190
Rich, Colonel, 26
Roach & Pilditch, 9
Roads Reconstruction Ltd, 135, 137, 139, 144 et seq., 153, 202
Robertson, J., 49, 53
Ruddick, J., 205 et seq.
Salisbury, 8, 20, 23 et seq., 30, 129
Sandy Park, 38, 50
Saxby & Farmer, 27, 203
Signalling, 27, 33, 41, 45, 61, 67, 74, 79, 92, 117, 161, 203 et seq.

Single Hill, 7
Smith, T.H., 16 et seq.
Somerset & Avon Railway Association, 5, 211,
Somerset & Dorset Railway, 8, 12 et seq., 29, 39, 81,97, 103 et seq., 115, 117, 129, 183, 190, 233
Somerset Central Rly, 12
Somerset Coal Canal, 6, 7, 9, 22, 26, 30, 93, 97, 103, 121, 219, 221
Somerset Quarries, 139, 140, 157, 195 et seq.
Springfield, 91 et seq.
Stanton Drew, 15
Storage & Transport Systems, 105
Stowey, 15
Strike, 39, 93
Sustrans, 211
Sweetleaze, 15
Temple Cloud, 87, 215
Thicket Mead, 93, 216
Thingley Jn, 8
Timetables, 34, 36, 37, 187 et seq., 223
Timsbury, 15, 223
Twerton, 8, 13
Twinhoe, 7
Tyning, 105, 112
Vallis Vale, 139
Vobster, 135, 139
Wagon Repairs Ltd, 105
Waldegrave Arms, 7, 15,22
Waldegrave, Lady, 9, 13, 17, 22, 103
Warwick, Lord, 13, 19, 22 et seq., 33, 69, 73
Weaver, Messrs, 135
Wellow, 6, 7
Welton, 15, 23, 27, 93, 97
Westbury, 8, 171, 179, 182, 185
Westbury Iron Co., 135
Westcott, Mr, 61
Weston-super-Mare, 175, 187, 189, 190 et seq., 215
Wethered, J., 35, 39
Weymouth, 8, 33, 35, 39, 175, 177, 187, 189 et seq.
Whatley Quarry, 41, 139,153, 157, 179, 183, 204,211,217
Wheeler & Gregory, 105
Whitchurch, 23, 39, 57, 191, 229, 233, 235
Whittenson & Hewits, 32
Willow Vale viaduct, 9, 157
Wilts, Somerset & Weymouth Railway, 7 et seq., 20, 31, 161
World War I, 23
World War II, 39,61, 129,201,209,217
Writhlington, 15, 17, 19, 44, 103, 105, 121, 129, 179, 185, 201
Yolland, Capt., 9, 24, 31
Yorke, Colonel, 67